FROCH

FROCH

MY AUTOBIOGRAPHY

CARL FROCH

WITH NIALL HICKMAN

EBURY
PRESS

3 5 7 9 10 8 6 4 2

This edition published 2014
First published as *The Cobra* in 2011 by Ebury Press,
an imprint of Ebury Publishing
A Random House Group company

The Random House Group Limited Reg. No. 954009

Addresses for companies within the Random House Group can be found at
www.randomhouse.co.uk

A CIP catalogue record for this book is available from the British Library

The Random House Group Limited supports the Forest Stewardship
Council® (FSC®), the leading international forest-certification organisation.
Our books carrying the FSC label are printed on FSC®-certified paper.
FSC is the only forest-certification scheme supported by the leading
environmental organisations, including Greenpeace. Our paper
procurement policy can be found at www.randomhouse.co.uk/environment

Designed and set by seagulls.net

Printed and bound in Great Britain by Clays Ltd, St Ives PLC

ISBN 9780091960360

For Rachael, Rocco and Natalia

CONTENTS

PROLOGUE

I had finally done it. I had crushed one of the best fighters in the world and won back my belt. I was the WBC Super Middleweight champion. As my fists kept finding a way through Abraham's guard the memories came flooding back. Me as a spindly youth at the Phoenix gym, me in my amateur vest when I represented my country, me as a professional in my first paid fight, winning the British title, defeating Jean Pascal for a world crown. It had all come full circle. It was only when I got back to Nottingham and watched the fight for the first time that it sank in. I was watching myself destroy Abraham and my career in the ring flashed by me.

As I watched the video of the night in Helsinki when I regained my world title and won every round against one of the legends of the ring, I started to reflect. As the TV commentators raved about my display and the newspapers and radio talked about it as a great fight, it made me feel super proud. I knew that night in Finland was good, but perhaps I hadn't realised quite how good. Now I knew.

It made me think back to where I had come from and when I first stepped into a ring as a youngster. It got me thinking back to the days when there was no TV commentator, no reporters, just me, my family and a few friends, driving up and down the motorways of Britain, fighting for the love of it.

I was like that as a kid. I just loved boxing so much. Mine was a meandering path to the top as I left the sport for several years, only to come back at the age of 19 as I was bored with my life and out of breath running up a hill. As I was watching myself smashing Arthur Abraham to pieces it made me realise that all the hard work, the dedication, the sweat, the blood, the smell of the gym – all of it was worth it. It was so worth it. I wouldn't have wanted it any different because boxing had given me so much. It had brought such value to my life.

I've always wanted to be the best from the day I really started to take boxing seriously. I always wanted to deliver a performance which would stay in the memory, not just for me, but for fight fans.

Perfection in any sport is surely impossible because there are always imperfections. There are always improvements to be made. But that night in Helsinki, for me, felt as close as I can get. And to think, as an aimless teenager just out of school, I used to spend my time collecting the toys out of Kinder egg chocolates. I was empty then. Not any longer. Boxing did that for me. It turned a little kid's dreams into the real thing.

CHAPTER 1

In 2008 the super-middleweight title was vacant, and the WBC ordered me to take on Jean Pascal for the crown. When Nottingham's Trent FM Arena was chosen as the venue I knew, just knew that I would win it.

I had first heard the name Pascal back when I was an amateur and he beat Paul Smith in the 2002 Commonwealth Games. I remember watching that fight and it was a close one. My promoter Mick Hennessy had said he would move heaven and earth to get the world title fight with Pascal in Nottingham and he delivered. Pascal clearly wanted it as badly as I did, and the negotiations were all pretty straightforward. It was a great match-up for both of us. Pascal was tough, no doubt about it, and I knew he would have a go. He was also quite flashy, but I didn't give it too much thought when the fight for the title was made, I just knew I was going to win.

I started my preparations with early-morning running and basic training in Nottingham, before heading over to Ireland for pretty much the rest of my training. This took place at the beautiful Breaffy House Resort in Castlebar, County Mayo, where they looked after my trainer, Rob McCracken, and me fantastically. Darren Barker and John O'Donnell were with us as well, which was great as they are terrific blokes and good mates. The idea of going to Ireland was to get away from it all, have no distractions and give myself the best possible chance of winning the world crown.

As I went into full training I was feeling super, super confident. I knew enough about Pascal from the amateur days and the videos I'd seen to know that I was going to be world champion. I just had to train properly, which I always do, and the title was mine. I certainly fell asleep every night just thinking and dreaming about being a world champion.

I should say that, although I do watch videos of my opponents, it is more just to see what they look like than to make a careful analysis. I never study fighters particularly closely before I get into the ring, because when I watch an opponent on video, it dawns on me that I will be fighting them and that makes me apprehensive and on edge, and I don't like that feeling. I will usually study them closely only a week or so beforehand and no earlier than that. So I watched Pascal's fight with Omar Pittman before we faced each other and that was enough for me. It was a clear points win for the Canadian, but Pascal wobbled a couple of times and I thought, great, he's a 'chinny' one.

I'm a big believer nowadays in the fact you can over-analyse as much as under-analyse, but it was a very different story in the amateurs. Back then, I used to watch all my opponents and video them with my camcorder. I even filmed some great stuff of David Haye when we were still in the unpaid ranks and now David is a superstar I might have to cash in on his fame! I also remember filming the Romanian Adrian Diaconu, who beat me in the 2000 Olympic qualifiers. Diaconu had a tight guard, was a counter puncher and, when I went in the ring to face him, I thought I knew what I had to do to beat him just because I'd videoed and watched him. It was rubbish – any game plan I had just went out the window.

When someone is coming at you wanting to knock your block off, you have to react instinctively and naturally. He'd be throwing shots I hadn't seen before and I'd be thinking, 'Hang on, you shouldn't be throwing that. That's not part of your repertoire.' When plan A doesn't work and you haven't got a plan B you have lost and so I never did it again. I prefer now just to rely on my own skills to overcome an opponent. I learned the hard way that you have to be ready for anything, not pre-programmed. You shouldn't be thinking 'He has just thrown a right hook so next up comes a left upper cut because I've seen it on video.'

Good boxers have different game plans for different fights. Anyone who has followed the fight game recently will tell you that Jermain Taylor looks a slick, superb, technical fighter, but he isn't always like that. Similarly, they have got me down in America as an Arturo Gatti or Mickey Ward-type fighter, an old-fashioned brawler. They have seen me with Pascal when we went toe to toe for twelve rounds and the same was true towards the end of my fight against Taylor. Though I can slug it out with anyone, I believe I have got slick boxing skills as well and I proved that on the night in Helsinki when I tore Abraham apart with my jab. With Pascal, I took him on because he was as hard as nails and he wanted that sort of fight. I was happy to go along with it because I knew it would be to my advantage. But I'm not always a no-holds-barred fighter, even though Pascal–Froch was a proper brawl all right.

I trained for a total of five weeks at Breaffy House Resort and, even though there wasn't a lot to do, the days went by very quickly. Gabriel Clarke from ITV came for a few days and did some filming, which broke it up a bit, and various press boys from the nationals and local papers also came over, but essentially it was just hard, hard work and plenty of rest. I would go down to the restaurant for dinner in the evening and make it last three or four hours, just hanging around and chilling, drinking a lot of mint tea. At 7 a.m. I was up for my morning run so I always went to bed early. Believe me, you need all the sleep you can get when you are in full training.

I am lucky because a lot of fighters get terribly bored when they are in full training. All they do is train, eat and sleep, whereas I have a few rental properties to look after so I have to be on the computer a lot checking things. If I had a choice, I would prefer to be at home in Nottingham in the build-up to any fight as I am more relaxed. But in Ireland at least I could go to my room, turn on the computer and take care of business outside of boxing. Then, more importantly, put in a couple of hardcore gaming hours on Xbox Live.

Everything was going smoothly in Ireland, until one thing after another started to go a bit pear-shaped.

The first thing that went wrong was when I was sparring with the Cuban prospect, Luis Garcia. He's a hugely skilful kid, very quick and very flash, and two weeks before the fight he perforated my eardrum. My head guard was not quite on correctly, as it had been jolted by a punch earlier in the round. Garcia threw a tiny little left hook tap right on the ear and, though he didn't hit me hard, it was enough. I couldn't believe it: it was the most piss-poor punch I'd ever taken and it popped my ear. You know when you are a kid, you get slapped around the ear and your head rings for a few seconds? Well, this was exactly like that. The second the punch landed there was an immediate ringing noise in my ear and I knew I had done some damage.

I went to see a doctor and he said, 'You know you have perforated your eardrum.' I replied, 'What? I can't hear you.' I said that about five times before he realised I was winding him up. The doctor said it would mend of its own accord, but only in about two weeks. Great, I thought. That's when I'll be in the ring facing Pascal. I felt a bit wobbly, but after a few days it improved slightly.

The day after perforating my eardrum, something even worse happened.

I was sparring with Paul David and Danny McIntosh, and Paul was wearing these old gloves: an ancient, really knack-ered pair with the thumb sticking out. We were knocking three bells out of each other when he nicked me at the side of my eye. It was only the tiniest of cuts, but I knew imme-diately that the skin had torn. But even worse was to follow. Still wearing those old gloves, Paul threw a big left hook and immediately my rib was really sore.

Only eight days before the fight and I had a perforated eardrum, a small nick by the side of my eye and a suspected broken rib. This was not good.

There was never any suggestion on my part that I would pull out of the fight. A few boxers always dive out of fights, but unless it is something really serious I never will. Up until my clash with Arthur Abraham years later, I had a proud record of never delaying any fight due to injury. My eardrum started to clear up in the week leading up to the fight, and though the rib was horrific at first and I couldn't sleep very well, I just faced up to it and accepted it. There was nothing I could do about it, and in the first rounds Pascal could have hit me with a great shot and broken my ribs anyway, so what's the difference?

I spoke to Rob and he said you have got to read what your body tells you. I took diclofenac every day, which is a painkiller as well as anti-inflammatory, and I had good days and bad. I couldn't get out of bed for a few mornings without feeling pain, but when I started walking around it loosened up a bit. I think if an X-ray had shown a definite break I just might have thought it was too risky, but because I didn't have that absolute proof, I went ahead with the fight. The way I looked at it was simple: it was painful, but Carl, you just have to live with it.

After all, as any boxer will tell you, you are never 100 per cent perfect going into a fight. Never. How you deal with these things, these little setbacks, is what matters. You can make excuses and you can pull out of every other fight if you want to, but that's just not me. Funnily enough, just as the doctor in County Mayo said, the eardrum healed on the morning of the fight, although Pascal slapped me on the side of the head in one of the early rounds and I knew it had gone again.

The little nick above my eye also opened up during the fight and afterwards I needed six stitches in it, which is very unusual for me. I'm from Eastern European stock and I reckon they just have tougher skin over there because I have hardly ever cut, either as an amateur or a pro.

The cut and the eardrum did not concern me before the fight but the state of my ribs definitely did (though only to the extent that I was worried it would affect my chances of winning and I felt really confident that the title was mine). The last thing I wanted was to lose the fight because I had hurt myself in sparring a few days before. But even with these concerns, by the time I had got back to Nottingham two weeks before the fight, I felt ready.

I always sleep well the night before a fight. I am so lucky to be able to blank everything out and not think about what is going to happen the next day. I watch a movie and just switch off.

I only really start to switch on when I am packing my kit before the fight. For the Pascal fight I did my usual routine, putting everything in place in my kit bag: boots, shorts, gum shield and my 'Cobra' cloak. That is when I know I am about to fight in the ring. It is not superstition or anything like that. I don't put my left boot on before my right or vice versa, but when I am sorting my bag I have to make sure everything is just so.

I tidied up my house, because I like it to be neat and clean for when I get back from the fight. I need to know the house is in order, with stuff put away on the shelves. I don't know why. That's just the way I am. I guess it's my way of coping with the pressure. I am not good to be around before a fight, because I often just like to be on my own, with my own thoughts.

Ever since turning professional, my best friend Adam Fukes has always tried to have a chat with me before every fight and the Pascal clash was no different. But by now he knows what I am like: a bear with a very sore head.

Adam has been my running partner for years. When I train in Nottingham he invariably turns up at 7 a.m. and bangs on the door, making sure when I am at home in Nottingham I am still bang on it, which is a blessing because it is hard to motivate yourself to get out of bed on your own.

In the changing rooms, just after the TV cameras left the dressing room, we were told by the TV producer that there were six minutes and then I was on. It was then that I could hear Jean Pascal and his team outside the door. He had an entourage of about twenty-five people: a dozen physios, dieticians and cuts men and trainers and whatever; the rest were his mates, his brothers and his family.

I was quite nervous as Jean and I had exchanged a few heated words at the press conference a few days before, so there was definitely tension in the air. I was just waiting for the door to open and the cameras to come back in, so I knew it was fight time. Pascal was outside the changing rooms for all those six minutes. His entourage started getting louder and louder with chants of 'Jean Pascal, Jean Pascal, Jean Pascal' and they were also banging the walls. I could see people's faces around my dressing room and they all looked a bit worried and a touch scared. I thought, if the idea is to get me really intimidated here, it has had the opposite effect.

It got me switched on and focused, and, rather than making me afraid, the banging and shouting came across as a sign of weakness. My stepdad Steve and one of my brothers Lee looked as though they were about to cry, but the chanting just made me even more confident. I felt at that moment I could not lose.

I knew when the fight got started, all his mates would be on the other side of the rope and it would just be me and Pascal in there. I don't have a massive entourage in my dressing room and that's one of the reasons. I just need to rely on myself, nobody else. As an amateur I was a very nervous kid, but not as a pro. In the amateur ranks I was a bag of nerves, often when I was sitting around waiting for my fight to start. Now it is a case of been there, seen it, done it. It just doesn't faze me any more.

Rob knew what I was thinking. Rob was good. He was cool. He is a man's man. You can't be soft in front of Rob because he will see it straight away, so when I climbed in the ring I was determined to show him the singing and chanting meant nothing.

I knew all I wanted to know about Pascal. He was a world-class athlete and he could fight. He punched hard and he had quick hands. This was his chance as much as it was mine and I am sure he wanted it just as much as I did.

As the fight started I felt in control throughout every round, even though I look back on it now and I can barely remember a thing. I just put it on him from the first round and he laid some good shots on me. Before the fight I was told he wasn't a big knock-out puncher, but that is doing him a bit of a disservice because Pascal could dig, no doubt about that. I took some heavy shots from him throughout the fight and vice versa. He never took a step backwards and neither did I.

I've got a great chin. I took a couple of big shots in the second round up close and I thought, yeah, OK, so you can punch. Saying that, it was the only fight I have ever been involved in when I basically can't remember anything from the second to the eighth rounds. I am sure there is a simple reason: I got smacked so hard in the second I have suffered memory loss ever since. So I'd love to describe the fight round by round but I can't. I can remember quite clearly all my other fights, but not Pascal.

I watched the fight back on video the next day and still couldn't recall a thing from rounds two to eight. At that point, I got cut and for some reason it must have woken up my memory senses again. But even after that, I was calling my best mate Adam Fukes the wrong name after the fight. He said I kept calling him Matt because I was still semi-concussed. There's a picture of me holding up the belt taken by the *Nottingham Evening Post* and you can see the vacant look in my eyes.

Although I can't remember two-thirds of the fight, I was aware enough to know that never at any stage did I think he was going to put me down. I always felt in charge, even after getting cut through a totally accidental clash of heads in the eighth. I was in a sort of comfort zone, if such a thing is possible in the ring. The eighth was a significant moment for me because I thought, I need to step it up a bit in case this is close. My corner was telling me I had bossed the fight, but with nearly five rounds still left in the middle of the eighth, it was there to win or lose. I wouldn't say I was worried, but your mind can play tricks on you.

I went back to my corner at the end of the eighth and my corner men put some adrenalin on the cut. Rob told me he had hurt himself more shaving, which was great. That took my mind right off it because if he wasn't worried, why should I be? I said I couldn't see anything out of my eye as there was too much blood in there and Rob just dismissed it as nothing serious, which was superb tactics. Rob was brilliant to have in my corner: he has done everything in the game and his help that night cooled me down when I needed it.

I got behind my jab in the last four rounds and used my right hand to get in some bombs of my own. Now and again Pascal would land a significant shot but, every time he did, I always felt I could hit him back with three or four of my own. Basically, my work-rate and accuracy were better than his. We had some great toe to toes in those rounds, smacking the shit out of each other. They were good, high-quality exchanges. In the latter rounds Pascal's legs were going a couple of times and I knew I had him. I couldn't really nail him until the later stages because he had such a good defence, but now I knew I was hurting him. I always finish strong, punching hard for the full twelve rounds, from first bell to last.

Straight after the final bell I had no doubts at all I had won it, none whatsoever. I could tell by the reaction of the crowd I had won and quite clearly.

It was a fairly wide victory for me, even though Pascal caught me with some belters. One of the judges made it 116–112, but I thought it was more conclusive than that.

The others made it 117–111 and 118–110, which I felt was about right. I think he might have nicked a couple of rounds out of the twelve but I had the rest. I'd fought a decent fight, even though I got caught more often than I'd have liked. Rob was telling me to tighten up, but basically I am the sort of fighter who is prepared to take a shot in order to get two or three of my own through. I think that is why I have been involved in two such fantastic match-ups with Pascal and Jermain Taylor. Looking back on the fight now, it was a great battle over twelve steaming rounds. I'm not convinced I got as much credit as I deserved at the time because Pascal was relatively unknown outside of boxing. But the fact that he went on to win the WBC world light-heavyweight title, beating Adrian Diaconu for the crown, shows just what a high-class fighter he is. Pascal then became the first boxer to beat 'Bad' Chad Dawson and I've not been remotely surprised at the success he has enjoyed in the ring after our battle.

When you are a puncher like me I think you have to be prepared to have a go and take a few on the chin yourself in return. When I was younger I wasn't so cocksure and I was a different sort of fighter, but after moving up to the pros I know my shots were hard enough. I might not be the next Julian Jackson, who according to Rob could punch like a mule, but I think my shots hurt fighters and they certainly hurt Pascal. When I hit anybody hard, it hurts them properly.

The bell went and my mum started crying in the ring. Anyone will tell you that when someone close to you starts bawling you never forget it. My mum was in bits because I'd finally won the world title. But even though I can remember that, there were interviews I did after the fight and the walk back from the ring that I can't recall at all. Even to this day it is all something of a blur. Fantastic isn't it? I'd won the world title and I can only remember about half of it!

I went to the after-show party at the Elewess Arms, a pub my mum used to own. One of my brothers bought me a pint of Guinness, but it didn't taste good. I had a few sips of it but I was very dehydrated and I didn't even get half way down the glass. I needed water. I had to do really shallow breathing to ease the pain on my ribs and after a short while I just wanted to go home.

I got back to my house and fell asleep for about an hour. I woke up very quickly but I couldn't get back to sleep. I dropped a few anti-inflammatory diclofenac pills and tried to go to sleep again, but it didn't really work. It was a bad night of getting up and down every hour or so, but the following morning I felt much better. The next day, as world champion, I took my family out for a meal. It was nice as we could all reflect on the whole event and talk about each other's perspective. I always like hearing my mum's version especially as she never comes into my changing room before any of my fights.

For the next few days, I tried to immerse myself in my properties. I did some tiling in the bathroom and I started building the new fireplace. I did the skirting boards after that. That's right. I was champion of the world and I was on my hands and knees doing a paint and grouting job!

The city of Nottingham held a civic reception in my honour a few months later. My entrance tune, Queen's 'We Will Rock

You', blared out across the council chambers. I ploughed through the heavy snow to get there for what was a cracking night as all my family and friends were in attendance as well as the ex-England and Nottingham Forest footballer Steve Hodge, who also grew up in Gedling.

I told the assembled crowd that I hadn't just won the world title for me, but the whole city of Nottingham. My mum also got a special mention. I think there were a few tears from her as I told her how special she was for bringing me into this world. I meant every word of that as well.

I have always been immensely proud of where I was born and brought up so when I was asked to help by the city council I jumped at it. The plan was to try and change Nottingham's image as the gun capital of Britain and I agreed to become an official ambassador for the city, which meant plenty of commercial and community work.

The honours continued to come thick and fast. I was made an Honorary Freeman of the Borough of Gedling, which was yet another very proud moment for this son of Nottingham. It means I can walk my sheep or carry my sword up to Mapperley Top, or something like that! A few days after beating Pascal I took my belt on to the pitch at the City Ground at the Nottingham Forest–Sheffield United game. Even the away supporters applauded so I must have been doing something right.

But all of the adulation and praise was put into context immediately after I had beaten Pascal. I was sitting in my dressing room after the fight when I was told Rob McCracken's mother Christine had died. I knew Rob's mum had been ill and in the couple of weeks leading up to the fight Rob was flitting between the training in Nottingham and Birmingham, where his mum lived. I was aware she was poorly, but I didn't know the extent of her illness.

On the morning of my world-title win, Rob had travelled over to Birmingham and was there when his mother died. In the build-up to the fight with Pascal he hadn't told me about what was happening as he didn't want to upset me before the biggest night of my life. That tells you all you need to know about the man. The fact that he was thinking of me, even when his mum was passing away, says everything you would ever need to know about Robert McCracken.

I look back on the night I beat Pascal now with one principal emotion: pride. I had done it. All those hours in the gym had been worth it. I also felt I had backed up everyone's belief in me, from my first trainers, my parents to my pals. They had all believed in me and I had done it. Nobody could ever take it away. I was a world champion.

CHAPTER 2

My surname, Froch, is a German name. I've looked it up on the internet and, as far as I can make out, there are no other Frochs in Britain, so if there is a Froch out there reading this, get in touch!

At some stage in the last century the Frochs must have moved from some part of Germany, where I am told they originated from, to Poland. My grandma Alexandra on my dad's side was from the Polish town of Tarnow and my paternal grandfather Wojciech – known to me and my brothers as William – was from Katowice in the south. Although both my grandparents came from Poland, they actually met at a boarding house in Derby sometime after the Second World War, both part of an exodus of Poles who came to Britain as their country had been flattened.

It came as a shock to discover that my grandfather was in Hitler's Nazi German army during the war. When the Germans invaded Poland, all those who could prove their German ancestry were told they had two choices: they could either join the army or be shot for being a traitor. My dad has told me his father didn't want to join up and had no interest at all in following Hitler or the Nazi party, but he was given that stark choice, and had no option but to join up.

It is weird to see pictures of my grandfather in his German uniform, and it was not a subject he was keen to talk about when he was alive. Granddad died in 1999 and all my dad has ever told me about his father's time in the war was that he had no wish to sign up for the invading Germans. All I know is that at the age of 21 he had to fight for the German army. He fought at some stage in the war in France and surrendered to the Americans on one of the beaches at Normandy during the D-Day landings. He eventually ended up at a prisoner-of-war camp in Scotland and when the war finished he went down to Ilkeston, where he found some work on a building site. Next he worked in a textile factory in Derby, which is where he met my grandma.

Grandma Alexandra was born in 1926, five years after my grandfather, in a little village called Lekawica, near the town of Tarnow, in Poland. All I know is she had a sister called Theodora and was from a very, very poor family. During the war, when Poland was invaded by the Germans, Alexandra was taken away from her family and went to Hanminden in Germany to work as a housemaid for a wealthy German couple, who had children, when the husband went off to fight.

After the war Alexandra made her way to England via a ferry which landed her in Harwich. She initially worked as a housemaid for two English ladies in West Bridgford and from there she went to work at a hospital in Nottingham. She was introduced to my grandfather through a Polish friend who lived in the same lodgings as William and they married in March 1951, living in a small terraced house in Nottingham.

My grandfather worked down the pit as a miner for twenty-seven years. Three months before he was set to retire and take his coal board pension he was spotted with a half-smoked cigarette in the lapel of his jacket. The manager caught him coming out of the lift and said, 'Because you've been smoking down there, you're fired.'

My grandfather had to work for years after finishing in the mines because he had no money at all. He didn't get his redundancy allowance or his pension and was left with nothing after twenty-seven years of hard labour. He did smoke, but never down the pit. He lost a mate down there when it caved in once so he knew how dangerous it was. Because he was Polish and wasn't very good at speaking English he was an easy target and couldn't easily defend himself. It was, for him, a bitter and unjust reward for all his years of service.

Many years ago my grandfather decided he wanted to go back to Eastern Europe to see one of his brothers (he had two brothers and two sisters), whom he had not seen for forty-seven years. My grandfather told my grandmother he had a big surprise for her, so he got the whole of the family together one Sunday afternoon, plonked his passport on the table and told them about his trip. My grandmother was shocked and couldn't believe it, but not half as shocked as when my grandfather placed another passport on the table:

hers. Grandma went wild and tried to tear up the passport, saying she would never go back to Poland again. She swore in front of the family that she wanted nothing to do with Poland because of her childhood, which I can only imagine must have been brutal.

My grandfather was determined to go ahead with the trip, so he caught a coach from Nottingham and found his brother somewhere in Germany. He rang my grandmother up after a couple of days and told her his brother had a couple of chickens and a tin bath in the living room, which he filled by boiling the kettle. He said, 'I want to come home' and promptly left.

As for my mum's side, her father came down from the north-east of England and worked at Gedling pit as a miner, just like my other granddad. Oswald Douglas, or 'Ossie', as everyone knew him, said the conditions there were awful at work, but that was the only regular employment available so he took it. My grandma Edith on my mum's side passed away only a few years ago of breast cancer. She very bravely fought it and eventually the cancer was beaten, but Grandma went into hospital for some treatment and caught septicaemia, which killed her.

They were fantastic grandparents and always looked after us boys. I was very close to my 'Nana Edith' and even to this day I miss her as she was so affectionate, helpful and lovable.

By all accounts Dad's upbringing with my grandparents was hard. They were strict Catholics and looking back on it now it is clear to see he rebelled, big time. My granddad used to hit him with an iron poker whenever he misbehaved and he got punished fairly often. He bashed him around on a regular basis and my dad first ran away when he was 14.

My dad Frank is a great bloke but he would be the first to admit he was a petty crook as a kid. He was always in trouble, although only for relatively minor crimes. Dad and his mates got caught for doing some fairly petty things as youngsters and the authorities, not half as lenient as they are today, finally had enough, so he got sent to borstal. He misbehaved in there, absconded, so they sent him to another more secure borstal, then it was prison. He was inside for minor stuff but because he kept absconding they kept increasing the punishment and eventually he ended up in the proper nick.

Throughout my dad's childhood and even when he was banged up he used to box and it is fair to say he was good at it, but he was far better at getting into scrapes than he was at fighting. Dad and his pals used to steal cars to go to Northern Soul dances all over Nottinghamshire and the East Midlands. He and his mates used to just nick a car and then drive it to clubs because they had no money at all. That was the only way they could have got there. He then did the odd robbery, mainly big factory warehouses. They got into one place and there was a load of cheques in this safe. Dad and his mates managed to get the safe out by pulling it out of the wall and they got it on to the roof. They chucked it on to the road but it embedded itself in the tarmac. By that stage Dad had an old Cortina, so he reversed his knackered old car over the safe. That worked. They emptied the safe of its contents and my dad and his mate then chucked it into the River Trent. So somewhere in the River Trent are the remains of a safe my dad broke open by driving a Cortina over it.

Dad was not very successful at being crooked and on one occasion he did a runner for about four days from one of his many penal institutions. He escaped with five other lads and ended up in Uxbridge, Middlesex, after nicking a car. The reason why they all went there was because one of the other inmates promised them some clothes and cash if they got him to his home in Uxbridge. Not exactly a master plan though, as my dad and the other escapees dropped the kid off near his house and that was the last they ever saw of him.

My dad decided to make his own way back to Nottingham and somewhere between Uxbridge and Nottingham he was walking along the side of a road when a car pulled up, with a police helmet visible on the dashboard, so dad dashed into some nearby woods and the police surrounded him. He knew the game was up so he sat down on an old tyre smoking a fag until the police found him and the great escape was over. The next day they took him back to Morton Hall borstal, in Lincolnshire.

When he was 18 Dad went to prison and did some time in loads of adult nicks, including the notorious Winson Green in Birmingham. He especially hated it in there and to this day says it was the most horrible six weeks of his life. He wasn't a proper criminal, just a confused, daft kid. He never did anything violent and he never robbed from houses, and his main crime was stealing cars to go to Northern Soul nights.

Being in prison eventually sorted him out, because he figured out he was on a downward spiral that would never end unless he started to think about getting a proper job. Dad used his time in the nick to work on his joinery skills and he continued to box. He had 20-something fights and he only ever lost one. He knocked out a lot of lads. He was, by all accounts, pretty good and it is a shame he didn't carry on.

My mum Carol is from Newcastle. She is a Geordie, although she hasn't got the accent as she left when she was very young. My granddad Ossie, on my mum's side, had a Newcastle accent, but my mum lost hers years ago I would imagine. She moved down to Nottingham when she was about four or five years of age. As I mentioned earlier, by an amazing coincidence her dad had a job in the Gedling pits, where he worked for many years. Strange, isn't it, that both my granddads worked at the same pit at the same time?

My parents met at a bowling alley in Nottingham city centre when Mum was 16 and Dad was 18. Mum had got a job there behind the counter doling out the shoes, while Dad used to fix the bowling machines. By all accounts they fancied each other for some time before Dad finally plucked up the courage to ask her out. My mum says she was warned off Frank, who had a reputation for being a bit of a toe-rag even then, but she ignored the warnings and they started dating properly.

In 2009, the bowling alley had a reopening as it had been refurbished so my mum and dad, despite being divorced many years ago, came along as I had been invited to do the honours at the official opening. The first person they met was an old bloke who had worked there for thirty-five years and instantly recognised them as Frank and Carol, the couple that got married so many years before.

My mum married Dad when he was inside and I remember (in fact, this is my earliest recollection of being a kid) going to the prison to visit him when I would have been 3 years old. Mum could not believe I could remember going, but years later I asked her if there was a park in the middle of the prison with a big climbing frame and she said yes, there was. She was amazed. I was barely out of nappies but I remembered it, possibly because she was crying and as a kid that would have stayed with me. I can recall it quite vividly.

What I also remember about going to see Dad in prison is knowing that he could not come back out with us. Prison sorted him out and he has never been in trouble since. Dad got his joinery qualifications and then he carried on boxing when he was let outside and in a way they both saved him. I have loads of newspaper cuttings, one that says 'Froch the Idol shows his power' from the *Nottingham Evening Post*. He knocked somebody out early on at Gedling miners' welfare and he was being talked about in local fighting circles.

While he was still in prison the authorities would let him out to box and he would try everything to spark out his opponent in the first round, so he could nip to the bar before the guards could get to him and have a few 'swifties'. He would have a skin-full in a very short amount of time then go back to prison and breathe on his cellmate to wind him up. My mum used to find out where he was boxing so she could go and meet up with him after he had fought.

From my earliest days I can always remember Dad used to train in the garage, where he would have a bag hanging from the ceiling. It wasn't anything flash, just a big bag full of sand. I think I would have been about eight years old and I would just hit the bag like a lunatic for hours on end. Dad showed me how to hit and I would ask, 'How do you do that?' I used to just swing at it as hard as I could, with no technique to speak of.

For whatever reason, maybe to toughen me up a bit, or maybe just because my dad was good at boxing, he took me and my elder brother, Lee, down to the local boxing club, the Phoenix ABC on Burton Road. I would have been nine years old and I loved it. I boxed down there for a few years before I could actually get in the ring and compete, but that didn't really bother me because two or three times a week I would get my kit bag and walk to the Phoenix and be a boxer.

Lee, who is two years older than me, wanted to fight as well and I remember him coming back one day crying his eyes out because he failed his medical to box. The doctors found astigmatism in his eye so he was banned from fighting. My mum has the same problem and that was enough to fail him. When I was going for my medical years later I was worried sick that I would fail it and I wouldn't be able to box, but fortunately I passed it with no problems.

When I was first at the Phoenix I was coached by a really friendly man Ray Windress but eventually, after maybe a year, he left the club and Dale McPhilbin took over for the rest of my junior bouts. Later I was trained by a combination of Dale and Dominic Travis through three ABA finals and the World Amateur Championships. I suppose the best way I can describe those early days is that I found boxing easy. I was very much a natural from day one. I had a lot of respect for my elders as I had been brought up in a home where there was discipline from my parents. Step out of line and I got whacked, simple as that. So I just did what I was told and got on with it. I enjoyed it, probably because I was good at it and I knew I was good at it, but when it came to taking instructions I would listen carefully and try my best. Of course, Dale and Dominic had to coach me certain things, but they have always told me I was an easy kid to teach. For the record, I won far more often than I lost and eventually ended up with an amateur record of 88–8. I won a stack of kids' competitions in places like Worksop, Leicester and Gainsborough and I even reached the quarter-finals of a national schoolboys' tournament.

I used to really enjoy going to the gym and the routine was twice during the week and once on Sundays. I never used to miss it because I was always really excited about going down to the Phoenix, which was, and still is, a very friendly club. It was never a chore for me. Whereas some kids have fads that last a few weeks, I stuck with boxing for years and years because it was so enjoyable and I used to love whacking away at the bags.

Unlike my brother, I passed my medical and at eleven years of age I made my debut against Radford's Jason Booth. Yes, Jason 'Too Smooth' Booth, a future British super-bantamweight champion and a top performer in the pro ranks. So good in fact he fought for a version of the world title in 2010, losing a close one on points to the Canadian Steve Molitor. It's incredible to think that the first fight I ever had as a little scrawny kid was against another little scrawny kid, and that we would both go on to make a success of the fight game in the pros twenty years later.

CHAPTER 3

At the age of six my world changed dramatically when, like so many others unfortunately do these days, my parents' marriage started to come apart. I can remember them arguing and splitting up, but then a few weeks later they got back together again. I recall the feeling of relief that it was all over, but this reconciliation was to prove short-lived, and they separated properly soon after that. Wayne was only a baby at the time, so he can't remember anything about the split, but Lee and I would stay up at night, listening to my mum and dad arguing about what was going to happen and where we were going to live. It was horrible, but at that age you don't really know what it means. My overriding memory is being sad, because I was close to both my parents and loved being with them.

It was my mum who finally left the house. Her leaving is not a vivid recollection, more vague, but I don't think any kid that age would ever forget the hurt caused by your parents moving apart. The agreement was that I live with Dad during the week and went to see Mum at the weekend. I think my parents felt we were settled in our various schools and therefore the easiest and most sensible option was for us to carry on living with Dad in the same house. As she left, my mum told me not to worry because she would always be there for us three boys – Lee, Wayne and me – and that if there was anything I ever needed from her, I only had to ask. I suppose looking back on it now it was clear that my parents weren't enjoying each other's company, so it was the right thing to do. But at the time, it was hard to take. All boys miss their mother and I was no different. I didn't cry myself to sleep every night, or at least I can't remember doing so, but I am sure there would have been tears, even though Dad was always a good parent. Over the years the three of us boys stayed together pretty much the whole time, which is a compliment to my mum and dad, who tried to make sure we had as 'normal' an upbringing as possible, despite their decision to split. We all went to the same schools and stuck together, which might explain why we are so close now, because we grew up a tight-knit family, despite my parents' parting of the ways.

Thankfully, when my parents split, they did it on fairly friendly terms and now, with the passage of time, they are great with each other. Over the years they have met at boxing shows when I have fought, and they and their respective partners have always got on really well. It wasn't always that amicable and for a while both sides weren't talking to each other, but thankfully those days are well over.

While Wayne was a long way behind us in terms of age, everything Lee had, I wanted. That's what it is like when you are a kid. We scrapped and argued every day, even when I followed him and went to my first school, St John the Baptist Primary School in Colwick. We were rough, tough kids and our dad brought us up like that.

Wayne used to cop the worst of it because he was so young. We would play fight with him, and sometimes quite heavily. We wouldn't do anything like bash him up and hit him in the face, but we would get him in a headlock and squeeze him until he started crying. It always ended in fits of temper and tears and looking back on it now, we were probably too rough with him. He is now a pretty hard, strong-willed bloke himself and I am sure that's one of the reasons.

My dad, a bit like his dad, was very tough and strict with us, but we always had a laugh. Maybe some of it was for his own amusement, I don't know, but we always had fun with my dad even though, boys being boys, it used to end up in tears on a regular basis. I loved just messing about with my dad, who would have made a world champion at mucking about in the outdoors.

Dad used to regularly take us to Colwick Hall when it was dark. It was an old wreck of a church and Dad would jump over the wall with the rest of us and take us into this creepy old building. Then he would do a runner. We couldn't get out of there because the gates were too high and he had helped us over them. He would come back five minutes later, creeping up behind us and shouting, 'Boo'. Maybe that's why I was so scared of the dark as a kid. Dad would find it all hilarious, scaring the pants off his boys, but at the time it used to give me the creeps.

Dad was always a big one for going outside and messing about. From a very early age he would take us into the woods at Colwick and we would spend a day making bows and arrows. He would cut a five-foot branch off a tree, an inch thick, and make a really good bow. He would screw the string into the bow and he was good at it. So from the age of about 5 years old we would make bows. Dad would bring along a load of canes as make-shift arrows and make an arrow-head around the end with a nail or screw, using insulation tape to secure the head. We would then start firing into the trees and from fifty yards these things were lethal. I remember not having the strength to be able to take the arrow-head out of the tree: they were that effective.

Dad would do crazy things like shooting them directly above us in the air and shouting, 'Run!' The amount of times the arrow would come down about five yards away from us all was countless, and again, it would scare the wits out of me and my brothers. Dad would never let us get hurt, but there was always an element of fear amongst all three of us. Which is probably why we loved mucking about with my dad so much, because all kids love being scared a little.

Another thing Dad liked doing would be to get his three boys on to a big wheel in the playground in the woods, but unlike other parents, who might be fairly gentle, he would spin it around like a mad thing, until we all fell off and couldn't stand up because we were so dizzy. On the see-saw he would bang it down so one of us would come flying off, but even though all these things sound a bit daft, he always looked after us and I never ever hurt myself badly playing with my dad.

I was always in the shed building things like go karts. I was mad keen on building anything and my dad and brothers would go into the woods to test things out. We would also make rope swings and build campfires in the woods. In the summer, we would camp out for the night, even though we were little boys, and cook baked potatoes and beans. We were like Rambo! I don't think we always stayed out all night as mostly we would come back in late at night, but on other occasions we would sleep under the stars.

There are some clay cliffs in Colwick Woods and I had a bad fall in there one day, which just shows how fearless I was back then. It was a fifty-foot drop. Lee and I went down there and I climbed up the side of the cliff. I was coming back down when I grabbed hold of a bit of a root, which came loose. I hit the side of the cliff and did a back somersault, landing on the back of my head. I cried my eyes out and thought I was about to die, before my brother came running over and took me home, hobbling back and feeling sorry for myself. Believe me, the side of a cliff does hurt if you land on it with your head.

One time my dad brought home these pellet guns, which, as you can imagine, to a kid is like heaven on earth. They only shot little pellets, like the ones you use at fairgrounds to hit the moving ducks, but naturally the boys all ended up shooting each other. They could take your eye out if you were not careful – and we were definitely not careful – so how one of us didn't get seriously hurt I'll never know. Dad used to come with us sometimes and we would play for hours, him giving us twenty seconds to run away before coming to find us with the pellet gun. If he caught up with you it would certainly hurt but you would be crying as well as laughing at the same time because of the thrill of the chase.

Name me a kid who doesn't love being chased and we were no different. Most of the time we would just shoot tomato cans on our own little gun range, but every now and again Dad would cock the gun and say 'Go on, you use it.' I'd then shoot Wayne on his backside and we would roll around laughing for what seemed like hours. Poor Wayne, being the youngest, often got the rough end of the stick.

Mind you, my dad tied me to a tree on one occasion and left me. Whether I had been cheeky or not I don't know, but my dad tied me to this big conker tree in Colwick Woods then said he was leaving. Of course, I thought it was all a joke at first, but then he didn't return. I started shouting and screaming for him, getting really scared, but Dad went round in a big circle and came up behind me. To say I was relieved would be an understatement, but I also found it funny. Eventually, anyway.

Another time my brother Wayne and his best mate Damien were messing around with the gun one night when the police came. Armed police appeared because somebody had rung the cops up and said there were some men in Colwick Woods with guns. The police shouted through a megaphone to place the gun down and put their hands on their heads. Dad replied that he was only in the woods messing around with his kids and there was no drama. The police, though, weren't having any of it. They continued to bark out these orders for them to all put their hands on their heads and for Dad to drop the gun. Dad didn't have a great deal of respect for the law in those days, having been banged up, so he shouted out, 'Are you lot just plain stupid? I'm here with my boys just messing about.'

Whatever the police tried, it didn't work because Dad, being a bit bolshie, just refused to put his gun down. He knew the police weren't going to shoot him and they could see his boys were with him. And if you wanted to practise firing real guns, you would choose somewhere a lot more private than Colwick Woods.

Dad kept hold of his gun. One of the policeman put his arm up his shoulder and it looked like he was going to get arrested. Dad, cool as you like, said, 'Look. I'm here with my boys just mucking about and as you can see it is just a pellet gun. Why doesn't everyone just calm down? This is nothing. We haven't just robbed a bank.' My dad was quite good at arguing his corner. I think the police knew all along that it was only going to be a training exercise for them because you'd have to be daft to shoot real guns in the suburbs of a big city, but it gave them a chance to wear all their gear and to pretend it was a real drama.

I stayed with my dad in Colwick until I turned 11 and went to senior school. Then I moved in with my mum because she lived nearer my new school. I went to Gedling Comprehensive School, and as Lee was already there it made sense for us both to live with my mum and walk to school together. That was hard for me because all my mates, every single one of them, from St John's went to Carlton le Willows Comprehensive, whereas I moved to Gedling, so when I landed at Gedling I knew absolutely nobody.

That's not quite true: I did know one kid. Nicky Roach was someone I nearly had a fight with one day at Victoria Leisure Centre. Who knows what the disagreement was about, but a few months before I started at Gedling Comp, we had a row which nearly came to fisticuffs. We were in the changing rooms and I think I spent a bit too much time looking at his skin colour. You see, I just didn't know any black or mixed-raced kids at school, so I was probably quite intrigued. He asked me what I was looking at, then we both puffed our chests out and had a bit of a stand-off. When I got to Gedling, Nicky came up to me and said, 'I know you. You're that kid from the Victoria who wants a fight.' I remembered him as well, but from that day on we were mates. We clicked straight away and spent hours on the bikes together and mucking around.

When I moved to live with my mum, she would get us boys around the settee and watch TV shows like *Bullseye* and 'Dusty Bin'. I remember not seeing my dad as much as I wanted to and that hurt. There were longish periods of time when I didn't see my dad and I often missed him. While my dad has always had a daft streak, my mum Carol is a very caring, affectionate person. To be honest, she spoilt us a bit, always getting her boys whatever it was they wanted. She would think nothing about getting an extra job in order to pay for her kids to have something nice. Mum worked at a pet care shop for years as well as behind the bars and Lee, Wayne and I very quickly sussed her out. We knew from a very early age that if we asked for something and kept the pressure on long enough, she would come up with the goods. Putty in our hands, she was.

I got new roller skates, a radio-controlled car, and all the things she probably couldn't afford. When Mum bought the little car, the shop wouldn't take her cheque without a guarantee card, so I had to wait there while Mum popped around to the bank to get the cash. I remember Wayne getting an Amiga 500 computer, the bee's knees, whereas I only had a Commodore 64. Being a kid, I wasn't really keen on waiting for the upgrade, so I pestered my mum even though she had only just bought me the Commodore. She argued that I had to make do with what I had got, but I played up so much I got one. Yes, I was spoilt, but you don't appreciate the worth of things when you are a kid.

I was a mixture of a lot of things at school. I had no interest in girls until much, much later. I was just a small, skinny kid with a ridiculously high-pitched voice until I was about 16 or 17. All my mates when I was about 14 seemed to have hairy chests and beards, whereas I was just a skinny youngster. When I moved to Gedling Comp, the only thing I was happy about was that you didn't have to have a shower after games. I was conscious that I was a late developer and hadn't started sprouting any hair anywhere other than the top of my head.

At 16, when my mates were going out trying to get into pubs underage I didn't do any of that for two reasons. Firstly, I wouldn't have got into a pub in a million years and secondly I had developed a fascination with motorbikes.

As well as the boxing, I became seriously obsessed with motorbikes in my teens. As usual, I knew the short-cut to getting a bike, namely my mum. My first road bike was a Kawasaki AR50 – but with an 80cc engine, so it was pretty fast. My mum eventually bought me my dream bike, a motocross KX80. It was my pride and joy. I would fill up a can of two-stroke petrol for about forty pence and then push the bike all the way through Gedling, on to wasteland in Colwick. It is an industrial park and shopping centre with the likes of Morrisons and B&Q now, but back then it was just an area of waste ground. Pushing my bike there took some doing and it was definitely knackering. I knew, though, that if I rode it on the main road I would have my little motocross bike taken off me.

The wasteland was brilliant for motor-biking as there would be ramps and turns all over the place. During the week, on Tuesdays and Thursdays, I would be boxing down the gym, but every weekend I was down there with the bike.

I would polish my bike all the time and keep it in great nick. I used to race others who had similar bikes to me, which was great fun. Bearing in mind this was a proper racing bike and could easily do about 60 m.p.h., you can see that I could have done myself plenty of damage, especially as the bike was bigger than me. I used to do some ridiculously big jumps, but back then I had no fear.

I only ever fell off really badly once. My friend Wayne Clothier, who passed away a few years ago in a car crash, was on the back at the time. As I did a jump in the air, he slipped off the back seat and starting grabbing me, pulling me off with him. We landed awkwardly and I cut my arm pretty badly. It was the only time when I needed stitches after a bike crash, but it was a small price to pay for all the fun I had.

Nowadays you can't do this sort of thing any longer. The health and safety brigade stopped it and you are not allowed to ride motorbikes on wasteland like I did.

But I have never stopped loving my bikes. I got my first road bike when I was 16 and in my garage now is a superbike, a Honda CBR 600RR. I have had it for a couple of years and I've only done about 500 miles on it. It does 0–60 m.p.h. in about three seconds! Funnily enough, years later when I joined the 'Super Six World Boxing Classic' I was flown into New York and spent a lot of time talking to Mikkel Kessler, who also loves his bikes. I am sure we spent a lot more time comparing bikes than we did talking about boxing.

I would genuinely describe my childhood as happy, although like all kids I had my ups and downs. There are gaps in my memory and grey areas, probably because the older you get the more you try and forget the bad days.

Growing up in Nottingham and being around my usual friends was a generally happy time, even though my parents had divorced. But all that was about to change: I was about to undergo a massive upheaval. It was one that I hated at the time and would also result in me giving up boxing.

CHAPTER 4

In my teens I went through a phase that I now call the wilderness years. My mum started in the pub trade when I was 14½, turning 15, and that's when I started to lose interest a bit in boxing. Not overnight, just over a few months. What happened was Mum moved to Newark, thirty miles up the road from Nottingham, for her first investment in the pub trade and took us three boys with her. Before that, Mum worked in various shops and factories and always made a living, but when she got offered the pub in Newark along with a friend of hers, she jumped at the chance of running the Plough Inn. My mum has always been very much a working-class girl and I think the opportunity to own her own business, as it were, was too tempting. Fair play to her though for taking the risk and, as events proved, she was to be a damned good landlady. She has a very warm personality and that's why she adapted so well to a new job. It was the first time we had left Nottingham and, even though the distance to our home city in miles was tiny, it could have been on the other side of the world. The Phoenix gym, which had been two minutes around the corner from our old house, had really become part of my life. The boxing club in Newark was completely different, it was literally a shed in the middle of a field. I had been spoilt with a full-size ring, loads of bags, wooden floors and a heating system that worked. The Newark club was nothing like that, and was a ten- to fifteen-minute drive away from where I lived: that was a pain in the backside. To make matters worse, my school, Grove Comprehensive, was new, living in a pub was new and all of a sudden I started playing pool, cards and the fruit machines instead of going down the gym.

The Newark boxing club was pretty crap, with no heating and lots of travellers down there who were always nicking your bike. They hung around in gangs outside and wanted to beat you up: not for any particular reason, just to have a fight. It was horrible and I stopped enjoying going training. I remember sparring with Esham Pickering and Carl Greaves while I was there, as both came from that area. They went on to do really well as pros, but I think I only boxed about two amateur fights out of the Newark club before I really began to give it up. My last two years at school were OK, but I did hardly any homework, paid very little attention and even though I ended up with nine GCSEs, most of the grades were Ds and Es. They could and should have been much better. I was never an unruly kid, but it was easy to skive off for a day or two here and there. Obviously that means your education suffers and mine did.

At school in Newark I never harboured any genuine thoughts of being a professional sportsman, although at one stage, as I got heavily into snooker, I wanted to be the next Steve Davis. All I knew was that I always wanted my job to be something that I loved doing. I was very sporty as a kid, and not just with the boxing. I would get stuck in playing anything from rounders to rugby. I was small, skinny and light and used to get flattened by the bigger lads on the rugby pitch, though I always scored a few tries. I was about five foot three inches tall until I was 17. Then I suddenly shot up. At a young age though I couldn't punch the skin off a rice pudding and maybe that's another one of the reasons why I gave up boxing at 15.

There was an almighty scrap in my mum's Newark pub one evening, which underlines what a rough area it was. Wayne, even as a kid, was brilliant at pool and snooker and would regularly beat the adults, even though he was only just about tall enough to play.

I was 15 and Wayne 11 when he cleared up one night against this bloke who fancied himself as a hard man. The next thing we know, the man has got Wayne on the pool table and is trying to take his trousers down, just to bring him down a peg or two. Wayne tried to push him off, but he had half his pants down and the bloke was pinning his head against the pool table, just because he had lost a game of pool to a cheeky kid. Then his other mate started to pour a pint of beer down Wayne's ear hole. Some of the beer went down Wayne's throat and he started choking.

I wasn't having that. I got the bloke by his shoulder and turned him around. I told him to get off my little brother but he grabbed hold of me and pushed me up against the wall.

I managed to let out a little wail as I was being choked and that's when Mum and Nana kicked into action. My grandma, Nana Edith, who is no longer alive, jumped on his back and stuck her fingers in his eyeballs. My mum then started to whack him. He was a big man, but he'd bitten off more than he could chew and eventually he let me go, mouthing a few obscenities about how he was going to burn the place down and beat the shit out of us all using his Newark muscle mates. Just to show how tough he was taking on an 11-year-old kid he put his fist through a window. My mum didn't let him get away with it. She punched him in the face and he went down on one knee. It was a solid right hook and I remember thinking, 'That's it, Mum, smack him!' He knew enough not to hit a woman, and a landlady, and left quietly, minus his pride.

We got that a lot in Newark. Because we were from out of town, we would regularly get punters saying they 'owned' this part of the county and what they said was the law. The incident involving Wayne pretty much finished the pub off because the locals decided to make our place off limits. They told all their mates that Mum's pub was now no longer to be used and sure enough, as the weeks went by, fewer and fewer people started to come in. All because one bloke lost a game of pool to a little skinny kid. It was downhill from that point and business was never as good.

By this point, I had pretty much given up on boxing. I finished school at 16 and moved back to Nottingham with Wayne, who also went back to Gedling Comp to finish his schooling, while Mum stayed in Newark for two more years.

I applied and got into Clarendon College in Nottingham to do a one-year business and finance course. I still use a lot of those skills to this day. Mind you, my lack of attention in class also came back to bite me on the arse as, years later, I applied to join the police force and got turned down as my letter was littered with spelling mistakes. During the course I lived with my late nana Edith and late step-granddad Brian. I really enjoyed her company and we would just sit down with the TV off and talk about anything and everything. I miss her to this day. Brian also taught me the basics of how to play the guitar and I still do a pretty mean version of Johnny Cash. Brian even left me his guitar in his will.

When I was 17, my mum bought me a car and I started picking my mates up, going here, there and everywhere, just looking for a bit of fun. We never got in any real trouble, but we did get up to some daft stuff!

Mind you, every time my dad came around he always badgered me about going back into boxing. He would never let up. Every time I met him, the first thing he would ask was whether I'd been back to the gym. He would tell me what I wanted to hear, saying I was so good at it I had to go back into boxing, but for whatever reason, I just drifted. I didn't go back to the gym. Something was holding me back, maybe just being a teenager. I suppose I started to think that I would carry on in the pub trade. My mum was earning a living in pubs and it crossed my mind that maybe I should go in that direction as well. For a total of four years I helped out my mum and, as such, working in the pub trade began to become something of an option. Did I wake up sometimes in the morning and think 'What am I getting up for?' Yes, I did. It would have been very easy for me to carry on like that, but there was always something nagging away at me, telling me there was more to life than this. I always knew that sort of life wasn't what I wanted. It wasn't good enough for me. I knew sitting around doing nothing constructive wasn't going to get me anywhere. I was never depressed, or down, but I did get to the point where I thought, I have got to do something about this because no one else will. I'm a big believer in making the most out of yourself. I could have either sat back and thought how crap my life was or I could do something about it. I was definitely in a rut at that time but I had a set of bollocks and I wanted to change my life. Only it took a while for that to happen and it eventually came through boxing. Bearing in mind I am a very focused and forceful person now, it's fair to say I have changed an awful lot since I was a youngster.

I tried for various jobs and eventually settled at a metal works company. I was an office kid, good with figures. I worked there while doing my business and finance course and got paid a tiny sum through the Youth Training Scheme. Unfortunately the business went bust and that was that.

I was made redundant at around the same time that my mum moved back to Nottingham in the pub business. She moved around Nottingham and a few places on the outskirts of the city to plenty of pubs, but the first pub she had in the city itself was the Rose and Crown and I moved in with her. Home was now a room above the pub.

The Rose and Crown, on Alfreton Road in Basford, was in an especially tough part of Nottingham: the area was rife with drugs. Needless to say I got involved in some scrapes even though I was just a tall and skinny 17-year-old kid. Not that I ever went looking for trouble: I just wasn't one to back down. The Rose and Crown was a run-down boozer that the owners wanted cleaned up. My mum was really good at this side of the pub business: she would go in, tidy the place up, get a pool and darts team going and try to turn the place around. She would upset a few of the locals by barring the rowdy ones, but it was all in an effort to sort the pub out and make it more welcoming.

On one occasion, I was working behind the bar when a bloke came into the pub, slapped a pound coin down and asked for a bottle of Castaway, an alcopop drink. I told him it cost £1.50, but he wasn't really looking at me, just around the bar, like he was casing the joint. When I said again that he didn't have the right amount of money, he suddenly pulled out a knife. It was shaped like a kind of mini-scythe and, as I could tell he'd had a few drinks, I wasn't going to ask him nicely to put it away. I picked up a long bar stool with four metal legs. We stood there looking at each other, him with his knife and me with my bar stool. I think he was trying to suss out whether I would use it. Believe me, I wouldn't have had any hesitation. Anyway, after a ten-second stand-off, he legged it and I was £1 up on the day.

The Rose and Crown was in a naughty area and I remember thinking, I can't believe a bloke has just pulled a knife on me for wanting a pineapple alcopop. I'm convinced he was in there just trying to rob the place and was building up the courage to do so. But his plans went a bit wrong the minute this pencil-thin kid asked him for the right money.

On another occasion, it was a fairly busy Friday night, and this guy, clearly off his face on drink or drugs or both, kept trying to get his knob out in front of these four women. He was so off his head, he tried it time and again. My step-dad Steve barred him and, after a bit of a jostle, he went outside with his mates.

Ten minutes after he left, some of the women went outside for some reason or other. I was looking outside the window, when I could see this bloke throwing shots. Sure enough, when I poked my head around the corner it was a scene of carnage. The guy had already knocked two of the women over and he was winding up to flatten another. I saw him punching this girl in the face and she then fell on the floor, next to two of her mates. He was beating the crap out of these women.

I shouted at him and he started coming forward towards me. I put my guard up and got into my boxing stance, even though I hadn't boxed properly for years. The bloke did the same thing, but he started doing it in a comical way, mocking me by taking big jumps from side to side. He was taking the piss, so I went bang with a jab. His head went back and a cut appeared above his eye. I thought it was a cracking shot and hoped that might be the end of it. No such luck. As he came back again I hit him with another jab and a right hand. He was a big bloke, probably about six foot two, and he had walked through both of my best shots.

I kept jabbing him but eventually he got me in a bear hug and rammed me against the pub wall. I could see my younger brother Wayne inside the pub with his best mate Damien at the first floor window laughing their heads off, watching me in a proper fight. Then Steve came out and, seeing what was happening, ran back inside to press the panic button for the police to come. I was still up against the wall, when my pal Nicky Roach, who I hung around with a lot in those days, shouted my nickname 'Froggy, Froggy.' The bloke let go of me and looked at Nicky, so I took my chance and whacked him with the kitchen sink, a right-hander, followed by a left and another right, which finally sent him down. He deserved it. He had been beating up these girls and that I can't stand. I am not a fan of bullying of any kind.

One of my right-handers had connected with his ear and blood had started coming out. As he lay on the floor I could have finished him off, but I have never, ever done that when someone is down. I just think it is the wrong thing to do. If someone's on the deck, kicking them is bad news. So I left him alone and he got up. He looked at me and ran. All his mates left as well. I thought that was the end of it, but the bloke only got as far as the kebab house about 100 yards up the road, where he collapsed. He was drugged and pissed out of his brain and he fell, lying in the middle of the main road. The police came but I went upstairs and cleaned myself up. Everyone scarpered off, although two of the girls were in a bad way, bleeding all over the place. They went to hospital and the bloke was picked up by the police and spent a night in the cells.

This was by far not the only ding-dong I had at the Rose and Crown. Another time, I was pulling out of the pub in my battered old knacker of a car, trying to pull into my mum's car park space at the side of the pub. I held up the traffic for my mum to come out, but then this bloke appeared in his car and started honking his horn. I tried to point out to him, by lifting my finger, that I would be one minute. He honked his horn again, this time a lot more aggressively. So I gave him another finger, this time the middle one. Next thing I know he gets out of his car with a steel baseball bat. Nowadays I would think, 'Shit, I should be a bit careful here,' but back then it was very different. I thought, 'The cheeky bastard' so I got out of my car and ran towards a rubbish skip next to the pub, where I picked up a half-broken pool cue.

I had a lot of front back then, so as he stood there with a baseball bat, I went up to him and starting swinging the cue at him, trying to show him I meant business. Sure enough, he dropped his bat and ran, leaving his car running in the middle of the road. My stepdad Steve gave chase and it was quite comical as he was soon chased back towards me by three blokes who came out of a restaurant that the driver's family owned. I thought, the odds aren't good here. My dad had always told me, if you can talk your way out of a fight, that is always the best option. So I picked up the baseball bat and said to these guys, 'Look, I don't know what is crack-ing off here, but I am just trying to get my car into my mum's space. She runs the pub here.' I gave them the baseball bat back as a sign that I was backing off and within about five seconds it was all over. The guy even apologised, saying, 'I've had a bad day, sorry.'

Another time I was working behind the bar and these three blokes, all in their late thirties and smartly dressed, were being really hostile. They started moving over to the pool table and, every time I looked over to watch them, I could tell there was something about to kick off. People who work in the pub trade say they can spot trouble a mile off. It is just experience I suppose, and to me these guys spelt trouble.

One of them slammed a pint down on the bar, really loudly. Then another said, 'Can we have the keys for the pool table as we want a free game?' I explained that it was fifty pence for a game of pool, same as for everyone else in the pub. I offered to give them change. The bloke said there was nobody else in the pub, so why couldn't they have a free game. Then one of them said something to Lee under his breath that was fairly nasty and we knew there was going to be a scene. I phoned my stepdad Steve up and told him to get down to the pub sharpish.

Steve was about ten minutes away in Gedling, so when one of the blokes starting swinging his cue around his head really aggressively, it was down to me and Lee until he arrived. I took my watch off and tied my shoelaces up really tight. Whenever I thought I was going to be in a battle I always did the same thing: the watch came off and the shoelaces were tightened! I didn't want to damage my watch and I always thought there couldn't be anything worse than your shoe coming off in the middle of a fight. Pretty strange I know.

The three men had another pint. Steve came in and said, 'You, you and you. You're barred.' He picked the biggest one of them up and literally threw him out. Steve pulled the cue out of their hands and that was it: the whole situation was defused in about twenty seconds. Like the guy with the alcopop, I really don't know what they were up to. They were probably casing the joint to rob it and to test the strength of the opposition. Anyway, when push came to shove they bottled it and I was delighted about that.

I was still pretty aimless at this time. I used to buy Kinder eggs all the time and put the toys in a row in my bedroom. This is how my life had turned out! I would go in the gym in the morning with my elder brother Lee, come back and go and buy a Kinder egg. This routine happened every day. That's how bored I was back then.

My mum moved to another pub thirty miles from Nottingham, at a place called Swadlincote in south Derbyshire. The Granville Arms in Swadlincote was a tough pub in a tough part of the world, where the mining industry had once ruled. There were a fair number of nutters in the town all looking for aggro. Pretty much every day there were people smoking drugs out the back so I'd have to tell them to stop. On other occasions they wouldn't want to leave at drinking-up time. Often the punters would say, I'll finish it when I'm ready, so there was always tension in the air.

Anyway, on this one occasion my mum was on the phone upstairs, when this bloke, in his late twenties and with a couple of mates, tried to make a call on the pub phone. He didn't realise that my mum being on the phone meant he couldn't make a call, as they used the same connection line. He was pissed, or off his head on something, and was trying to order a taxi. I looked over and could see he was getting more and more irate.

He started swearing and I told him he would have to wait two minutes because my mum was on the phone. He began to hurl a bit of abuse my way, so I was short with him as well. Next thing I know he is starting to threaten me, telling me to come over to this side of the bar, and let's sort it out. He told me I was from out of town and that he 'ran' Swadlincote. Then he aimed a pretend gun at me and said, 'I'll shoot you between the eyes if you mess with me.'

I walked out the swing door from behind the bar to get out to the main drinking area and as I got there he threw a massive haymaker towards me. Needless to say, he missed by about three yards. I ducked and whacked him with a big right hand myself and his legs buckled. One of my brothers booted him up the arse and he fell on to the floor. He was down there on the deck and, again, I couldn't hit him while he was defenceless. It's just not my way.

The bloke got up, but he was OK, even though he was bleeding heavily from his nose. I sat him up on a bar seat and he looked at me and said, 'So, do you do a bit of boxing then? That was quick, I didn't even see the punch coming.' I told him that I did use to box, but had given it up a few years before. I wasn't going to make any small talk as he had just gone for me, so I said he was barred and had to leave. He looked a bit pathetic as he asked if I had anything for his nose, so I gave him a beer towel to stop the blood going all over the place.

From 17 to 19 I lived at my mum's various pubs with my younger brother Wayne, with Lee sometimes also in tow. I used to write Wayne letters to his school to get him out of class. I was like his dad. He always used to tell me I was dead strict because I always told him he had to be back in bed by 10 p.m.

My brothers back then were a major part of my life and they are to this day. I'll try and describe them as best I can. For starters, Lee and Wayne are very different. They were different back when we were kids and they are different now. Lee is a Gemini. If you don't know what that means, I'll explain. Lee is a soft, lovable bloke, who is very loving and very generous but, if you cross him, he is like an elephant: he never forgets. That, apparently, is a classic Gemini trait. There are two sides to Lee, the good and the bad. He will do anything for anyone but if he catches anyone yanking his chain, he will cut them off.

From day one when I went back into boxing, Lee was always my number-one fan. He wouldn't miss a fight for anything. He would help promote it and nothing would be too much trouble, getting a thousand tickets off Mick Hennessy and moving heaven and earth to sell them. Lee told anybody who would listen I was going to be Nottingham's world champion so they had to be there. Lee worked his knackers off to get my name out there and even to this day I know how grateful I am for his efforts.

Lee has always been the softest one of the three of us. I would have been six years old and Lee eight when we sat down one day and watched *King Kong*. At the end of the film when the stuffed gorilla falls off the skyscraper to his death, I looked around and Lee was crying his eyes out. I thought it was all a bit silly, because quite clearly we weren't talking about a real fifty-foot gorilla here, but a fake. But Lee was inconsolable. He cried for a good few minutes and even though Mum told him time and again it was only a story, that didn't do any good at all. He just cried some more.

Mum always says I have got a heart of stone, whereas Lee would blubber over anything. I don't know about that but when Lee split up from his first proper girlfriend, the tears flowed again. That is Lee. There is definitely a bit of a split personality going on. He is someone who is not afraid to show his emotions, but cross him and he will never ever forget. Lee is a grafter and he owns his own building business, which means we spend a lot of time together. I wouldn't have it any other way. His wedding in Cuba in 2009 to Emma was a fantastic occasion, especially because the family all spent some time together.

Wayne could not be more chalk and cheese compared to Lee. When I was growing up, Wayne was always the little kid brother. He is a lot more reserved than Lee and I, and he keeps himself to himself. When he was little I used to beat him up all the time. It was only play fighting but it would always go too far and eventually Wayne would end up crying his eyes out. He was a mini-Bart Simpson, always into trouble and basically just a toe-rag. He has grown up to be a great bloke and is very reliable and hard-working. He gets the job done. Whereas Lee is something of an open book, you never really know what Wayne is thinking. He was the same as a little boy and he is the same now. I love both of my brothers equally and we are very close. We were close as kids and we are close now and I'm thankful it will always be that way.

As a kid I didn't really get into any major trouble, but there were a few fights here and there. At the weekend, on Fridays and Saturdays, I used to work like a dog at a nightclub in central Nottingham called Pieces. I worked from 10 p.m. to 3 a.m. on the third floor. I would have to go down to the cellar with all the beer then walk up with crates of the stuff. It certainly improved my fitness levels! After the club closed you had to sweep the whole place, clear the toilets out and stock the bar up. I did all that for £20 a night: in other words, £40 a weekend, which at the time seemed like a lot of money. In fact, it was bloody hard work for very little pay.

During these years, my mates would be going out clubbing and drinking and yet I always had a bit of a problem. I never looked anything like 18. I couldn't get in anywhere because I looked about 13. It meant I couldn't really get into clubs as the doorman would clock me straight away so I didn't even try and anyway, while some of my mates were big drinkers who loved a pint, I was never really that interested in booze. On the day I turned 18, I was asked for ID by a shop owner while buying a lottery ticket. I told him I was 18 that day, but I certainly didn't look it, even though I could prove it.

I started to change my life when I got a job working for NTL when I was 19. I was in the accounts department, sorting out direct debits. There was a bit of responsibility involved and basically I think I just began to grow up. Eventually, though, Dad's persistence about the boxing paid off and thankfully it did. I had always told my dad I would think about going back into boxing for years but never had. Then it just happened. One day, I had to pick something up from a shop about half a mile away up a hill and I ran there. By the time I got to the shop on Gedling Road, I was wheezing and out of breath. I was in bad shape. When I was boxing I would have done that run without even breaking sweat because I was always super fit. I had always been the kid who was the fittest in the class. I had prided myself on working out and feeling good about myself. Now I was the kid who wheezed when he ran to the shops. Thankfully, it was just the wake-up call I needed.

CHAPTER 5

I finally returned to the Phoenix gym and it just felt right. At first I went back purely to get fit, not to start boxing. But I had my same amateur coach again, Dale McPhilbin, and pretty soon I was loving it. At that stage I used to train in the gym, but I never really used to run much. Maybe a few times around the block but that was it. I used to do a circuit, which involved press-ups and squat thrusts and that sort of thing. Dominic Travis, who was four or five years older than me, also trained me a lot and we ended up sparring frequently. He told me that I should go in for the ABAs – the Amateur Boxing Association Championship – but I didn't have a clue what he meant. That's how little I knew about the fight game. Anyway, he said he was going to put me in the ABAs, so I said fine. It is difficult to analyse why my coaches rated me so highly because it sounds boastful and I'm not like that, but I'll be as honest as I can. I wasn't the most obsessive trainer back then and I didn't have any pushy parents telling me what to do all the time.

Other kids in the gym had both, but whenever I sparred with them in the ring I would just play with them. I realised, and I think everyone else in the gym realised, that I was naturally very good at boxing. I could hit hard, I could take a shot, my movement was good, my technique was OK, everything just came very easily to me. I knew myself that I was better than anyone else but ask me why and I don't really know. I had been hitting bags for so long, it came as naturally to me as walking. My dad never stopped harping on about how good I was and I can only thank him for continually badgering at me to go back into the gym. My other coaches also told me I was a level above everyone else and so it started to filter in that I was a decent young amateur boxer.

Gradually, I got really back into boxing and started taking it more seriously. Dominic was there when my comeback started with the ABA Midlands finals in March 1997. I won it with a majority points win over Grantham light-middleweight Roy Watson. I went to Birmingham for the national finals and beat Albert Coates in the quarters and Clint Johnson in the semis. Now I was up against the Army's Chris Bessey in the final, who had won it seven years on the trot. I'd heard his name and thought, 'Hang on a minute, this Bessey is like a *real* fighter.' I started to get a bit nervous, especially when I found out it was to be shown live on BBC television. As it turned out, I actually dropped him in round one and again in round five. Chris, though, had bags of experience and legitimately beat me 9–7. He went to the Commonwealth Games two months later in 1998 and won the gold medal.

During my comeback, I had some real humdingers with various other amateurs. The Francis Doherty fight will always be in my memory bank. In one Midlands final, I knocked him out cold with ten seconds left in the last round. Just as it looked as if it would go the distance I'd jumped on him and sparked him out. Doherty was part of a travellers' family and during the fight I thought I had probably lost this, as there were seemingly hundreds of travellers in the crowd at the Regency Rooms in Ilkeston. But Doherty walked on to an uppercut and his eyes rolled to the back of his head: he was out on his feet. His arms dropped and he was gone, so I lined up another shot and bang – he was down. For about a minute, he didn't move and just lay there on the canvas.

The fight was over but I thought another one was about to begin as we walked outside. There was just me, my dad and his old pal Johnny Greenwood, heading for our car when the Doherty fans walked out at the same time towards their minibus. Johnny picked up a big concrete slab off the top of a wall outside the club, to use it as a weapon if needed. He was carrying it above his head, to make the intention clear. But at that precise moment when it looked likely to go off, one of them suddenly collapsed, with what looked like some sort of epileptic fit. This kid was rolling around on the floor, so Johnny put the slab down, we got in the car and drove off as fast as we could. It was a hairy situation.

After boxing Bessey in the ABA final, I obtained a copy of the fighters' bible *Boxing News*. I flicked through it, but it was only later when one of my friends said, 'Have you seen, you're the number-two amateur in the country?' that I opened it up again and there it was. I couldn't believe it. I was the number-two amateur middleweight in the whole of Great Britain! Bessey was a proper fighter, but with a bit more experience and nous, I felt I could have beaten him in the ABA final, which would have made me number one. Even to this day, I cannot get around the fact I wasn't really aware of how good I was. I just assumed, wrongly, there were loads of other amateur boxers out there who were better than me.

There was another reason why I came back to the world of boxing. This reason was a spindly little kid from Sheffield and his name was Prince Naseem Hamed.

Even to this day I am a massive fan of 'the Prince' and back then he meant everything to me. I was absolutely in awe of him. I even tried to box like him: people are amazed when they see old video footage of my early fights in the amateurs because I based my style on his. It changed when I got in the pros, although I still naturally keep my hands low, but back then I just wanted to be like Naz. I watched all his fights on the box and I loved everything about him: the entertainment factor, the way he smacked people around and spoke about how he was the best. Naz was pure excitement for me and the only fighter I really closely followed.

His performance in beating Steve Robinson for the WBO world title on a rainy night in Cardiff was just incredible and that period was certainly his heyday. Robinson took a fake jab then Hamed had him with two lighting-fast punches. They were so quick, I don't think many people at ringside would have seen them, let alone Robinson. I watched him take apart Jose Badillo in Sheffield on TV in a mesmerising display and get up off the deck to beat Kevin Kelley on his

American debut. Nobody could live with him. Wayne McCullough went the distance with Naz, but the Prince dropped pretty much everyone else, including Paul Ingle, Wilfredo Vázquez and Vuyani Bungu.

A couple of months before the World Amateur Championships in 2001, I saved up every penny I had to go and see Naz fight against Marco Antonio Barrera in Las Vegas. I lost my life savings on him, though at that stage they wouldn't have amounted to much! I went with my brother Lee and my best friend from my amateur days, Jason Yarnall, and we stayed a cheap hotel on the Strip. When it was built it would have been the bee's knees, but it is a bit tatty around the edges now and it was back then, but it was on the Strip and that's all that mattered.

I'll be perfectly honest: I didn't really like Vegas. We had a week out there and Lee, who loves his gambling, lost most of his money in a few days. Jason and I wanted to go home after about day two, but, as Jason was there, between us we made the most of it and had some real laughs. Only the fact that we were just counting down the days to the fight kept Jason and I from packing our bags and leaving. I so desperately wanted to see Naz fight in Vegas against the great Mexican Barrera that I stuck it out.

There are a great many things to see and do in Vegas, but I didn't do any of them. We didn't see any shows or travel out to the Hoover Dam or anything. We went to a dodgy nightclub in a casino one night and this girl came over with a bottle of champagne. We all thought we had pulled, but you don't have to be a genius to work out what happened next. The bill came over and it was 300 dollars, about £200 then, so I made it plain that under no circumstances was I paying for that. I thought it was a joke. She ordered the champagne when she came over to our table and sat down. I hadn't even drunk any of it, so when this bloke came over asking for the money I told him he had no chance. I said to him, 'She ordered it, not me and I'm not getting hustled.' Don't ask me how, but I think this bloke took me seriously and we got away without paying.

I don't know what happened to Naz, but his sparring in preparation for the Barrera fight was apparently atrocious. Maybe he had made so much money from boxing that he just didn't want to be involved any longer. Whatever was the case, he wasn't training properly and as we all know now, it showed in his performance. We had tickets to watch the fight in the cheap seats, but it was chaos that night at the MGM Grand Garden Arena and so I managed to get a seat quite near to ringside, simply because no one moved me out of the way. I shouldn't have bothered as Naz took a pasting. I have still got the signed programme from the fight as I got to meet Naz a year later: oddly enough, bearing in mind what was to happen in the future, Jermain Taylor fought on the undercard.

My amateur career continued to flourish. After getting beaten by Chris Bessey in the 1998 light-middleweight ABA finals, I went one better the following year, winning at middleweight against Mark Redhead, in Barnsley. I missed out in 2000 through injury but won the ABA middleweight title again in 2001, this time overcoming another Army fighter, Dean Frost, in the final.

I also picked up a bronze medal for England in a Multi-Nations tournament in Liverpool. As the newly crowned ABA champion I was beaten 7–6 on points by American Randy Griffin in the semis, who was ranked number five in the world at the time. I boxed badly in that semi, but I was up against a class opponent and still though I thought I might have nicked it. In 2000, I was one of two British boxers picked to fight in the European Championships in Finland and I got to the quarter-finals, where I lost on points to Stjepan Bozic. The Europeans are a real test for any fighter as all the super tough, former Eastern Bloc countries are involved. Although I had lost, the experience I gained was invaluable.

I left NTL when I started boxing for England. I think this showed, more than anything else, that I wanted to make something of my life. Basically you get paid a pittance in lottery money when you become an England international, but I was so determined to make it I thought the only chance I really had was to become a sort of professional amateur, if you see what I mean. I gave up the job with NTL, which I liked, because I wanted to devote myself to boxing and to become a full-time athlete. I was absolutely adamant that the only way I could be a success in the ring would be to leave my job, even though that meant I would lose out financially. In fact, I took a substantial pay cut, but I think the fact I was prepared to do that showed just how convinced I was that I had to give boxing my best shot. It paid off in the long run. So I gave up working in the direct debits department at NTL in Nottingham, work which I liked. I am really into maths and numbers and so it was a bit of a wrench to leave. But looking back on those amateur days and working for NTL, I must have always had professional boxing on my mind because my password whenever I logged on at work was Naseem Hamed, or Naz1, Tyson1, or ThomasHearnsbox, Haglerhit or RayLeonard.

Actually, while I was at NTL I managed pick up an injury, which you would have thought was just about impossible working in an accounts department. I used to sit there with my calculator for hour after hour and I got so good at it I would process the bills and tap out the payments on the calculator without even having to look at it. I did it for so many hours I built up a kind of fatty deposit in my wrist called a ganglion. It was a massive lump of fat and eventually I had to go to hospital and get it burst. It comes back now and again and that is all because of the way I used a calculator at NTL!

I was hoping to make the Olympics in 2000 but events were to take this dream away from me. The powers that be set up a very tough qualifying system, much harder than it is now, where the odds were stacked against me. I reached the semis of a Multi-Nations tournament in Liverpool, losing to Adrian Diaconu by a wide margin. The same Diaconu who has since lost twice to Jean Pascal as a light-heavyweight. I was 10–0 down going into the last round and eventually lost 14–1. The winner and runner-up in Liverpool made it to the Olympics, so I had just lost out.

As luck would have it, both semi-finalists were then handed a last chance saloon reprieve: the boxing authorities said we had to take part in a box-off for one final Olympic place. The other Liverpool semi-finalist was the Pole Pawel Kakietek. I travelled to Venice for the fight with huge hopes. I'd watched Kakietek on Merseyside and was convinced I had the beating of him.

I am absolutely certain to this day that I beat Kakietek in Venice. I beat the crap out of him and he never even managed to lay a glove on me. The judges, though, just did not score my best shots. They obviously didn't like the way I boxed and I don't think they scored any of my body punches. I'm a big believer that when you lose, you lose and you take it like a man, but on this occasion I know I beat him hands down. Yet after the fight, I was told Kakietek had got the nod 3–2. For a while I was inconsolable. I told everybody who would listen that I was robbed and looking back on the fight something smelled pretty rancid. The upshot of it all was I wouldn't go to the Olympics and that summer it was Audley Harrison and not me who became a national hero for his exploits in Sydney.

By the 2001 ABA senior championships, I really felt I had matured as an amateur. I showed it by knocking out Dan Guthrie inside less than a minute and beating David Frost in the final. I was now rated the number-one middleweight in Britain and that meant I secured a pretty decent lottery grant. It wasn't a fortune by any means, but it meant I could train every day and in my spare time I started a course at Loughborough University.

I'd changed a lot since my 'wilderness years' and was becoming much more switched on. The course I enrolled on was a sports science and physical education two-year diploma course at Loughborough University. In my first couple of years as a pro I would go to classes in Loughborough on a Monday and Tuesday and then drive down to London. I certainly clocked up a heck of a lot of miles up and down the M1. Why did I do it? I always felt it would be crazy to only have a plan A without a plan B to back it up. When I turned pro I didn't think for one second I would hit the heights that I have, so I always felt the sensible course would be to have another string to my bow.

I have always been interested in the physiological side to the human body and all the other aspects to the course such as diet, how to train properly and first aid. I didn't study anything like hard enough when I was a kid taking my GCSEs so Loughborough was a chance for me to redeem myself. Most of the course was home-based so I didn't have to spend too much time with my tutors in Loughborough but it was very enjoyable and when I got my HND I was very proud.

Whereas a lot of fighters these days have massive entourages, with experts in diet, nutrition and physiotherapy, I just do it myself. I know which foods I should and shouldn't eat and I know my own body better than anyone. So why would I need someone else to tell me what I already knew? I have always been that way since I turned pro. It makes me cringe when some boxers hit the big time and all of a sudden they have a person there to wash their kit, another to towel them down, another to put the kettle on. Believe me, boxing attracts a lot of people who are just in it to make a few quid before moving on to the next sucker. I don't have that and never will.

*

In June 2001, I joined the likes of David Haye, Steve Foster and Courtney Fry in the team for the 2001 World Amateur Championships in Belfast. Although ultimately I had to settle with 'only' a bronze, I can look back on it now and take great pride in the fact that I became the first English fighter to win a senior World Amateur Championship medal. Just think, in all those years, no one had ever done what I had achieved. Mind you, I only became a 'first' by about twenty minutes as David Haye's fight was straight after mine and he won a silver in his division!

In the first round I had a really good opener, winning by 21–12 over the Olympic bronze medallist Vugar Alakbarov, despite trailing 6–2 at one stage. It was a massive win for me against a recognised world-class opponent who won bronze in the Sydney Olympics in 2000. In the latter stages, I felt I pulverised him. I was feeling super confident about my chances when it was announced I would be coming up against a high-class Russian by the name of Andrei Gogolev in the semi-finals.

I was devastated when I got beat 28–16. Immediately afterwards, I was inconsolable as I just could not believe I had lost. The truth was I had suffered with a really sore right thumb for days, having caught it in one of my earlier fights and, having had four bouts in four days, I was jaded going into the fight. The annoying thing was I had Gogolev out on his feet in the first round and if I had been even remotely fresh I would have taken my chance and polished him off. But I just did not have the conditioning and towards the end he had too much experience for me. I was gutted that my fitness hadn't been good and the really annoying thing was

Gogolev went on to win the title. I had won a bronze medal at the World Championships and all the other fighters congratulated me for becoming a 'first', but I didn't really feel like celebrating. I had been so close to winning it and I had blown it. I know that sounds a bit over-critical but it was how I felt. I had got the bronze, but it still didn't make up for the fact it could and should have been gold.

Right before the World Amateurs I was on a great run and my reputation was growing. It was enhanced further when I not only took middleweight gold for England in a Multi-Nations tournament in Copenhagen, but was also voted the best boxer in the event. David Haye and I both won gold in the tournament and we were competing against each other for best boxer prize. I won it, which was great because I got one over on David, but he soon got me back when I only won a bronze in the World Championship and he won a silver. It was a memorable tournament because during it I came up against a vastly experienced amateur 'legend', Sweden's Roger Pettersson, who had won something like over 200 amateur fights. Pettersson won the Swedish title every year and had also boxed in the 1996 Atlanta Olympics, but I hammered him. It was like fighting an old man and I felt like it was just a quick and easy workout for me: I won at a canter, 17–4. I couldn't believe how straightforward it was to beat someone who had such a massive reputation in amateur circles.

I was beginning to wonder whether the amateur code was still for me. Dale McPhilbin weighed it up and thought the best option could be to stay as an amateur and go to the Commonwealth Games in 2002. I think it is fair to say I would have been a hot favourite to take gold. The problem was that my amateur contract was renewed every six months, so I didn't have any real long-term job security. Also, I was becoming increasingly angered by the computer scoring system in the amateurs, which, for me, often doesn't really work: a great shot carries just as must weight – a point – as a fairly gentle tap.

Over the years, plenty of people have asked me whether I regret missing out on the Olympics. If I had gone in 2000, I'm pretty sure I would have won a medal: maybe not gold, but certainly a medal of some description. The truth is that I don't look back at anything with regret really and the Olympics, or failing to reach them, is no different. I don't think the timing was quite right either. I had only just won the ABAs and a year before that I went to the ABAs and lost in the final. So even though I think I would have come back with at least a bronze or a silver from the Sydney Olympics, at the same time I don't think I was ready. After all, I had gone a very long way in the amateurs in a very short space of time. One minute I was nothing, then suddenly I was number two in the country, before going on to win the ABAs and fighting and beating some of the best in the world. All of that happened in the space of a couple of years, after not lacing a glove for so long.

Also, I was very nervous whenever I boxed for England in those days. Although I am a pretty confident sort of bloke nowadays, I wasn't always like that. I think sometimes I just felt it had all happened so quickly and that somehow I was going to get found out, fighting way above my level. My nerves and lack of confidence meant, not to put too fine a point on it, that I used to box absolute crap in an England vest. I would hardly throw anything I was so wound up and nervous. The worst night I had fighting for England was losing to Denis Inkin 7–6, when I should have hammered him (yes, the same Denis Inkin who was to surface again in my career many years later as I was chasing down a world title). I was not remotely convinced of how good at boxing I was back then and the England coaches used to make me more nervous, not less. I suppose I just didn't really click with their way of doing things. I had loads of the coaches in my corner for the Inkin fight, shouting and swearing away. That kind of thing just didn't work for me at all.

I was so eager to do well, I was putting too much pressure on myself. Putting on an England vest turned me into a nervous wreck and, suffice to say, I just didn't perform as well as I should have. The main coach Terry Edwards tried to gee me up on one occasion, saying I didn't deserve to wear the national shirt, and other coaches said similar things. Edwards also called me a disgrace and on one occasion said I hadn't even earned my flight ticket to get to a tournament in Europe. I guess he was trying to get me to shake myself out of it, but it didn't work. That attempt at getting me fired up just had the opposite effect. It was a useless piece of psychology on a kid who was a nervous wreck and couldn't find a way out. Those comments have stayed with me for a long time.

Before I had even got into the ring, I was often a mess: I was just not used to dealing with pressure and no one on the coaching side was able to help. They hadn't got inside my head. The politics involved in amateur boxing didn't make things easier, either. It is immense and everywhere I looked there was politics poking its nose in. Some fighters got picked and others didn't. Why? Half the time there was no reason and no explanation given. I felt I was getting the rough end of the stick with some decisions and I am sure I wasn't the only one.

CHAPTER 6

I never had any intentions of turning professional when I started boxing in the amateurs. That was the furthest thing from my mind. All I wanted to do was get fit, fight a bit and carry on working outside boxing. I used to watch Robin Reid, Nigel Benn and Chris Eubank on TV and I would think, 'No chance. There is no way I am strong enough for that.' On television, they looked so much bigger than I did. Chris Eubank, with his muscles on muscle, looked particularly huge. But my days as an amateur were coming to an end. It was time to start taking this boxing lark seriously.

It was after doing so well in the world amateurs in Belfast, that it dawned on me that there could be a living to be made from boxing. I was approached by the promoter Mick Hennessy, in a hotel bar in Belfast. I had seen him before at various shows, often wearing a green wax Barbour-type jacket, which I used to take the piss out of mercilessly. Matthew Thirlwall, who I had boxed with as an amateur for

England, knew Mick well and he said he was a sound bloke, very reliable and very honest.

Other promoters like Frank Warren and Naseem Hamed's Prince Promotions were interested in me, although I only went up to see Naz because I wanted him to autograph my fight programme from the Barrera clash! When Mick and Rob McCracken sat down with me, there was an instant rapport between us.

Mind you, that first time I met Rob, I thought he was pissed. He has got a pretty strong Brummie accent and is very laid-back. I mistook that for being a bit tipsy, so when Mick made the introductions I said to Mick, 'Hey, Rob's had a few hasn't he?' Mick thought it was really funny because he knew Rob doesn't drink. The accent had fooled me and I had properly put my foot in it.

At the time I just went with my gut instinct. I checked up on Rob on the internet and as a fighter you didn't have to be a genius to work out how good he was. I spoke to a few people in boxing who have been around some years and they told me the same. Rob always struck me as being painfully, 100 per cent honest and it meant a lot that he was so completely sure I would be good enough to make it in the pro game. In fact, he had a lot more faith in me than I did. I began to think there could be some truth in this. I liked him and trusted him immediately, simple as that. I take my time over decisions and on too many occasions to mention, Rob said it was my choice, but I would be daft to stay amateur and wait for the next Olympics. Rob was convinced my style was perfect for the paid ranks. He said I needed to turn pro and he was right.

I've always been a cautious bloke when it comes to money and contracts, so took my time to make a decision. Also, through doing so well in the World Amateur Championships, I knew I had been promised category 'A' lottery funding, which was good money, maybe £1,500 a month. After a while I think Mick was beginning to lose his stack with me. Eventually I got something of an ultimatum from him, which was fair enough. He had a host of boxers ready to put on the BBC but the deal was subject to me signing with Mick, so the pressure was on. I was offered a decent signing-on fee from Mick which was pretty damn good. I thought, if I turn pro and it all goes tits up, at least I can say I gave it a go and I've got that money in the bank. The key to the decision, though, was Rob, who kept saying, 'You'll be surprised how easy it is in the pros, as long as you train properly.'

I said that I would train with Rob and see how it went in the gym before putting pen to paper. I had a couple of months with Rob before I made my pro debut and it must have been murder for him, because I would make his ears bleed by nattering on. I would drive to his house in Droitwich, on the outskirts of Birmingham, which is seventy-odd miles, then we would drive down to London and the Lennox Lewis College where Rob's fighters were based for another three and a half hours in his Jeep. On the way back I would be constantly asking him questions. Shall I really turn pro? What about this? What about that? For months we had the same conversation and he answered me again and again with the same answers, never putting too much pressure on me at all.

When I first started training at the Lennox Lewis gym in east London I would stay down there from Monday to Thursday, or occasionally Friday. It was a bit like when I used to go to Crystal Palace to be coached when I was an amateur fighting for England. My life revolved again around training, driving back to Nottingham for the weekend, then more training and more driving back. I never had a home in Nottingham to call my own at this time: I'd just live with my mum. I would come home and dump my stuff in a room above Mum's pubs, often a different one every few months. I was never homesick. I loved the training and the camaraderie of being with other fighters almost non-stop for five days a week. The other boxers were, almost to a man, a pretty decent bunch of blokes and that made things easier. Homesickness never came into the equation. I love my hometown of Nottingham and always will, but being in London was not a chore. I wanted to be there and I wanted to get better at boxing. Being under Rob was the only way. Also, I have always enjoyed my own company. I had plenty of nights in London where I would go up to my tiny bedroom and just watch the TV, or read. Even to this day I don't surround myself with hundreds of hangers-on because that is just not me. I like my own company and always have.

Rob advised me that I could stay amateur for the Olympics, as that was always an option. But the way he argued against it made sense. He pointed out that I would be 26 to 27 years of age by the time the Olympics came around and what if I got robbed in the games or didn't even get there due to a bad decision? I had got one already in an Olympic qualifier so who was to say it wouldn't happen again? If that happened, I would have been coming out of the Olympics, already past my mid-twenties and with nothing to show for it. Rob argued that by the time I would have been fighting in the Olympics, I could have turned pro and have already made it to British champion. He also insisted that my style was perfectly suited towards the pro game, where I could be successful and make a few quid.

Rob was convinced I was coming into my own as a fighter. He always had more faith in me in those days than I did. Don't ask me why, but Rob was just convinced I had the 'star quality' that it takes to get to the very top. He was also absolutely certain I would learn quickly as a pro and as such would continue to improve in the paid ranks. I think Rob could see I was a bit raw and naïve, but the basic speed and strength were all there. I just needed careful coaching. Rob would tell anyone who would listen that I had the potential to go a long way in the fight game. Whether he thought I would make a world champion I don't know, but he was adamant I had the tools to become a high-class fighter. When I lost in the World Amateur semi-finals, both Rob and I were convinced I would have won had I been better conditioned, allowing my extra power to take effect in the later stages. My style and stamina levels, if developed, would be perfect for a pro career. Amateur fights only lasted eight minutes. Sometimes the bout would be over and I would be back in the changing rooms without even sweating. I lost a close points decision in the World Amateur semis when what I needed was a few more rounds and better stamina. That told me it was time to turn pro and Rob just cemented my opinion.

*

Even with Rob's persuasive talents it still took me ages to decide. But I made the decision. I signed. I left the unpaid ranks with a proud record and also a very unusual one: not once as an amateur did I ever hit the deck. As anyone in the fight game will tell you, that is pretty rare and even to this day I am proud of having never touched the canvas with an amateur vest on. Even in my early days in boxing it showed I had a resilient chin. It would be 2009, seven years after turning pro, before I first tasted what it was like to go down, but that was one hell of a fight on a night when I had to come from behind to keep my world title.

I started my new life down at the Lennox Lewis College. I sparred for round after round with Peter Oboh and others down in the gym like Wayne Alexander, Costas Katsantonis, Matthew Thirlwall, David Walker and hard nut Valery Odin. That toughened me up a heck of a lot and Peter especially could really whack. Darren Barker, now a real prospect, was a bit younger but he was always around as well. A lot of fighters used to travel into the gym every day from various parts of London, but I stayed on the floor above, with Rob. For four years we did that. I had my own little room and I'd squirrel myself away, coming out at night to play pool and table tennis. They were great times and we used to have a real laugh with everyone winding each other up.

On one occasion we all went to a Chinese restaurant on Islington High Street. There was me, Rob, Mick, Matthew Macklin, Matthew Thirlwall, Lee Meager, David Walker and his cousin Steve. David and his cousin left early while we carried on eating for an hour or so. It seemed strange because David was always a pretty sociable bloke, who loved to chat about the fight game. When we eventually left the restaurant, it all went quiet, then wham! Eggs started raining down on us from all angles.

I looked up and saw David and his cousin Steve standing next to their car with row upon row of eggs on the car bonnet. They were both firing eggs at all of us as we were walking out of the restaurant. It was like the final scene from *Butch Cassidy and the Sundance Kid*. At the time Rob had a protective plastic cast on his nose as he had just had an operation to fix it. We all scarpered in different directions. If anyone reading this was there on that day in north London I can only apologise, but it was hilarious and quite what the punters would have made of it, especially with Rob wearing his nose cast, is anyone's guess. David just did it for a laugh and there must have been hundreds of broken eggs dripping down us following our ambushing.

The amount of times we used to nick Mick Hennessy's clothes when he was in the shower are countless. He would come out of the shower with a tiny little towel just about covering his nuts up, having his arse flicked by the rest of us. Sometimes, probably once or twice a week, we would all nip into Islington and go to an Italian restaurant which did a very top-notch pasta. We would spend the evening just chatting away and generally talking boxing: if it wasn't boxing it would be football. I really enjoyed those early years as a pro. They were some of the best times I've ever had.

I didn't really ever hit the West End. Rob wasn't into that kind of thing and to be honest neither was I. Our social life wasn't exactly a whirlwind. We always had to be up at the crack of dawn for our morning run so that tended to put the kibosh on late nights. I like my kip, so it didn't take a lot for me to hit the sack and go to bed. Rob and I got on like a house on fire from pretty much day one. He is a very straight-talking, no-bullshitting kind of bloke: a bit like me. And he has got a sense of humour too, which I like. The fact that he cleaned up domestically and fought at elite level also helped our relationship develop. He had the knowledge, simple as that.

Other good fighters were in the gym in those days and that helped. When Mick signed Howard Eastman, it was a big thing for me. I used to spar a lot with Howard, who was at the top of his game back then and a world-class fighter. He would give me plenty of digs and I'd start very nervously, but when I relaxed I realised, and I think Howard did too, that I was heading for the top. We would have some right ding-dongs over eight or ten rounds, really throwing leather at each other. Sometimes the sparring was a lot better than my fights. Even to this day I would say I used to take command over Howard in the later rounds, although he might disagree!

The whole package that came with Rob was perfect for me and it is fair to say I flourished in that environment. I loved the training and I loved boxing and I had a great coach. I also had a few pounds to spend. What could be better? On top of all that, Rob always spoke really highly of me, not just to big me up, but I think he genuinely felt I could make it. He always said there are great fighters out there, the likes of Roy Jones Jr and later on Floyd Mayweather, but they were flesh and bone just like me. They started at the bottom and worked their way up through hard work and dedication and I could do the same. Because this came from Rob, I believed him.

I have so much respect for the bloke that if I even think of cutting corners in training, I always feel guilty. If I don't do my runs in the early morning, eat something which isn't right for me, or don't give it everything in training, I feel terrible. From the day I turned pro, I didn't want to let him down. We are mates, too, but there is a line drawn. You can mess about with your best mates by slapping them around the head every now and again or just taking the piss. With Rob it is a bit different. He has real and genuine boundaries, not just with me but with all the fighters he trains.

When I first started at the Lennox Lewis College, some of the other boxers and me were constantly pissing around. Myself and David Walker were always having a bundle, rolling around on the floor and rabbit punching each other. We were just mucking about play fighting and nothing other than a bit of fun. I did it with Rob once and once only. I got him in some sort of head-lock and immediately he grabbed me by the crown jewels. He clamped me on the floor and I was tapping on the boards saying enough, enough, I submit. But he wouldn't let go and it hurt. Rob might not have fought for some years but he is still a strong bloke and when he had me by my Jacob's, it was like a clamp. From then on I knew there was no fucking about with this geezer. He was on a pedestal and nobody was going to take him off it.

Rob loves a laugh and a joke, but it only goes so far. I never did anything like that again and neither did any of the other fighters. It was in my character, certainly at that time, to take things as far as I could, if I could get away with it.

But Rob obviously felt it was important to gain our respect and play fighting with him wasn't part of that deal. For what it's worth I agree with him. Just that one incident there put me in my place and I knew where I stood with him straight away. I had over-stepped the mark. Basically, Rob tells me things, I listen. It is as simple as that.

Technically, Rob is simply excellent. At the start of our relationship he spotted very quickly that I had to keep my weight in the centre otherwise a lot of power was used up for no effect. He taught me so much about throwing my shots properly and we would slow it down to a snail's pace in training and practise it time and time and time again. Practice does make perfect and I must have thrown millions of slow-motion shots with Rob in the gym. I often over-reached with my punches: it was a real fault of mine but over many, many hours we managed to correct it.

Over the course of our time together, I cannot remember the amount of occasions when, at the end of a round, either in sparring or a proper fight, Rob has spotted something that I was convinced he would miss. It could be something very small, like I had a tendency to drop one shoulder when I threw a particular shot, or my feet weren't in the right position. It could be tiny things, but sure enough, at the end of a round he would say, I saw that. And he did. He never missed a trick and that's why he is such an outstanding coach.

I have still got a low guard, though I have got a low one for a reason. I have always boxed that way and it would be daft to tear that up and do something completely different. Keeping my hands low, came from my desire to be the new Prince Naseem Hamed. It is a Brendan Ingle style and I have always boxed like that in the pros. Rob realised very quickly there was no point in trying to fix something that didn't need changing. I've been criticised for that by some sections of the media, but most of them have never laced a glove in their life, so what would they know? Don't get me wrong, I'm perfectly happy to take criticism on board, but only if it is from someone who knows what he is talking about. I wouldn't tell Stephen Hawking how to improve his theories, so why some critics think they know better than me is just stupid. They don't.

I often haven't got the patience to really slow things down to that level and get everything technically just right, but Rob certainly has. It is an attention to detail, which is vital. Even minute things he would spot and say they needed correcting. In the early years he would train me at 10 a.m., then David Walker at noon, then another fighter would walk in and he would be just as keen to get it right with all of them – there were definitely no favourites. He wouldn't talk to me while he was training someone else and that's important as well. It means the fighter who is being coached gets complete attention. He wanted all his fighters to win, not just me. Nothing would be left to chance.

I don't know what would have happened to me had I never met Rob. I know for a fact I would not have been as good a fighter, but how high I would have gone is anybody's guess. I like to think Rob has been good for me and vice versa. We have had some great times together and that will never change.

Certainly in our early days together Rob was very careful about whom I went up against. He was always convinced I had what it took to make it, with a bit of thought and consideration over the choice of my opponents. I got whacked hard in some of my early fights. Varuzhan Davtyan springs to mind, but because Rob schooled me properly, when I went up against seriously good fighters like Jermain Taylor, I could dip into my bank of experience and come out the other side. Only a trainer who knows what he is doing could do that, bringing his fighter on at just the right pace.

As well as a great coach, Rob was a decent amateur and a top fighter who loves the world of boxing. He is always just himself, whoever he meets, and I like that about Rob. There is nothing false about him at all. You meet a thousand people in the boxing world and they will all say the same thing: Rob is a sound, likeable, very approachable person. There is no bullshit about Rob. He is straight with you and I am convinced that is why I reacted to his teaching much better than I ever did in my amateur days for England. I've never in all my time heard anything said about him that has been derogatory.

It was Rob who I can also thank for coming up with the 'Cobra' nickname. Rob said I needed a moniker and we sat around one evening talking about a few possibilities. Then he said he always liked the name 'Cobra', which was the nickname for the great Don Curry. I still don't know an awful lot about Curry, other than he lost his world title in a famous fight against Britain's Lloyd Honeyghan and that he was considered, for a while, to be the pound-for-pound best boxer in the world, but that didn't matter. I loved the name. The second I heard it from Rob I knew that's what I wanted for a nickname. Carl 'Cobra' Froch just sounded right to me then and it still does to this day.

I was with Rob one time when he went through a red light, although he swore it was amber. We got stopped by the police and, next thing you know, this young officer was slapping a pair of handcuffs on to one of his wrists after doing a license plate check on his car. Rob, very coolly, said, 'What exactly are you doing?' He remained very calm and said quite simply, 'You're not putting the other one on me. That's not going to happen.' I thought the copper would call for back-up, about five of them would put him in an arm lock and that would be that. But Rob just stayed cool and basically asked the copper, 'What seems to be the problem?' The situation was defused very quickly and I was impressed with the way Rob calmly conducted himself. That's him down to a T.

I suffered from a few nerves in those early days, but Rob insisted I was beating myself up when there was no need. His psychology worked. He told me I was good enough not to worry about my opponent, to let them worry about me, and he was right. Terry Edwards's efforts at getting rid of my nervousness hadn't worked for me, but Rob's approach fitted my psychological make-up. He doesn't get angry and start shouting and showboating for the cameras when he is in my corner. He assesses a situation calmly without bellowing in my ear. If I've done something wrong in a fight he will let me know, but he will do it very rationally. He will call on me to use my own boxing intelligence to work the situation out and that is much more my way.

Rob's idea of a bollocking is to say something like, 'I told you not to sit on the ropes because you were always going to get caught with that shot.' There is no don't fucking do this, don't fucking do that: none of that at all, although Rob, like anybody, has been known to swear occasionally. The last thing you need in the ring is some old duffer or a bloke who has never laced a glove in his life yelling at you in between rounds. I suppose some fighters might go with that, but not me.

I think when I first met Mick there was a lot hinging on my signature. The BBC, who had just returned to boxing on the back of Audley Harrison's incredible Olympic success story, really wanted me as part of Mick's so-called 'Class of 2002'. I have stayed loyal to Mick and let's face it: there has never been a great deal of loyalty in my sport. But Mick gave me the opportunity to fight on TV and I have appeared on both BBC and ITV, as well as Sky.

It is just a shame that I became a world champion when the bottom fell out of the market. ITV pulled out of the sport and Setanta went bust. Therefore it was a job choosing the best path for my future on British TV. I am happy with what I have earned from boxing, bearing in mind I love what I do, and I know Mick has made a few quid as well.

CHAPTER 7

For my pro debut I didn't exactly go for the easy option. Michael Pinnock had been floating around the cruiserweight division for most of his career. He operated almost exclusively at light-heavy and cruiser and was always thirteen stone plus. Although he had lost a lot more fights than he had won, the thing that stood out about his record was he never really got stopped.

Out of his sixty-odd fights, Pinnock had only not gone the distance four times. I thought, this guy must be tough and can clearly take a shot. Rob, Mick and I decided to start me going with a six-rounder as we all felt there was no point in bothering with just four rounds. It was more Rob's decision but I agreed with it completely. I thought it gave me a better chance of knocking out my opponent and back then, just as today, I am gutted if I don't stop a fight early. I think it is the mark of the really great fighter that they can stop their opponents. On all the occasions I have gone the distance, I'm not overly happy, although that probably didn't apply to my crushing win over Arthur Abraham many years later. My knock-out ratio is pretty good and, although I admit it is a bit silly, stopping my rival is really important. I love fighters with high knock-out ratios – Naseem Hamed, early Mike Tyson – and they were the boxers I wanted to watch.

I took a lot of confidence from Rob into the ring that night in March 2002. The fight was televised live from Bethnal Green's famous York Hall venue by the BBC. I felt there was a real need to impress, not just for the watching punters at the venue but also those sitting in their armchairs at home. Rob was my wingman and he just said trust me, you'll be fine against Pinnock.

My immediate family all went in a minibus from Nottingham and there was another coach load, about fifty friends and relations, who all travelled down from the East Midlands. I would say about sixty or so people came from Nottingham to see me. As I walked down the stairs and into the ring at York Hall I had a little look around. Even with Rob's calming influence, I was a bit nervous and I could see my brothers Lee and Wayne in the crowd, just telling me to take it easy, work him out and finish him off. Easier said than done: Pinnock was hard and I knew he would take some stopping.

I was very dependent on Rob that night as the adrenalin really started to kick in when I stepped through the ropes. He could tell I was nervous, but then something just happened: I went into fight-time mode. I love fighting, always have done and I knew I'd be OK. Once the bell went I knew everything would be fine, though as I was being introduced to the crowd, there was definitely some jelly building up in my legs.

The nerves were still there as the fight started, but they evaporated completely the moment Pinnock tried to hit me. I'm not being disrespectful to Pinnock when I say he was a journeyman pro. He took poundings every time he went in the ring and it takes a brave warrior to do that. Michael's a great bloke, but he'll be the first to admit he has his limitations: the moment I realised the pro world was not something to be feared was the exact moment he threw a punch at me. His double jab was slow and ponderous, and he was half looking away as he threw it. I thought, is that it? I had been fighting at world amateur level where the fighters were fast, slick and quick, and with good pros in sparring. This, though, was nothing of the sort.

Don't get me wrong. I admire Michael Pinnock for standing there for round after round as he took a hell of a pounding. In rounds three and four, I was getting through almost at will and I think the ref should have stopped it earlier than he did. Having said that, Pinnock always threw something back at me and that kept him in the fight. I hit him around the body and head, but whereas in the amateurs he would have got a standing eight count every day of the week, in the pros he just took it and kept coming back for more. He might have been painfully slow and hopelessly outclassed but he was a hard bastard!

In the fourth, Michael was getting tired. I had properly worked him over and got a great pro debut under my belt when the end came with a double jab right hand. I slipped out of the way then caught him with another straight right. I lined up an upper cut, bang, and I was ready to throw another when the referee dived in. It was quite a brutal stoppage but it was all great experience for me. Rob had chosen my first opponent brilliantly. The emotions when I got back into the dressing room and saw my family were fairly mixed. I was pretty pleased with my night's work and had got my debut out of the way, but I didn't really feel I had been tested enough. This was all part of the learning curve of life with the paid boys, I suppose.

Two months later I was back in the ring again. In 2002, my first year as a pro, I had five fights in all. That was deliberate as Rob, myself and Mick agreed I needed the time in the ring. I had turned pro at a relatively late age, so there was no point in hanging around. While other prospects fought a fairly high proportion of deadbeats, I never did. I had a few blow-outs in thirty seconds, but not many, which shows that the quality of my opponents, even in those early days as a pro, was pretty good. All of my early fights served a purpose, to get me used to the pro game and in fairly quick time.

I felt my second test in the pros would be a stiff one as we chose Ojay Abrahams, again at York Hall. I had sparred a lot in the gym with Ojay, so I knew he could handle himself. He had been British Masters champion and had been around for years so when the fight was made I was very excited. OK, he'd lost a few as well, but everyone in the industry knew he would be a good examination for me.

Ojay was a pal of Rob's and mine and before the fight he promised he would keep me in the ring for all six rounds, without much of a problem. Rob told him that if he accepted the contest all the playing around stuff we had done in sparring would be put to one side. Rob told Ojay I would go in there to bang him out in double-quick time and I would hit him very hard in the face: there wouldn't be any messing about. To his credit Ojay took the fight and in the weigh-in the day before, he told me I wouldn't lay a glove on him. He was going to show me a few tricks of the trade and bring me down a peg or two.

It lasted a round. I meant business and I wanted to do damage. At the start of the first round Ojay was pulling faces to the crowd trying to get a laugh. At one stage I had him in a kind of head-lock and he pulled a face, as I could hear the crowd at ringside beginning to roll around laughing. I thought, this doesn't look good if he is getting the fans to laugh at me, so I pushed him around until I got him in a corner. I let go a double jab and a straight right hand down the pipe caught him, as sweet as you like. The moment he went down I knew he wasn't going to get back up again. He went over, got up at eight but his legs were all over the place and the referee, Lee Cook, stopped the fight.

He may have been a bit of a journeyman but Ojay Abrahams was still well respected in boxing and I had walked through him. I had clocked up a couple of respectable wins and I felt I was on my way. Three months later, in August 2002, it was Darren Covill. Covill was half my size and limited and Rob could have been arrested for making this match. I looked at him and he appeared to me like a welter-weight: I just knew I couldn't lose. That was probably the nearest I came to facing a hopelessly outclassed opponent. Covill had a decent record but he looked so small when we got in the ring.

Mind you, the fight nearly didn't happen. I had a chest infection leading up to the bout and it was almost called off. Unbeknown to me, I had an allergy against dogs. Whenever I stayed in Nottingham, I always looked after my dog, a Yorkshire terrier crossed with a Staffordshire bull terrier called Sam. He was a right little bastard, angry all the time, and would invariably bite everyone who came to the house. I would say, 'Sam, attack!' and he would have a right go. The 'Staffie' in him meant he loved a good fight and he would never back down with other dogs three times the size of him. I loved that little dog and would take him on runs whenever I could. He lived until he was 18, though sadly not with me.

At this time I was training in London and living in my house in Nottingham at the weekend. Every weekend when I went back home I would be wheezing all night long, then when I went down to London it would mysteriously clear up. I thought it might be the carpets and never considered it could be Sam. But sure enough, after undergoing a load of tests it turned out Sam was the culprit. I had to move him out and I never suffered from chest problems again. I missed him. He died partially blind and in really poor health and it really hurt when he passed away.

I was kept busy with another fight two months later in October 2002. This time I was up against another tough nut, the ex-rugby league player Paul Bonson. Bonson was huge, much bigger than me when we weighed in. It was my first fight to go the distance and even to this day it really does my head in that I couldn't stop him. I had been nervous before the fight, even more so when I saw the size of him. But after the first couple of rounds I was wondering, what is all the fuss about this guy, as he was just taking shot after shot from me and not throwing anything much back.

After three rounds, I thought it was a walk in the park and he was about to fold. Instead, I discovered the hard way just how difficult it is to put opponents away in the pros. Bonson, as game as they come, just hung in there. He was like a human punch bag but he wouldn't go down. Every now and again he would even throw a punch or two of his own.

As the fight wore on towards its end, I started really letting go, whacking him with big digs, mainly to the body. Bonson started to use his professional nous, ducking low and grabbing me. We had what could basically be described as our own little rugby scrum for two or three rounds. At the end of the fifth round, the ref came over to our corner and said, 'I know what is happening. I can chuck him out and have him disqualified if that's what you want because of his persistent holding.' Rob, though, insisted he was left in there. He wanted me to get in the rounds, whereas I stood there thinking no, let's go home and get out of here. He was so big and strong that I just couldn't flatten him, however hard I tried.

The last round was the same as the fourth and fifth. Bonson held on at every opportunity and I wasn't able to send him packing. At the bell I was gutted but Rob kept saying it would do me good to have got the rounds in. He was right, the experience was beneficial to me, but the highlights of the fight were shown on BBC and it was pretty dour stuff. Though you could see straight away it was my opponent and not me that was doing all the holding.

I finished off my first year as a pro by fighting Mike Duffield, a Midlands area champion, just before Christmas. For the first time in the paid ranks I moved away from York Hall, this time a few miles east to Goresbrook Leisure Centre in Dagenham. The venue meant next to nothing to me, but it was more difficult for my supporters to come down from Nottingham.

Duffield was a step up, as it was the first time as a pro I had fought anyone with 'champion' written after their name. He was a tall, skinny kid who looked very awkward. He was a Brendan Ingle fighter and as such he prided himself on the Ingle gym's famous elusive style. He was also a bit mouthy and my first opponent who you could really class as cocky. We got into the ring and he brushed up against me as we were both pacing around. He puffed his chest out and looked at me, just staring. I walked away and Rob, who never misses a trick, told me to ignore it. He insisted Duffield wouldn't be so tough when I started hitting him on the jaw.

Rather like my pro debut with Pinnock, as soon as Duffield threw a punch I just thought, is that it? Without being disrespectful to him, it was useless. He was a very limited fighter and the moment I watched his first punch go sailing by, I knew that I would have him. I thought I needed to get him out of the ring before this starts looking bad, so I double jabbed him, backed him up and kept jabbing away, having a look at what his response would be. Every time I threw the jabs he was reaching for it, trying to get my fist out of the way by pawing at it with his gloves. I noticed he kept his chin up way too much as well: he was just screaming out to be flattened.

I got him in the corner and the second I did that I knew I had to throw a big, looping overhand right. So that's what I did. I threw a double jab and bang, let go with the right over the top. I knocked him down in just over a minute and he was counted out on his arse. He was on the floor sat down and tried to get up, but the referee stopped it straight away. Job done.

I didn't exactly celebrate Christmas like a wild thing – I probably had a pint of Guinness on Christmas Day – before it was back in the ring again, this time at the end of January. On this occasion Rob and Mick had chosen Valery Odin, my first opponent with a winning record.

The Odin fight was my debut in Nottingham, which made it extra special. Odin was also at the Lennox Lewis College so I had sparred with him a lot before we fought. He was a big, strong, tough fighter who would hold his own against anyone in sparring. Two days before the fight was due we still didn't have an opponent as a couple of fighters had looked at it, looked at the money on offer for taking me on and cried off. Rob told me it was going to be Odin, which I had no problem with, even though I knew how hard he would be to stop.

As usual, Rob just insisted I would be fine and would handle him without any real problems. I knew I would win – or at least I was very confident – but stopping a massive bloke like Odin wasn't going to be easy. I also knew that in the gym in sparring he could be very reckless with his head and elbows. There was no sweet science in Valery Odin.

I had sparred with Valery plenty of times with sparring gloves, 16 oz soft 'pillows' and a head guard, but it would be vastly different with tiny, little 10 oz fight gloves which could really cause damage. I was desperate to put on a show, this being my first time in Nottingham, and the fight was held at the city's new arena and ice-skating rink. Although I was training in London I had built up a pretty decent following of mainly friends and family and, although I didn't tell Rob, I would probably have preferred an easier opponent so that I could look good in front of my home fans.

The fight wasn't massively promoted, just a few bill-posters around the city, so we did about 1,500 tickets. Those hundreds of fans were certainly loud and it was busy enough that night on what was my homecoming. All my old school-mates from Nottingham were there and every person I grew up with seemed to be in the crowd that evening. All the nerves built up, but Rob and I had a chat in the dressing room, just prior to going into the ring, and that calmed me down. I suppose because I had sparred with him I knew he was dangerous and Odin had a habit of leaning in with his head, which was a pretty fearsome weapon.

I hammered him for round after round with those 10 oz Reyes gloves. Those gloves were deadly. I used to wear them all the time until my hands started getting injured later in my career, but believe me, with a heavy hitter the Reyes gloves could be seriously dangerous. In a street fight, if I had the option I would much rather wear horse-hair Reyes 10 oz gloves than just bare knuckle, bearing in mind you would want to do some damage to get the bloke down, then keep him there.

Back then, I was using Reyes gloves, which was as hard as bare knuckle, just with a bit of protection. During the fight Odin nutted me a few times and he even screamed at me at one point, I think in frustration because he was getting nowhere, but by round six he was tiring and I put it on him with a fast combination. I broke him up with some powerful shots, one of which, an upper cut, nearly raised him off the canvas, and he just couldn't keep me off him any longer. When Odin was showing no signs of punching back, thankfully the ref jumped in, which left me probably as relieved as Odin was. After the fight I felt on top of the world. I am a proud son of Nottingham and so to hear every single fan assure me it was only a matter of time before I became world champion, while being premature, was also very flattering. That night after the Odin win, on my home turf, was fantastic as I celebrated with my family and friends. The 'Cobra' was beginning to make a name for himself.

Two months later at York Hall, my opponent was Varuzhan Davtyan. He had just beaten Tony Dodson, so I knew it was another tough one. I was thinking along the lines that if he had just beaten Dodson and Dodson was knocking on the door for a British title shot then I wasn't far away myself. I knew he would be decent, but Rob gave me plenty of advice saying I would beat him, which I did over five rounds of my first scheduled eight-rounder. I was 25 and wanted to move on quickly so we both felt there was no point in staying down to six rounds. I was very fit anyway and would make the weight easily, so moving up to eight rounds was never really an issue, just another step in the right direction.

I watched the fight back on videotape afterwards and being such a massive Naz fan, I was pleased with what I saw.

I kept my hands down my sides and hit Davtyan with a perfect upper cut. I looked really super confident, loose and threw shots from all sorts of crazy angles: all the classic Naz traits. Mind you, I will never, ever forget Davtyan and for this reason: it was the first time I had ever been hit hard on the chin. Seven fights in and it was my wake-up call to the pros.

In round four, I backed him up to the ropes. He put his head down and must have shut his eyes as I had him into a corner, but the overhand big right punch he delivered landed flush on my chin. It was right at the end of the round and it shook me to my boots. I backed up and had a momentary, very slight wobble. He noticed as well and stuck about four shots on me in quick succession, throwing two, then rolling off and another pair. They all missed as I had the sense to back up and slip out of them. The bell went and I moved back to my corner. Rob had seen what had happened and calmed me down. I recovered in the interval quickly as I had been more stung than genuinely hurt, but I will never forget Varuzhan Davtyan, as he whacked me in the chops and made me realise I was now in the big boys' league.

Davtyan's punch would probably have laid out most people, but thankfully I have always been blessed with a tough chin. I learned a lesson, though. My chin was in the air and I was wild so it was totally my fault. These are the things you have to learn in the pros and I had to learn them fast. I started the next round very quickly, backed him up again and on this occasion I took my time. Referee Ian John-Lewis halted it half way through the fifth round with Davtyan well beaten, but for me it had been a night to remember.

It was back to Nottingham a month later, where Michael Monaghan was waiting. It was my second time out in my hometown and this time I wanted to spark my opponent out in the early rounds, having taken six to get the better of Odin. I got what I wanted as fellow Nottingham boxer Monaghan, a slick, super-confident Brendan Ingle fighter, was not in my league.

Before the fight, Michael asked – well, demanded to know – whether we could do it at twelve stone two pounds. I told him I was a twelve-stone fighter and I made the limit easily, so why should I give him any advantage? He said he couldn't make twelve stone, to which I said that we couldn't make the fight then.

In the end, when Mick was negotiating to meet Monaghan, I said I would give him the extra two pounds because there was no one else out there I wanted to fight. But then, after all that, by the time we met he came in light anyway! He came in a few pounds under and made the weight easily, which shows he must have taken me seriously and trained very hard.

Before the fight he started bigging himself up, saying he was going to knock me out and make me look a fool in front of my own fans. The reality was somewhat different. He still says he was robbed, but for me that is just a joke considering I bounced his head off the canvas. Michael Monaghan has always had a big mouth and when the fight started I decided I was going to inflict some serious damage on him. It was never really a contest, whatever he says to the contrary. From the very first bell, the fight was one-sided: by the third, he had been knocked down and was taking a pummelling.

The memorable thing about that evening was that in the process of flattening Monaghan, the referee Terry O'Connor was also sent tumbling to the deck in the third round. I caught Terry as I was whacking away at Monaghan and as the ref was in the process of stopping the fight, he jumped in and lost his footing. Thankfully, the official was all right, although he looked a bit shaken up. Terry then stopped the fight – he didn't really have any option as Monaghan was not even defending himself – but it gave Michael the perfect opportunity to go around Nottingham saying he was robbed. I wish the ref had let the contest carry on so I could have done some serious damage and shut Monaghan up once and for all. There is nothing worse than a bad loser and Michael Monaghan was certainly one of those.

I then had a six-month break from the ring, due to a really painful knee injury that wasn't diagnosed at the time. All I knew then was that it was hurting. Not a constant pain, but a sharp jab in my knee whenever I twisted my leg in the wrong direction. It was to be another four years before the knee would be properly diagnosed and I would spend eight months out of the ring in recovery.

As it was, I spent a few weeks on crutches after sparring against Andrew Lowe. As soon as I threw the punch I knew there was something wrong in my knee. I had twisted it and it felt bad, but all the scans I had failed to show the real damage. Without the concrete evidence that later showed I had torn my anterior cruciate ligament, I thought I had just twisted my knee badly. When I got rid of the crutches and went back into training, I did hours and hours of physio to get my leg back into something like shape. It continued to feel unstable for the next four years, but I just didn't realise the extent of the injury. Had I known, I would have had an operation and been out of action for several months, but without the proper proof I just dismissed it as a training injury and something that would go away of its own accord.

Typically, when I returned to the ring six months after dismantling Monaghan I had another stiff assignment: Vage Kocharyan. Just eighteen months after I had turned pro, I was facing an opponent who had only recently lost to former WBC super-middleweight champion Glenn Catley by a point. Catley won the title in 2000, beating Markus Beyer in Germany and a couple of years later had only just got the nod over Kocharyan. I knew I was in for a hard night against the big, tough Armenian and that's exactly what I got.

It was my first fight back after such a long gap and Kocharyan took me the distance over eight rounds. He had killed himself getting down to the weight as he usually boxed at light-heavy, and felt extremely strong not least because I had given him a bit of weight away (just over three pounds). Three pounds might not sound like much, but it felt a lot on the night, especially when he caught me with a big hook over the top in round six, and perforated my eardrum.

I learned a heck of a lot that evening. Although Kocharyan was a journeyman, he was also very good at tucking up on the ropes and taking shots. For the first time since turning pro I felt I was not powerful enough to do any real damage to my opponent. I was lining him up and hitting him with some great shots, but he took them and came back. During the bout my knee definitely felt dodgy, but I dismissed it, knowing that all fighters get pains and aches. You have to put up with it and get back in the ring: if you waited to be exactly 100 per cent you would never lace a glove. After so long out, it was good to have got an eight-rounder in the bag. Rob was convinced I was now ready for my first real title fight.

Seven weeks later in November 2003, I travelled along Brian Clough Way from Nottingham to Derby, to face Alan Page at the Derby Storm Arena for the English super-middleweight title.

I was supposed to fight for the Commonwealth title but that fell through, and I was offered the English title instead. Page was unbeaten and ambitious, but I had got in my mind now that I wanted to be British champion and I was in a hurry. To get the British title I had to win the English first. I was growing in confidence and feeling good, apart from my knee, and I was happy to fight Alan. I knew him from my days in the England amateur squad and I was convinced I would beat him.

The atmosphere that night in Derby was electric. Half of Nottingham seemed to have come out to support me and I will never forget what a brilliant evening it was. Before the fight started I noticed there was a big hole in the changing-room wall where someone, presumably, had hit it with a mallet. You couldn't exactly call it glamorous, especially as you could see the car park through the brick wall. It was freezing too: so cold, I think I have only just started thawing out. To make matters worse, I had to walk though the main bar to get in the ring, through the smoke and all the rowdy punters.

Alan Page was a great fight for me. Funnily enough, as an amateur he beat Mikkel Kessler, who I was to face many years later. Alan was a top amateur and a very proud fighter, but he only ever boxed once more after that night. For three rounds he meant business and was tough to nail, but I really felt in the flow. Afterwards, I found out that one of the commentators, Duke McKenzie, had given Page a draw in the fourth round, but how he came to that conclusion I will never know: Page barely landed a punch of note.

I was so confident I started to put on a bit of a show, winding my right hand up before hitting him with the left, Sugar Ray Leonard style! Page was a standard come-forward fighter who never moved his head much, so when I threw my trademark upper cuts they were often landing. But he was a game opponent and lasted seven rounds, which shows just how hard he was in the ring. I will never take anything away from Alan, because I pounded him for round after round, and he took it until he had nothing left to give. Towards the end, it was getting ridiculous. An upper cut from long range nearly lifted Page off his feet. Then three big rights in the seventh round rattled him. Page turned his back and referee John Keane rightly called the fight off.

I had my picture taken afterwards with my best pal and training partner Adam Fukes with the belt and a massive bruise on my lip. I had been in a fight all right. The snap is still on my kitchen wall because it made me so proud and happy to have won something in the fight game, something that could never be taken away. As the fight was being tele-vised, I joked afterwards into the microphone, saying, 'I know I told everyone I would stop him in six, but I had to get my air time in on the BBC.' I hope Alan didn't think I was being disrespectful. I then went back to my mum's pub and celebrated with half a Guinness: nothing more than that. Well, I might have gone wild and stretched it to a pint!

There was only a two-month gap before I was back in the ring again. Dmitry Adamovich had been sparked out by Robin Reid inside four rounds a few months earlier. Although he had a winning record, the match-up didn't seem to ignite much interest in the fans as the Goresbrook Leisure Centre in Dagenham was half-empty that night. A couple of body shots put paid to Adamovich and the fight was over inside two rounds. The best thing to say about that night was that I had got rid of him quicker than Reid had managed. I had moved to 11–0 and, although my knee was still a concern, it wasn't painful enough to stop me fighting.

All the signs were that my twelfth pro fight would be facing Tony Dodson for the British title, until he pulled out with an injury. Whether or not he was really injured I don't know, but Mick and Rob scratched around for an opponent before they chose the Ghanaian 'King' Charles Adamu for my first scheduled twelve-rounder. If I thought Adamu was going to be a step up in class, I was right. He had just beaten Matthew Barney a few months previously so I knew exactly what I was up against. He was much better than Alan Page, which is probably right because we were boxing for the Commonwealth title. Commonwealth is supposed to be higher than the English and Adamu was certainly much tougher than Alan Page or anyone I had faced up to then.

I was still a little naïve for a pro, which was hardly surprising bearing in mind I had only been doing it for two years. Could I do twelve rounds? Could I beat someone like Adamu, who I had a lot of respect for? He was a rough, rugged African who could take a punch, so my game plan was a simple one. I had to be careful not to burn out because I suspected this would go to the later rounds. In front of about 3,000 fans in my native Nottingham I started fairly conservatively, saving myself for the later part of the scrap. After six rounds, Rob was pretty adamant with me that I had to pick up the pace because it was a close one. He told me to start letting my shots go and really build up the pressure.

I did as I was told. Round seven went well, but round eight was the turning point for the fight. We were in a clinch and the referee Marcus McDonnell called for us to break. Straight away Rob shouted out, 'Back at him, now!' As we pulled apart on the break, I dived back towards Adamu and caught him a bit unawares. I connected perfectly to his chin and he went down on one knee. Fight over, I thought. I gave Adamu no chance of getting up, but he was saved by the bell for the end of the round. I still didn't think he had a hope in hell of getting out for the ninth, especially as he had a blazing row with his corner man. But out he came, showing just how hard he really was.

I was well on top for the last four rounds. Bearing in mind I only won the fight by three points, I must have been losing it up to the eighth, but I felt by the end it was becoming fairly conclusive. Adamu tired fairly badly in the downward stretch, though I was on a steep learning curve: no matter how hard I whacked him, I couldn't put him away. In retrospect,

Adamu might have been a couple of fights too early for me, but Rob had so much confidence that I would win, more even than I had in myself, that the decision to face him was the right one. I did twelve rounds for the first time in my career, which showed that my stamina was not in question. And I got the Commonwealth crown as well.

Again I was kept busy and three months later I was defending my Commonwealth title against Mark Woolnough, a big bruiser of a bloke who really should have been a light-heavy. Straight after fighting me, he went the distance with Otis Grant so his credentials have never been in question. Woolnough was hard and could take a shot or two, but he had limited skills and I don't think the outcome was ever in doubt. Although, again, I took my time finishing the job. I punched him to a standstill in the eleventh round and referee Dave Parris dived in to save him from further punishment. It was a correct call from the official, though some people at ringside thought it was a bit late.

The Woolnough night was memorable for Rob and former world champion Duke McKenzie having a bit of a barney afterwards. Duke, who was commentating on the fight with Jim Neely for the BBC, said Rob had been wrong to tell me to go for the knock-out. Duke was convinced I was winning the fight hands down, so why put that in jeopardy? Rob, though, was sure I had it in me to finish off Woolnough and told me so. Regardless of their spat, my reputation had improved as Woolnough was a well-respected operator in the super-middleweight pro scene.

I was also getting myself another reputation: for knocking over sparring partners. Being such a heavy hitter, I was struggling to find good sparring partners in London. Basically, I tried to kill my opponent every time I put on a pair of gloves, whether in a proper fight or in training, and as such, the offers of sparring were going into a steep decline. Not only was I hurting everybody I sparred with, I was also having problems with my hands and not really learning much. Rob hauled me up and told me it had to stop: sparring should be about fine tuning, not knocking the other bloke's head off. He was right of course, and from Woolnough onwards I started to calm down whenever I sparred. The result was that I began to learn a lot more about my own technical abilities, instead of just whaling away. I still like a dust-up in sparring even now, but nothing like what I was in those early years.

I'm a bit of a traditionalist at heart and the fact that I won the English, Commonwealth and then the British title is the way it should be done. Don't get me wrong, other fighters can do whatever the hell they want, but it always rankled with me that I never fought for the European title before winning my world crown. At the time, I never really got the chance for a shot at the European crown. The various opponents just did not want to know and that is something I regret. I wanted to fight for it, but every time a European title shot got close, the holder would just relinquish it.

Boxing should be about winning titles and the fact that so many fighters these days skip the British title is sad. Many past and present world champions never won the British title, and I think that's a shame. It is wrong in my book. I think I did it the right way, although I wish I had also fought for the European. I think a European crown entitles you to think you are in the world top ten and a legitimate contender for the global title. And doesn't it sound great? Can you imagine the ring announcer booming out, 'And in the blue corner, the former English, British, Commonwealth, European and world champion!' Surely that has to be the dream of any domestic fighter?

Anyway, what happened next was another massive disappointment as Tony Dodson yet again pulled out, claiming another injury. This time I had had enough and gave Dodson a load of stick in the papers, telling him to fight me or give up the belt. I also questioned whether he really had an injury or not as he kept pulling out of our proposed fight. Later, I discovered that Tony had been involved in a car crash and had hurt himself so I probably shouldn't have said what I did. At the time, though, I was angry because I felt he was making excuses.

The British Boxing Board of Control obviously felt the same way as me, as they made the British title vacant and ordered a box-off between me and Damon Hague. Hague was a good friend of mine back then and has remained so ever since. He was an Ingle gym product whom I knew well and, needless to say, I really fancied my chances, so much so that I told my two brothers to lay on bets for me to win in the second round. I just could not see any way that Hague could beat me.

Mick sorted the money out and I got about £35,000 to fight for the British title: a pretty good payday, though as it turned out I didn't spend long in the office. There was a fantastic atmosphere in Nottingham that night as Hague, from Derby, had brought hundreds of his fans and I had sold 800 tickets to my supporters. Ronnie O'Sullivan and I had met a couple of times in London as we used the same physio, and he also came along. Just before the start all the fans in the arena held an impeccably observed minute's silence for football legend Brian Clough, who had just died. Suffice to say, supporters from Nottingham and Derby showed their adoration for one of the greatest and most inspirational managers in the history of the game.

It was electric in there as Damon and I entered the ring and the hostilities started the moment the first bell went. Damon came at me like a man possessed and we stood toe to toe for the first minute, whacking lumps out of each other. He went down early on after I had cuffed him around the back of the head, but I think it was a slip. Then a solid right hand to the top of his head sent Damon to the canvas, where he took an eight count from the referee. Damon recovered, or to be more accurate, he tried to recover. He got up and with just seconds to go in the round Hague started beckoning me forward as if to convince the referee his head was clear. I caught him again, with a straight right and a left hook that sent him back to the floor. This time there was no way he was coming back. He'd taken a sickening couple of shots and the referee Mickey Vann picked him up as he called off the fight.

I couldn't quite believe it. I was the new British super-middleweight champion, thirteen years after another Nottingham fighter, Fidel 'Castro' Smith, aka 'Slugger O'Toole', had won the title. I'd spent a lot of my amateur days with Fidel learning a few tricks and sparring with him. My head nearly exploded, I was so overcome. First and foremost, I checked to see that Damon was all right and then, when he got to his feet, a wave of relief washed over me. That is always the principal emotion the moment a fight is called off. For weeks and weeks as a professional boxer all you have thought about is your opponent. He is always in the forefront of your mind, so that when the fight is won, the relief that you have done it is immense. It was even more so that night as Damon is a great bloke. I was also naturally concerned about Damon's health because I liked him so much. I was always pretty certain I would win the fight, but I was surprised because I didn't think for a minute it would be that easy. I did not want Damon to get into any sort of rhythm as he could be a tricky customer, so I jumped on him. Every time I connected, I could see my shots were hurting. I would have preferred it to have been Dodson, but that didn't happen, so Hague had to take it like a man. If winning the title wasn't enough, there was another dollop of icing on the cake as Darren Barker, whom I had sparred with many times, made his pro debut that night, easily out-pointing Howard Clarke.

Since the fight, Damon has seen the light and found religion. About two weeks after we fought for the title, I was down in London for light training when Damon rang up and invited me over to his flat near Victoria. He is a bit of a chef and he knocked up a fantastic chicken salad with pasta, while we nattered about the fight, which just shows what a great bloke he is. Damon told me I could go the whole way, just as Rob had always predicted and I was beginning to think he might just have a point.

In the ring, straight after I had won, I was handed the British title belt and was disappointed to discover it was, not to put too fine a point on it, a bit knackered. The bronze parts were fine, but the red, white and blue bunting was basically tatty and falling off. I remember thinking, 'That's not right,' and a few weeks later the BBBC chief Simon Block took it off me and got the belt cleaned up.

After the fight I went to my mum's pub, the New Engine House in Carlton, and celebrated with family and friends. The place was packed and I had my usual, a pint of Guinness. Whether I finished it or not I can't remember, but it was an incredible feeling as I walked in there with the belt slung over my shoulder. All the hard work and dedication had paid off and I was the British champion, the best twelve-stone fighter in the land. It made me quite emotional to think that this achievement could never be taken away from me.

The other way I celebrated was to buy a new car: a VW Golf R32 with a V6 super-charged engine that went like shit off a shovel. It was my first really big payday since I had got my money for turning pro and so, being a bit of a speed freak, I thought a new car was in order. I bought the Golf, the car of my dreams back then, and started haring around Nottingham. About a week after I bought it, I was driving back from training in London and got stopped by the cops on the M1, just south of Nottingham. I was lucky. It was about 3 a.m. and I was busy clocking up about 140 m.p.h when I spotted the police car in the far distance. Thankfully I have got decent eyesight: I braked like a maniac and the officer pulled me over. He knew who I was and asked for my autograph, so I began to think I might just be about to get away with it. No such luck, as he showed me that my speed over fifty seconds, the legal requirement, had averaged out at 97 m.p.h. In a sense I was fortunate as anything over 100 m.p.h and I would have been taken back to the station and probably had my licence taken away. Because it was just under, I bagged three points and a whacking fine. Speed limits are right, of course they are, though I cannot see the point in having a speed limit at 3 a.m. on an empty motorway. The cops thought it was all pretty funny and just said that if I carried on like that, they would one day be scraping me off the road.

I may have had points on my licence, but I was the new British champion. I could scarcely believe it. I turned pro in the hope of maybe one day becoming the best in Britain and I had done it in just two and a half years. Perhaps this wasn't my limit. Perhaps Rob and Mick and all the other fighters who told me I could go on to the world level were right after all. I still pinch myself, even today, but winning the British crown made me realise that I might be on to something. The rest of the journey had only just started.

CHAPTER 8

The plan after winning the British title was to head to America. Mick had done a business deal with Oscar De La Hoya's Golden Boy Promotions organisation which allowed Mick to showcase some of his talent on Oscar's shows: perfect for his fighters to gain considerable coverage in America and also some useful experience.

A proposed fight with the Mexican Librado Andrade fell through, as Rob was convinced he was too tough a test for me. Years later Andrade lost a world title bid to Mikkel Kessler, so he went on to become a genuine force in the fight game. Rob just did not like the look of what was being put in front of us in an eight-round fight. Andrade was in Oscar De La Hoya's camp and it was on a De La Hoya card. Rob was concerned that if it was close over eight rounds, the kid from England was not going to get the nod. Although I trained at the Warrior gym in Fort Lauderdale, Florida, in the run-up to Howard Eastman's world unification middleweight title clash with Bernard Hopkins,

I didn't get to fight on the undercard, which had been the original plan.

While I was out there, I sparred with Howard Eastman at least three times a week and really enjoyed the experience. Howard was at the top of his game back then and Hopkins was easily the biggest fight of his career. The sparring opened my eyes, because I could handle Howard without too much difficulty. OK, he was only a middleweight, but even so, the sparring was pretty easy for me. Howard is a very laid-back, chilled person and that came out in his training. So I wasn't surprised when he lost to Hopkins at the Staples Center in Los Angeles. Yes, it was close-ish, but Hopkins did out-box him, without ever delivering a real beating. It was a typical latter-day Bernard Hopkins performance, in other words. He might go down as one of the modern-day greats, but entertaining the fans has not recently been top of Hopkins's agenda. Only late in his career has the American legend been more cautious in the ring. He is now a clever mover and hustler, but in the early days 'B-Hop' was exciting to watch.

Because I didn't fight on that undercard, I had ended up spending six weeks in America for no real reason. Mick pulled all the strings he could but another opponent just did not materialise. I went back to Nottingham, only to get a call a few weeks later saying there was another fight deal set up with the Costa Rican boxer, Henry Porras. It was to be in April 2005 at the Avalon club in Hollywood.

Porras was a perfect test for me as he had only lost a couple of times in over forty scraps. He was a decent opponent, having lost to Otis Grant in a twelve-rounder and lasting nine against Kessler in a world title eliminator.

Porras was rated number eleven by the WBC and was a step up for me, no doubt about it.

I flew back over to America and trained at a rough gym in LA South Central, in the famous Compton suburb. I am a big fan of the film *Boyz n the Hood*, so it was all a bit surreal driving around and seeing all those houses with bars in the windows and boarded-up homes. LA is a massive city, but apart from imagining I was an extra on one of my favourite films, I didn't think much of it. My dad and brothers spent a few days desperately trying to find a half-decent pub, or bar, but to no avail and they had to settle for the very average one in the hotel. The beaches in LA were a bit livelier and I enjoyed jogging along there as the air was fresh and the girls were, well, I don't really need to explain that.

Training went perfectly and I was dying to get back into the ring after such a long lay-off. Because I was a bit ring rusty I started the fight cautiously, just snaking out my jab. But at the end of the first round a big right hand almost finished the fight there and then as Porras crumbled, returning to his corner on shaky legs.

The bout was going according to plan. I was enjoying beating up my opponent until I wound up a big punch in the fourth round, and smashed into Porras's elbow with my right fist. The middle finger of my right hand had been splattered by the impact on the very corner of Porras's elbow, and the pain was immediately sharp and intense. If you want to get technical, the extensor hood over my knuckle was torn, but I didn't need any jargon to know that I was in agony. I looked up the injury on the internet after the fight and the most common way of getting 'Boxer's

Knuckle', as it is sometimes called, is when kids ride their bikes into a lamp-post and jam their knuckle between the handlebars and the post. Ouch.

Back to the fight, and I felt I could barely carry on. As usual, Rob just said I would be fine and not to worry about it. It was true that the padding on the glove took away some of the sharpness of the pain, but it still stung. My right hand now hurt whenever I threw it, so I was very much a left-sided boxer from there on in. I caught up with Porras towards the middle rounds of the fight and in the sixth and seventh delivered some pretty good left upper cuts.

By now, Porras was taking a heavy beating and I just wanted the fight to end. I was looking at the referee as if to say, let's stop this, but Rob told me to stop bleating to the ref and quietly bollocked me at the end of the round. I went out in the eighth and put it on Porras. He had clearly run out of gas but the ref, having heard me begging him to stop the fight, wouldn't do so. It was left to Porras's brother in his corner to throw in the towel. They do like their pound of flesh in America.

I was interviewed at ringside immediately afterwards and told the commentator that America was waking up to a new talent. As the show had been broadcast live on HBO Latino, it didn't do my profile any harm at all to have beaten someone as good as Porras so convincingly – and with only one hand.

All of which meant it was something approaching a small miracle that I was back in the ring just three months later, to defend my British and Commonwealth title against Matthew Barney. I refused to pull out of it because I did not want to be forty years old, looking back on my career and thinking, why did I do that? Having got used to fighting so regularly, I also didn't want to slow my momentum. But most of all, I took the fight in order to shut Barney's big trap, as he gave some interviews to the media saying there was no question he would beat me. I didn't want to miss that opportunity, just because my hand was hurting.

To get through the fight I had two pain-killing injections put into my hand, and getting my fist into the glove was difficult. I had put extra padding inside the glove and as a result there was an air pocket in there: it took all of Rob's heaving to get it in there. In fact, I boxed with so much padding that it felt as if I was hitting Barney with a pair of pillows.

The fight was one of those horrible, boring, dull occasions where one boxer is holding on for twelve rounds and the other can't put him away. I reckon Barney's always had a bit of an inflated opinion of himself and yet, a bit like Andre Dirrell a few years later, he spent the entire night running and holding. I knew he was the kind who would jab, wrestle and run all right, only not at the same time. I just cannot give that kind of fighter any sort of credit and I have absolutely zero respect for him. Part of boxing is to hit and not be hit: you are taught that from the moment you first lace on a glove as a youngster. But what is the point in going into the fight game if you are just going to spoil it?

In the early stages of the fight, I tried to cut off Barney's escape, but he did more running than Paula Radcliffe. I stalked him and Barney ran. In the sixth I caught up with him with a cracking right hand and Barney's response was to run even faster, just throwing out the occasional flicking, ineffective jab. In the eighth and tenth rounds I thought I had him down, but he lasted until the end by holding on whenever I got close. A bit like the Dirrell fight many years later, Barney was finally docked a point for persistent holding in the eleventh round. Why the official didn't punish Barney sooner is beyond me: had he done it in the earlier rounds and warned Barney to stop or be disqualified; it might have been a far more entertaining fight. Whatever the rights and wrongs of the officiating, I won by stacks: the referee's scorecard was 118–110, which tells you how easy it was. It was, however, a fight I'd sooner forget.

I promised Barney beforehand that I would unleash hell on him and it was hell all right – to watch. In my view he came only to survive and to make me look bad, and he certainly managed to do that. By the end of the fight, my face was marked: I didn't look too great as he used his head to butt me to good effect a few times. But at least I had got another win under my belt against a different type of opponent, although with the possible exception of Dirrell, Barney was the most negative fighter I have ever shared a ring with.

Immediately after the Barney fight I had surgery on my knuckle. The operation was at the Park Hospital in Nottingham under a surgeon called Nick Downing, who did a fantastic job in making sure it would not become a long-term injury. Despite Barney being a crap fight, I felt I was still making good headway and, more importantly, I kept winning. I fought Barney in July 2005 and by the end of the year a few of my injuries had time to heal, including the knuckle I had hurt against Porras. Just before Christmas, I was scheduled to face Ruben Groenewald, again at the Ice Arena in Nottingham.

There was a bit of needle as I had sparred with Groenewald in London a few times. I don't think he liked me because in sparring I nearly dislocated his head off his shoulders a few times, but he didn't stretch me. The fact we had sparred helped to sell the fight to the public and the tickets went well: there were just over 3,000 fans there on the night, even though my last performance had been only very average. I told everybody who would listen that Groenewald would go down in round five, which meant that Nottingham was swamped with bets on the fifth, including my brothers, who put a pile of money on it. Basically, I knew I couldn't lose: Groenewald was a streetwise, strong kid, but he was limited and coming up from middleweight. He said all the right things about how overrated I was, but if I ever knew I was in a different class to an opponent, it was this one.

I started fairly cautiously to see what Ruben had got. It wasn't much, so I gave him a taste of my power towards the end of the first round with a clubbing right. At the start of the second, Groenewald came out like a threshing machine, but I knew that wouldn't last. He tried to make a big deal of a couple of slaps I gave him to the back of the head, gesturing to my corner that I should have been thrown out the ring for illegal punching. The ref, though, was having none of it. In the third, I should have finished him off as I had him in real trouble on the ropes but Groenewald got lucky and he was saved by the bell. I held him up in round four and my friends and family all cashed in when Groenewald finally went down in the fifth. I hadn't really caught Groenewald with anything particularly effective, but the ref had clearly seen enough. Groenewald was just a punch bag: there was nothing coming back from him, so the referee waved the fight off. Afterwards, Groenewald complained that the referee had stopped it early and he wanted a re-match. Even now I chuckle at that. Groenewald was certainly brave, but another fight would have been a waste of time.

After the Groenewald fight, I headed for Los Angeles to spend New Year's Eve with three of my best mates: Adam Fukes, Scott Denby and James Bennett. Adam reckons he is a dead ringer for Nick Lachey, the former partner of the American singer Jessica Simpson. He never used to miss an episode of *Newlyweds: Nick and Jessica*, a reality TV programme a bit like *The Osbournes*. Adam is a good-looking bloke, with dark hair and a chiselled chin, and fancied his chances with the now single Jessica Simpson. There was a party in LA on New Year's Eve and Adam went on the internet and bought four tickets, costing about £150 a head. He did it just because she was there and he wanted to try and meet her.

The party was to be held outside at Universal Studios, with all sorts of cardboard cut-outs of New York skyscrapers. With our VIP tickets, we were all revved up for it and got ourselves dressed up in an effort to try and catch Jessica Simpson's eye. But when we got there in our taxi all we could see was a security bloke on the door saying move on buddy, the party's off. It had rained all week in LA for about the first time in 200 years or something, and because the party was outside, the organisers just cancelled it.

I pissed myself laughing, as did Scott and James, although Adam was gutted. We went to Hollywood to go to a nightclub and all his dreams of meeting Jessica Simpson were blown away by the weather. It was a great trip out there, despite the weather. We went to the famous 'Muscle' beach on Venice beach and that was an experience not to forget: there were more bodybuilders out there, both male and female, than I ever knew even existed.

We hired some bikes to go riding along the boardwalk and, although we were told the brakes were on the opposite handle to bikes in Britain, James clearly didn't listen. He was riding past some girls trying to look cool with his new Tiger Woods TAG watch, and attempted a big skid to show what a catch he could be. He pulled the front brake, thinking it was the back brakes and went over the handlebars, smashing his face on the floor. James's new watch was bent and scratched and he also hurt his knee, while we just stood watching and cracking up with laughter. The girls didn't think much of him either. Every day of the trip was like that: one of us being a bit of a dickhead and the others all taking the piss. None of us four were drinkers – we had the odd one here and there – but we partied for England, well into the small early hours most nights.

If I thought I had the fight game sussed, I was about to get something of a wake-up call. My next opponent was Dale Westerman who, a bit like Groenewald, I just didn't rate. All right, he had an OK record, but I just didn't think he stood a chance against me. Arriving back in Britain from Los Angeles, I didn't really train properly. Rob was warning me all the time, saying I was just going through the motion, and he turned out to be right. I went into that fight unprepared and unfit, and I paid the price.

My grandfather Wojciech Froch, or 'William' to us, was forced to serve in the German Army in the Second World War after the Nazis invaded his home town, Katowice in Poland.

Me, Wayne and Lee with Dad on a ferry to the Isle of Wight.

Looking angelic in a
school photo, aged five.

Lee and I with Dad
on the dodgems.

With one of my first
trophies for boxing,
aged 11.

My amateur days. At the Crystal Palace
Sports Centre. From L-R: Audley Harrison,
Me, Gary Jones, Courtney Fry and coach
Ian Irwin.

With my best mate Adam Fukes after beating
Alan Page at the Derby Storm Arena in 2003.

Fighting Charles Adamu in my first scheduled twelve-rounder after turning pro.

With the Commonwealth belt around my waist and the English title belt over my shoulder after beating Adamu in Nottingham.

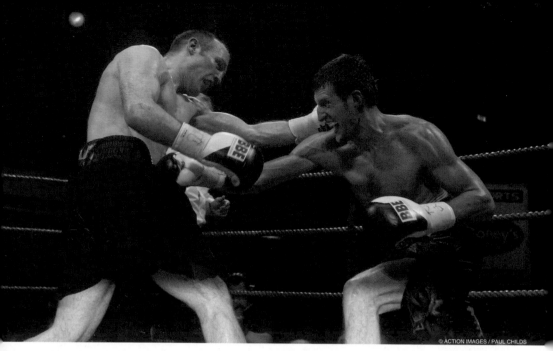

Beating Brian Magee at York Hall, Bethnal Green, despite breaking my hand.

Fighting Jean Pascal for the vacant WBC Super Middleweight title on home turf in Nottingham at the Trent FM Arena.

In the corner during the Taylor fight.

Celebrating my emphatic win over
Jermain Taylor.

A quick bit of patching up after the Taylor fight.

Against Mikkel Kessler in Denmark in 2010.

Early in the second round, I thought I had Westerman out of there as I hit him with a great upper cut and I was convinced it would be an easy night's work. But my lack of conditioning came back to bite me on the arse as I then tore my bicep muscle really badly, throwing a big right-hand shot. There are pictures where you can see how my arm went bright red and purple, from the shoulder to the hand. Luckily, the bicep muscle had not detached itself from the rest of my arm. If it had, I would have been pulled from the fight to avoid any further damage, and lost my winning record as a result.

I was in agony and had only myself to blame. Westerman was a brawler, short and stocky, but he was very limited and although I put him away in the ninth round it should have been a whole lot earlier. The pain was horrific in my right arm, but any thoughts that I might get some sympathy just didn't happen. Rob did the 'I told you so' after the fight and of course he was right. I also copped a load of stick from the main Sky commentator Jim Watt, saying if I fought like this in my next fight, I would get my head taken off by Brian Magee. Westerman had a go as it was his shot at the Commonwealth belt, but if I had been fully focused on the job, he wouldn't have lasted a couple of rounds.

But I wasn't fully focused: my mind was elsewhere. Even my ring entrance that night at York Hall was to a Biggie Smalls song that I had been partying to in LA. I was always going to beat Westerman but, looking back now, what I did was stupid. I thought I had all the answers and I didn't. I take no pride in being so daft and Rob, as usual, said all the right things to sort me out. I'd got away with it this time, but if I was going to continue to cut corners, eventually I would come a cropper, especially given the calibre of who I was going to fight next.

Westerman was a warm-up to the big one: Brian Magee. Up to that point, I had been going through the levels since turning pro: Alan Page for the English title was the first step up; Charles Adamu for the Commonwealth title was the next; Magee, though, was the first really world-class fighter I had faced. This was a fighter who had enjoyed a humdinger with Robin Reid when Reid was in his prime. He had only recently lost a European title challenge against Vitali Tsypko on a wafer-thin points decision – a fight that, in fact, I thought he had won. Magee was a whole new level for me and was gunning for my British title. Such was the interest in the fight that the promoter Frank Maloney beat Mick on the purse bid, and the contest took place at Bethnal Green's York Hall.

Despite not being able to fight in my hometown, things started well for me, when I dropped Magee in round one with an upper cut. Backing me up to the ropes with a flurry of shots, Magee walked straight into my trap: there was a huge gap in his defence as he motored forwards and I sent an upper cut through it. He went over and bravely got up to continue. By the second round, I started to get the measure of his rough, dirty tactics: Magee would throw a shot, lead in with his head and hold. When he clinched hold of me, he would whack me on the side of my head on the opposite side to where the ref was standing. Even so, I was catching him with big shots and it looked only a matter of time before I would finish him off.

I felt so confident in that second round that I threw a big missile, a right-hand haymaker over the top. It was the shot which Robin Reid used to such good effect against him in their scrap. A couple of stiff jabs opened him up and there was my chance, so I threw the big right-hander. By my own admission I threw the punch badly. Instead of the force of the shot landing on his head with the front of my knuckle, I glanced him on the side of the head and all the force of the blow went down my thumb.

Boxing fans might not know it, but not all gloves are the same, far from it. On this occasion I was wearing a different set of gloves to my usual Reyes as Maloney, because he was promoting, had the authority to insist that I wore BBE gloves. When I put them on they felt like pillows and the thumb just did not sit right. There was probably nothing wrong with the gloves, but they just felt completely different to my usual pair. I didn't want to kick up a big stink before the fight so just said this would be the first and last time I ever wore that make of gloves. Little did I know I was about to pay a heavy price.

The second I hit Magee I felt it crack. I knew immediately what had happened. My hand had gone. Afterwards I was to discover that it was the first metacarpal which attaches itself to the thumb that was broken. In the medical trade it is called a Bennett's fracture. The bone was completely broken and I felt sick as the pain throbbed inside my glove. As usual, I sat in my corner, told Rob and guess what? As usual, Rob just said don't worry about it. He had never been one to use excuses and he wasn't going to start now.

From rounds three to about the seventh, I felt really drained, probably because my body's energy was all directed towards my bad hand. Also, I knew that if I threw another right hand I could have done some real damage. I had to be really selective with my right hand because if I had caught him on his elbow while throwing a body shot there is no way I could have carried on.

Magee was able to get back into the fight using his experience and dirty tactics. After all, that is how he fights. Magee head butted me loads of times throughout the fight and I have still got the scars to prove it, so I did what I have always done, I head butted him back. I caught him once under the eye with a beauty. In round seven, I also caught him with a big left-handed body shot and Magee wobbled, eventually going down on one knee. The commentary team were asking if it was a legitimate knock down as his hand and knee touched the canvas, but the referee Richie Davies made the right decision. A punch was thrown and his hand touched the floor, which in my book makes it a knock down.

I could see that the pace was beginning to tell after about the ninth round and I hurt him badly in round ten. In the next round I knew it was over. I caught him sweetly with a double jab and Magee dropped his arms: he held on to me, but I shrugged him off. I had my arms down and threw a long, left upper cut that caught him under the chin, lifting his head up. I went bang with a right hand that was as painful for me as it probably was for him. I don't know how for the life of me he didn't go over, but somehow he grabbed hold of me again. There was nothing left in him now: in every sense, he was hanging on. Another overhand left and I had

Magee in the corner. I lined him up and as he came to grab me again I sent another upper cut on to his chin. It landed with horrific force and sent the blood, spit and snot flying into his corner. Magee collapsed on my left foot. I can be a spiteful bastard at times, and I was that annoyed with his constant head-butting and holding tactics that I wanted to stamp on his face. Being honest, I had totally lost my cool and all I wanted to do was inflict some real pain on him. Maybe it was the broken hand that made me so angry, I don't know, but I guess that sums up your emotions when you are in the ring. It is dog eat dog in there and pretty much anything is fair game.

At the time, just for a few seconds, I could have done anything and it was all I could do not to stamp on Magee. I was properly wound up and I am just thankful I didn't: Magee needed oxygen when the ref called it off and thankfully he made a quick recovery. I am glad he was OK and that he was healthy because I now have a lot of time for Brian. I might think he's a dirty fucker in the ring, but out of it he was a top bloke and I respect what he has done in boxing, whatever my opinions on his tactics being close to the edge of what is allowed.

Despite the two knock downs, two 10–8 rounds, I was amazed to find out afterwards that two of the judges had it quite close when I stopped Magee in the eleventh. It was a Frank Maloney show and whatever politics was going on I didn't want to know or care, but how two judges had me winning by a single round when the fight was stopped, I do not know. The other judge had me ahead by five points, which to me was about right.

Magee and I weren't the only ones the fight had taken it out of. The referee Richie Davies had a lot of work that night and after our clash, in the changing rooms, he looked pale and ill. He told Rob he didn't feel well, which wasn't a massive surprise as Richie had spent the best part of eleven rounds pulling us apart. Richie was almost as involved in the fight as we were and Rob handed him a litre and a half of water. Richie drank it down in one go and didn't even come up for air. Within two minutes he looked better but he was obviously dehydrated from the fight.

A day or so later I went to A and E and got my hands sorted at the Queen's Medical Centre in Nottingham. Because it was deemed an emergency operation, I had it done straight away: strange, isn't it, that you can wait months and months for a routine operation, but if it is considered an emergency you go to the front of the queue. Apparently a thumb is regarded as a limb in the medical profession, which is why I was classed as an emergency. You can break a finger in an industrial accident or whatever and it could take months for an op, but break a bone that disables the use of your thumb and you are in there the next day. The surgeon, again Nick Downing, put pins in the first metacarpal and it was all over in about twenty-five minutes, done and dusted.

I had the pins in for about six weeks and when they took them out I was still a bit cautious. It was a full six months before I fought again. When you think about it, I have had a terrible run of luck with injuries over the years, which is probably because I hit so hard. They always say the bangers in boxing hurt their hands so much easier and I think I follow that rule.

*

Little did I know at the time that an even worse injury was to come, but after I had recovered from beating Magee, I was finally set to face Tony Dodson. He had pulled out three times before, with one injury after another, and it was getting on my nerves. Anyway, at last he said yes and the date was set for Nottingham in November 2006, in another defence of my British and Commonwealth crown.

I knew Dodson was rough and tough and would come and have a go, but he was too limited for me. In the first round I had a look at him by letting him work and put his shots together. I allowed him to throw shots as I kept my defence tight, blocking his best efforts. I do that sometimes because I want to see what the opponent is bringing to the table. It might have cost me the round, I don't know. I was speculating to accumulate in the belief that the one round I may have lost could help me win. I could see he was a bit wild and had a habit of keeping his chin in the air when he threw a right-hand shot, and I felt that there was no real method to his technique. In the second round I hit him with a couple of little ticklers and started to measure him up. My jab started firing off and I began to feel comfortable.

It turned out to be an easy night's work in front of a big crowd, which was a bit disappointing. All the build-up had been suggesting it was going to be a barnstormer and Sky had it down as a brilliant domestic dust-up. In fact, it was all over very quickly. I got him in range in the third round and I finished him off. I cranked it up in that round and put together a few shots to see how he coped with it. I threw a double jab right hand and then a left hook to the body that landed sweet on the ribs. Dodson went over and I was thinking, brilliant, I'm going to have some fun here. I was bitterly disappointed when he failed to get up. I've heard since on the grapevine that Dodson went around telling everyone for two rounds he gave me a boxing lesson. It's funny the reasons you hear after the event, but the truth of the matter is, Dodson was outclassed.

Immediately after the fight, there was a proper full-blown riot. There were some disgraceful scenes as chairs went flying everywhere. Millwall had played Forest that day so they had a load of fans there and Dodson's supporters came down from Liverpool too. About twenty-five or so police officers came in and started charging the crowd. I got out of there as soon as I could and the scenes were shocking. There were women and kids in the crowd and all these dickheads were trying to prove to their mates how hard they were. It was stupid and thankfully nothing like that has ever happened again in one of my fights and I hope in the future it never does. I've watched the scenes on YouTube and, to be perfectly frank about it, they are disgraceful. Boxing should have nothing to do with the sort of idiots who want to have a punch-up, just because someone else is from another part of the country. Who really cares? What if a chair leg had hit a little kid in the eye, or an old lady going out there to support her local boxer? It was mindless stuff.

Sergey Tatevosyan had been in with some proper fighters and he was my next opponent. Just before I met him, he had taken future world champion Lucian Bute the full twelve rounds and a few years earlier lost a European title shot to Howard Eastman, again on a twelve-round points decision. So he was right up there in terms of class. Magee and Dodson were a move up and so was Tatevosyan. I was now on the fringe of world class and if I could win this fight in style I would both look good and show the public that I could be a dominant force in the twelve-stone division. However, if I struggled to beat this big bear of a Russian I would probably never become a world champion. That was my mentality.

At the time of the Tatevosyan fight, I was beginning to get a feel of where I stood in the boxing world. I watched my training team-mates like Matthew Thirlwall, David Walker and Lee Meager and though I have nothing but respect for them as boxers and people, I think they all had limitations, which I am sure they would agree with. All of them tried their absolute best, but in the end it is down to ability – punching power, skill, stamina – and the determination and willingness to work hard to maximise those attributes. All of them have found their level, which is domestic. I would not want to give any of them stick because if it had been me, I would have said fine. That's my level. You have to live with what you have been given.

Take away anything in a boxer's make-up and that can mean the difference between winning and losing. If you haven't got any real punching power you will struggle at the top and the same is true if you haven't got the heart for it. And if you don't like getting punched in the face, then boxing is a difficult sport to excel at, because you are going to get punched. And those punches will hurt.

There are so many different factors which make up creating a world champion and, if you are short in any of them, you will not make it. I felt Tatevosyan was another question being asked of me. Could I take his best shots, because he could dig? As I found out after Dale Westerman taught me a lesson, there are no short-cuts in boxing. There is no cheating way to do it and get to the top. You can have the best promoter in the world who will get you hand-picked opponents but eventually, in order to reach the top, you are going to have to face someone who doesn't mind getting hit hard and will be happy to answer back.

I like to think I am the consummate professional, having learned the hard way. Howard Eastman had everything in his locker to be a world champion but he didn't make it and I reckon the reason is a simple one: commitment. He used to go back to his birthplace in Guyana and party and I honestly believe that is the reason why he never made it to the very top. OK, he went the distance with William Joppy, Bernard Hopkins and Arthur Abraham but he never won the big ones. I don't know what he used to get up to in Guyana but he would always arrive back badly out of shape and I just don't think you can do that.

I trained like a maniac for the fight. This was not going to be anything like the Carl Froch who turned up for Westerman. Mind you, I was a bit shocked when Tatevosyan came into the ring with two wolf skins, with the heads draped over either shoulder. It looked a bit bonkers. As I got over the ropes I remember thinking, I wonder if he killed them with his bare hands somewhere in Siberia. He's not the only one to go in for this sort of thing of course: 'King' Arthur Abraham wears a crown and comes in on a throne for his fights, which again, could be a bit unnerving for a young fighter. Me? I just think it looks plain silly. Though I loved Prince Naseem Hamed's showmanship and he came in on a fake flying carpet once! I don't suppose you can get more showmanship than that.

From the first bell I just felt totally switched on, as if I knew I was going to knock him out early. There were no injury worries and after beating Dodson and Magee I felt ready for another fight that would get me ever closer to the world title.

The Tatevosyan fight was over nearly as quickly as it began. I put it on him right at the first bell and he was in trouble in the first round. I had him in a neutral corner in the second and unleashed shot after shot until the ref jumped in to save him. He was gone and the referee made the right decision: you could see Tatevosyan's eyes, as well as his legs, were all over the place.

After beating Tatevosyan, I only wanted to fight the man I regarded as the best in my weight division: Joe Calzaghe. I was convinced that I would beat him: he was a southpaw who came at you in straight lines, and I thought I would knock him out. I was super confident in my ability and I thought I had been brilliantly brought on by Rob and Mick. It was a great team effort: Rob did the matchmaking, Mick the promoting and I did the fighting and winning. I'd moved through the gears in terms of opponents and was matched very well. I'd won my English title in my tenth fight, Commonwealth in my twelfth and British in my fourteenth. Tatevosyan was my twenty-first professional match-up, and I felt I was ready to move up and fight for a world title.

I had been having trouble with my knee for several years by this point, and although it was just uncomfortable, it never felt quite right. Every time I stretched it a little too much the pain would be intense. After the initial injury and inconclusive scan I had another couple of scans on it and the doctors thought I might have torn my anterior cruciate ligament. The doctors couldn't be sure and I convinced myself it would be OK. After all, some people can function without a cruciate, although not usually sportsmen.

Six months before my next fight, this time with Robin Reid, I was having a kick around with some mates in Nottingham. I was playing on a pretty poor AstroTurf surface in Nottingham in studs and the local Wayne Rooney and I were having a bit of a battle. He was nudging me and I was doing it back to him. Then we both went for the same ball at full sprint. My foot got down there to the outside of the ball and I got there first, but as I stopped dead all I could hear was crunch, click and a horrible ringing noise. My whole body felt in shock. Then I started to feel sick. I was on the floor and I remember thinking I don't really want to look at my foot because I had seen another kid do that, only to look up and see his foot facing the wrong way to his leg. I didn't want to see that.

I needed the cruciate ligament to work for me much more for football than for boxing as footy involves a lot more stretching and sprinting. Although I didn't know it at the time, my cruciate had in fact been torn many years before so it was very much an accident waiting to happen. I did a grade-two tear to all my other knee ligaments and on the scan I had, the anterior ligament didn't even show up. The doctors said there was a gap where the ligament should have been, which meant that this was not a new injury. It had actually been damaged ages before and had tried to heal of its own accord.

In other words, my knee was a mess. I had torn ligaments all over the place and had no ligament in my anterior where a ligament should have been. You didn't need to be a doctor to work out it wasn't looking good. I went to Nottingham Forest Football Club and got it looked at by their physio Steve Devine, the old Derby County and Northern Ireland footballer. He had a high-quality scan done and said it could be fixed, but it would take maybe a whole year. Six months later I fought Robin Reid.

My surgeon Derek Bickerstaff got me in quickly. He performed an ACL reconstruction using my hamstring tendons. The new ligament then starts to get bigger and stronger over time. Thankfully we are all made with extra hamstring tendons that can be used in these types of operations.

As it turned out, I got lucky because I refused to have morphine as a painkiller. I hadn't taken any as I don't agree with putting things like that in my body: I'm a big believer in the fact that your body treats itself. (I do take diclofenac tablets as a painkiller but it is also anti-inflammatory so it is also helping the body to recover.) Anyway, the machine which the hospital put me on bends your leg every few seconds, so that straight after the operation the rehab starts. Except that, in my case, the machine didn't work. Had I been zonked out with morphine I dread to think what would have happened.

The metal pins which held the machine together were faulty, which meant that every time the machine bent my knee, I was moving further up the bed. Instead of bending my knee forty-five degrees, it was starting to bend the knee more and more and if I had been comatose I wouldn't have known anything about it. My knee would have been way over-flexed and untold damage could have been caused. Fortunately, I was awake and knew instantly that something was wrong. I stopped the machine and told the nurse, but she had no idea how to fix it. The nurse said the bloke who was coming to fix it would be an hour, but it was crucial at that stage to keep the knee moving to try and get the blood circulation going. I saw that the metal pins weren't in the right place, and that they had popped out of their grooves, so I did it myself. I played around, got the pins back into the grooves and it worked.

I don't take any type of drugs to this day. I am convinced that antibiotics result in more long-term problems for your body than you get out of them in short-term gain. If you get an infection or a cold or whatever, the first thing a doctor does is give you antibiotics. To get rid of an infection, the antibiotics will get rid of the bad bacteria but they will also get rid of the good bacteria. They write off your immune system totally and that is clearly bad for you. You need good bacteria to fight off infection, but taking antibiotics results in your whole body having to start building its immune system up all over again from scratch.

All you need for colds and infections is loads and loads of water and lots of vitamin C. You need a week or two weeks of rest and your body will recover a lot stronger and more naturally.

Anyway, the Forest physio said I was going to be out for twelve months before I could really start using the knee again. I asked him what that was based on and he replied it would be that long before I could safely play football again. However, you don't need your legs as much for boxing. Yes, you need to be able to run and turn, but there is nothing like the twisting and turning at high speed that a footballer requires. I was told I would be able to run again in three to four months, but I was giving it a go in two.

I wasn't on crutches even for a day. I thought the longer I was on crutches, the longer it was going to take to come back. The problem was that the muscle above my knee had just wasted away because of the operation and so building that up took a while and mine, even to this day, is still pretty small. The rehab on my knee was a full-time job. Building the muscle up from nothing meant exercising for hours and hours every day. After two months, I tried running again and the pain was horrendous. My kneecap was all over the place because there wasn't enough muscle around it to provide for it a solid support. I would try walking up and down stairs for hours and eventually the strength around the knee started to build up. It was hard work, but six long months after the initial injury I was back in the ring, defending my British and Commonwealth title.

In his prime, Robin Reid had won the WBC title. He was past his best when I fought him, but he was still a formidable fighter and I know he trained right because he was a very proud boxer. He didn't have as much in the can as he used to but he still had enough to have stopped Jesse Brinkley before facing me. Before that he had been stopped himself by Jeff Lacy, but even so, I was under no illusions: Reid was still a high-class fighter.

That said, the Robin Reid that I beat in five rounds was not the Robin Reid that narrowly lost to Joe Calzaghe in 1999. In fact, I thought he beat Calzaghe hands down, even though the judges gave it to Joe on a split decision. I have watched the fight a few times and I thought Robin caught Joe lots of times with great shots and had him in trouble. I gave it to Reid by two rounds. I am not just saying that because it is Joe: the judges were very mixed in their scoring, with two of them making Joe an easy-ish winner and the third giving it to Reid by a similarly wide margin.

My own fight with Reid was negotiated very easily as he could see me as a way back to the top flight and I saw it as a stepping stone up. As fight night neared, I was warned by both Rob and plenty of friends within boxing that Reid would still be dangerous. As it turned out they were absolutely right. Even though the statistics suggest it was a straightforward win inside five rounds, that doesn't tell half the story.

There was a noisy, partisan crowd of about 6,000 fight fans in the arena that night. I settled into a pretty decent rhythm early on and put Reid down with a flurry of shots in the second round. As he went to the canvas he grabbed hold of both my legs, which hurt my knee. I went down with him in order not to twist my knee, but in doing so I over-flexed the knee and it bothered me. I was still thinking about my knee when Reid caught me with an absolute haymaker in the third round. Reid was someone I had always watched growing up through the amateurs so I had a lot of respect for his power. It's the last thing a boxer loses: the reflexes go first, then the stamina, but the final thing that goes for any fighter, especially the top ones, is the ability to punch very hard. Reid still had that, and yet I'd got a bit too cocky and over-confident and paid the price.

When Reid sent over a big right hand towards the end of the third, I saw it coming. I thought there was no way that's landing so I pulled out, just what Rob had taught me not to do every day in the gym. Unfortunately for me, Reid cleverly stepped into the shot, closing the gap by moving about two feet towards me. The first I knew about it was when it landed flush on the jaw. His eyes were shut when he threw it so there was an element of luck, but the way he stepped in was very unorthodox and the second the punch made contact it rocked me to my boots. I stood there thinking, what the fuck was that? I just didn't think the punch was going to land but he connected perfectly. A few days later in one of the boxing magazines there was a great picture of me at the split second I was caught by Reid and my eyes have gone all boss-eyed. I was pulling a hell of a face as my neck muscles had been almost torn.

Anyway, Reid backed me on to the ropes and went for it. He hit me with a couple around the side of my head just as the bell went and those sort of punches can tend to make you a bit dizzy. I walked back to my corner in a straight line, or at least I thought it was. At the time I could see my corner, but I couldn't really focus on it. I kept stumbling towards it and the TV replays show that I did meander a bit! I could see where I wanted to go but my legs were deceiving me.

I was all right and my legs weren't shot to jelly, but obviously there had been a central nervous system breakdown. My brain was telling my feet to go to the right places, but my feet weren't necessarily doing as they were told. When I sat down in my corner, after about thirty seconds I could feel a strange pinching sensation on the calf of my left leg. I looked down there and it was my good mate Lee Meager, pinching my leg. I asked him after the fight why he did it and he said it is an old way of waking you up. He said it was the sixth time he had pinched me really hard and only on the last one did I notice it. He said he knew I was back in the land of the living on the last one, because I said, 'Oi! What the hell are you doing, Lee?' It was like a bee sting and the fact I hadn't felt it just underlines the way your brain is not in tune with the rest of your body.

I certainly felt that Reid shot but I think I have got excellent recovery powers and that night I showed it. After a minute's rest went by I got back in there and vowed it wasn't going to happen again. Rob said Reid had got away with one, but there was no way I'd let him get a second big dig in. Years later when I went down for the first time against Jermain Taylor I was nowhere near as hurt. That Taylor knock down was more about me losing my balance than anything else, but Reid's whack really stays with me as the hardest I have ever been hit in my professional career.

In the fourth round, I was a bit tentative as I jabbed and moved and lined him up, but by the fifth it was time to pull the curtains over on this one. I had him in real trouble throughout the whole round and dropped him midway through with a single punch to the temple. Reid sat down on his stool at the end of the round, and didn't come out for the next, having realised he was fighting a losing battle. Reid complained of an elbow injury but the truth was he was only going to get hurt, although his elbow was swollen when he came into the changing room after the fight.

It was quite emotional for him as he announced his retirement after nearly a decade at the very top of the sport. Reid's a very decent bloke and he did everything you could ever hope for in a career. He won a 'legitimate' world title and mixed with the very best. I thought he was robbed against Calzaghe and let's not even start about the Sven Ottke fiasco: the referee all but stopped Reid punching Ottke, yet who got the nod in Germany? Reid was a proper champion who fought the best and always gave them a tough night's work, including me. And whatever the history books say, I still think he did enough to win the Calzaghe fight.

Following the fight, the knee swelled up again and, although I hadn't done any ligament damage, I had over-stretched it and was in some pain. My surgeon Derek Bickerstaff looked at it and said it would heal, though it took some weeks to feel right again. But after so many months out of the ring, I was just happy to get some more rounds under my belt against a high-class opponent. It was a good comeback fight bearing in mind how long I had been out of action. I was very happy when I got back home and so was Mick: the promotion had been watched by easily my biggest crowd to date at the arena. I felt I was beginning to catch on with the public, who could see I was a hungry, all-action fighter who also fought to entertain.

I had been ranked with the World Boxing Council at number two and number three for so long, it was only a matter of time before I got my shot at the super-middleweight title. I had seemingly spent my entire life chasing Joe Calzaghe, the unbeaten WBC and WBO champion, and in 2008 Joe was finally on my horizon. I beat Robin Reid a week after Joe Calzaghe defeated Mikkel Kessler, so I naturally assumed I would be taking on Calzaghe for the title. But rather than fight me, Joe vacated his WBC title instead. When I first heard about his decision, I couldn't really believe it: the news hit me like a bombshell.

It all very political, as boxing can sometimes get, but I'll try and explain what happened as I see it. I was supposed to have been taking on Denis Inkin in a final eliminator for a shot at Calzaghe and the WBC title but Inkin, claiming an injury, pulled out for a second time. With that contest cancelled, I obviously thought I was going to get an automatic title fight with Calzaghe. But then Joe went up to light-heavy to face Bernard Hopkins, and relinquished his title.

I was hugely disappointed, as the only person I really wanted to get in the ring with was Joe. At the time I went to the papers and gave Joe a bit of stick to try and goad him into fighting me. But it was never anything personal against him: I just wanted to get the fight going. It would have been a fantastic occasion: over 50,000 people roaring us on at Cardiff's Millennium Stadium, and the chance for boxing fans to discover which one of us was the better fighter. Even now, I feel that fight should have happened.

I often wonder what the outcome of a clash with Joe Calzaghe would have been. I think I showed in wiping the floor with Arthur Abraham that I have got the technical skills that would have been needed to beat Joe. I lost a close one to Mikkel Kessler and Joe won a close one against the

Dane, but that doesn't mean to say Joe would have got the better of me. He fought Kessler in front of 50,000 Welshmen, whereas I went to the lion's den of Kessler's home fans and even to this day I thought I won. It goes without saying that I'm convinced I would have got the better of Joe. Yes, Joe was a great champion who held his title for many years, but if there is a criticism of him it's that, while he went up against some good fighters, I also think Joe fought some absolute no-hopers. I mean, who the hell was Tocker Pudwill? Or Evans Ashira? Or Mger Mkrtchyan? All were World Championship title defences!

I read the statement Joe made after the news had filtered out that he admitted using cocaine following his decision to hang up his gloves. I have no intention at all of kicking a man when he is down and I have a degree of sympathy for Joe, but that doesn't make it right. It was not only the fact that he admitted taking cocaine, which is bad enough, as an example to the many thousands of kids who look up to him, well, I don't know where to start. He complained that he was the victim of a sting operation, but for what it is worth, my opinion is that if you don't want to get hustled, don't do anything to get hustled for in the first place.

Anyway, back to the WBC situation. I was his mandatory, and if you win a title, you should defend it where it counts. I suspect Joe fought Hopkins for money – an understandable reason – but even so, I still can't get used to the simple fact he voluntarily vacated his world title. I don't think it's right for a boxer to give up their belt. Especially when it was to move up a weight and fight an old man in his forties, albeit one of the all-time greats.

Joe, if you're reading this, you should have fought me, and I think it's something deep down you probably agree with.

After the knee calmed down I went to Tenerife to do some warm-weather training, which was a fantastic two weeks of running and sitting in the sun. Next up would be the fight against Denis Inkin, who had beaten me in the amateurs. Except, of course, Inkin wasn't going to play ball.

After beating Reid, the WBC announced that Inkin and I would fight as a final eliminator for Joe Calzaghe's WBC title. The fight was made for March, but Inkin pulled out, claiming an injury. Mick went to the WBC and told them the situation was getting ridiculous because it looked like Inkin didn't fancy it. The WBC came back and gave him one last chance. The governing body said if Inkin pulled out again, I would be made Calzaghe's mandatory challenger for the world title. It was at this point that Calzaghe announced to the world that he was moving up to light-heavyweight to take on Bernard Hopkins because he could no longer make the twelve-stone super-middle limit. But, as he kept his WBO super-middleweight title, a clash with Calzaghe was still on the cards, as long as I beat Inkin.

I was already super fit but the work I did in Tenerife at altitude was superb. If it was designed to give me a bit of a boost, it worked. I felt in great nick and when I came back from Tenerife I was ready for Inkin. Having landed back in London, I was on the Gatwick Express when Rob told me Inkin had pulled out again. I was boiling and I could barely contain myself. A fair few people would have seen me going bonkers on the phone near my flat just outside Turnpike Lane tube station that day.

I was so angry, I forgot one of my bags: the one with all my kit in and my laptop. I got back to my flat in Hornsey, north London, when I realised I had left the bag on the train. I turned around and went straight back to Victoria station in the middle of the rush hour and found the train guard. I told him I had left my bag on the Gatwick Express about an hour ago. He said, 'You're a silly boy, aren't you? What did you do that for?' I couldn't believe I was about to get a bollocking off the train guard, but then he just started laughing. He told me to follow him and there was my bag, with thirty kilos of gear: head guards, sparring gloves, training kit, a portable DVD player and my laptop, which was more important to me than anything else. I nearly kissed the bloke.

With Inkin pulling out about two weeks before we were set to meet, I was without an opponent and my new television deal with ITV looked to be set to start with more of a whimper than a bang. I ended up fighting Albert Rybacki as a late replacement for Inkin. Rybacki might not have been a great name but at least he was unbeaten (he had a 15–0 record, which just goes to show how these things can be deceiving), but a fighter who has never lost is always going to be confident. Mick had done a brilliant job considering he only had a fortnight to find a suitable opponent.

Rybacki was Polish and when I looked at him on the videotapes, I didn't think I would be stretched. I was right. I was whacking away at him from round two onwards and there was very little coming back. I told my brothers to put their wagers on the second or third rounds, so as the third round ended I am sure I could hear plenty of groans at ringside. I managed to finish him off in the fourth and unfortunately my older brother Lee, who loves a flutter, lost his money.

From being in a disastrous situation with my new broad-casters, Rybacki had at least stepped up to the plate and fought. I wasn't kidding anyone though, because he was obviously second-class, whereas the Inkin fight had been the real deal. ITV were naturally disappointed and so was I that Inkin had pulled a flanker on us all. After the Rybacki fight, Mick started the negotiations to finally get me in the ring with Calzaghe. The WBC ordered purse bids to be made, and Calzaghe was pushed into a corner. He had to fight me or relinquish his title, and he chose the latter. I'll let you decide on that. Though personally, I think it was a bottle job.

CHAPTER 9

Then of course came the Jean Pascal fight, and I finally had the super-middleweight title. At this point in my career, Rob and I were in full agreement that we had to keep the ball rolling: there was no point, at my age, in going backwards. So when the offer came up from Mick that he could make a fight with Jermain Taylor, my WBC number one-ranked mandatory challenger, I jumped at the chance.

Robust and powerful, Taylor was my kind of fighter. And yet I fancied my chances from day one when the scrap was being made, even though in America, as I was to discover, I would be second favourite all the way up to the bell. I also accepted Taylor because I had fought long and hard to win my title and I didn't want to be remembered as someone who bottled it when the big names approached me for a match-up. Finally, I felt I needed to get out of the 'comfort zone' in Nottingham and try and take my road-show over to the United States. I also felt that going over to fight was the only way I would crack it with the American TV market, which remains very lucrative. Mind you, my mind wasn't always focused from day one on my next fights as something else happened to me just a few weeks after I had beaten Pascal. I fell in love, and I mean properly.

I've not exactly been Nottingham's answer to Don Juan over the years. I suppose I'm pretty old-fashioned when it comes to girls in that I've never had them dripping off me because I've never remotely wanted that. Also, boxing has, for so many years, been the most important part of my life. I've actually only had a few 'proper' girlfriends.

There was a girlfriend from when I was in my teens, who was into going out late and partying. She smoked weed and was pretty wild. I suppose we just drifted apart. A lot of teenagers like to go out and get pissed a lot, but I didn't. Maybe that's why we split, I don't know.

I was with my next proper girlfriend for four years. We started going out after I won the British title. She was a student at Nottingham University and worked part-time as a waitress in Nando's, where my best friend Adam Fukes and me at that time used to spend half our lives.

I met her there after having been single for a few years. We got on very well but as soon as we started living together we were really incompatible and we both realised we weren't right for each other. Basically, it just didn't work out.

After we split up I was single again until a friend of mine, Adam Harris, who works for Mick Hennessy's company in Canada, rang me up. Adam is a top bloke who I like a lot and he called me out of the blue to ask how I was. Off the cuff he said he knew somebody who I would really get on with. I said I was happy staying single for a while. I'd just become the world champion, was very focused on boxing, and I wasn't really interested in going steady with anyone.

I was and have always been pretty content in my own company, but Adam had other ideas. He got hold of Rachael Cordingley's number and I got it off him. I suppose I was intrigued more than anything because Adam seemed so certain we would hit it off. I eventually plucked up the courage to send her a text message, just to introduce myself. I then phoned her and after speaking to her for what seemed like an age I thought how easygoing she appeared on the end of a phone line.

We talked about various different things and how she knew Adam through her modelling work. I think she had done some PR stuff for a company Adam had worked for. Adam is a real people person and he just said time and time again, 'I know she is the right girl for you.' I thought 'What's the worst that could happen?' so I caught a train to London to where Rachael lived.

I had a sneaky look at Rachael on the internet and, without stating the blindingly obvious, she was definitely worth a £50 railway ticket to London. I went down there also to meet a sponsor of mine, Joe Upchurch, and his girlfriend Renee and him double-dated with Rachael and me.

We all went out for a night on the town in London and ate at one of Gordon Ramsay's restaurants. It was a cracking meal and it was followed by a casino and then a nightclub. Rachael and I had a dance and we just laughed all night long from start to finish. It was absolutely memorable and we ended up at the Lanesborough Hotel in the West End on Hyde Park Corner.

We stayed the night there, in separate bedrooms I might add, then the next day I woke up and was chuffed to bits as she hadn't done a runner! I certainly had no intention of doing a runner either and we spent the day in the West End, shopping and going to the cinema. It was just us two and we had another great night. As we left the next day I kissed her on the cheek and said I'd be in touch.

I wanted to try and play it cool so I waited a while and a few days later I called her and she said she had been waiting for me to phone. Little did she know I had been itching every hour to ring her. I invited Rachael up to Nottingham and she came up to my house.

Instead of staying a day or two, she stayed for a couple of weeks, meeting my friends and my family. For years my mum had told me I had not met the right person yet, but when I did she was going to tell me. When you meet the right person, my mum said, you will be relaxed and everything will just flow so easily. She met Rachael and within a couple of minutes she pulled me to one side and said, 'That's the one.' It sounds a bit soppy but I was so happy. Suffice to say, it was an amazing and incredible experience.

Rachael and I are very compatible and I love her to bits. In fact, you'd have to be bonkers not to love Rachael as she has no side to her at all. She treats everybody the same and that's another aspect of her character which I love. I am not into these people who smile for the cameras then bitch about each other. Rachael says what she thinks and I invariably agree with her. I don't think we have had a proper row since I've met her because she is that easygoing. I just think I'm the luckiest bloke in the world to have Rachael beside me.

While my first WBC super-middleweight title defence was being made against Taylor – and the negotiations were pretty straightforward – I decided on my training programme. This would be two weeks in Nottingham, just ticking over and getting back my fitness levels, then seven weeks in Loughton, Essex. Three weeks before the fight, I would move out to Canada to acclimatise: the fight itself would be held in a massive hotel and casino in the wilds of Connecticut.

In Nottingham I started doing a bit of running and shadow boxing, but the real hard graft was done at Tony Sims's gym in Loughton, on the outskirts of London. I would go down on Sunday night and stay in Loughton at the house of a friend, Mark Seltzer. Mark has done my corner for years as an assistant so staying with him just a few minutes away from the gym was perfect. I trained in Loughton from Monday to Friday and sparred a lot with then-Commonwealth middleweight champion Darren Barker and super-middleweight prospect George Groves.

Whenever a fighter comes out and says he is in the best shape of his life you can often take it with a pinch of salt but in the build-up to Taylor, I had the evidence, in black and white, to back it up. Since turning pro, I have kept a little diary to mark down every aspect of my career. That means every training run time, every sparring session and every gym visit were all logged in a book. At the weekends in Nottingham, I went for the same six-mile run I had done for years and normally I did it in thirty-five minutes, which is under six minutes a mile. Anyone who runs regularly will tell you that is a decent lick. I was shocked to break my best time in the run-up to the Taylor fight, but a few days after the high of that achievement, my world then came crashing down. I may be a proper anorak when it comes to recording my training runs, but that doesn't mean a thing if you don't look where you are going.

A week before flying out to Canada, I turned over on my ankle doing something very, very stupid. I went for a quick run in Nottingham with Adam, just a little jog around to get a sweat going, but I momentarily didn't look where I was going. I went over a kerb as I crossed the road, did a mad somersault and ended up on my arse. A car pulled up and a bloke asked if I was all right. I replied that I was in some pain and couldn't walk, and bless him, the guy offered to give me a lift to hospital. I took him up on that as I couldn't actually put any pressure on the injured ankle.

My foot had instantly swelled up like a football and I was convinced I had broken my ankle. I went for a scan and in fact I had torn a load of ligaments in my ankle. This was only four weeks before the fight: for the rest of the build-up to the Taylor bout, I couldn't go running anywhere and had to make do with swimming and cycling, which aren't really my cup of tea at all. I'm not making excuses for anything, but I know my own body better than anyone and I was not as fit for the Taylor fight as I would have liked to have been. I wasn't exactly out of shape, but I couldn't run in the four weeks leading up to it. It's true that the treadmills at the gym in Canada were fantastic, top-of-the-range stuff, and I could do a bit on them. But as any fighter will tell you, treadmills are no match for proper, hard graft on the roads.

We went over to Canada and I trained near Niagara Falls at the White Oak Resort and Spa. It was a five-star palace, so my little brother Wayne, who travelled with me along with Rob, didn't know he was born. I don't think he had ever stayed anywhere quite as plush and I'm not sure I had either. It was magnificent. The fillet steaks were about four inches thick and there was something called a 'Belgian bomb' on the menu, which was basically a chocolate cake about the size of Nottingham. Wayne probably had two of them every night as he is a chocolate fiend and must have come home several sizes bigger. Rob loves his sweets as well, so he dived into a few while the rest of us weren't looking.

The food was unbelievable, but of course I looked at the menu and could barely eat anything on it. Anyone who has ever travelled to Canada or America will tell you the same thing: the food portions are about three times bigger than ours and they don't exactly go a bundle on health food either. I had porridge every day, which was OK for me, and a lot of Caesar salads in the evening, with the occasional pasta dish thrown in. The nearby gym and the hotel were tremendous and the Canadians were so friendly and helpful. Nothing was ever too much trouble. Mind you, the hotel was situated on Taylor Road, which made me laugh.

I got into serious sparring and although this might come as a shock, bearing in mind I had just beaten him, I did a lot of spar work with Jean Pascal. Jean and another boxer, the American amateur light-heavy champion Lennard Thompson, were perfect for me. I also sparred a bit with

Pascal's elder brother, who was pretty basic but very strong. The camp went really well and the fact that Jean was generous enough to spar says all you need to know about him. We had so much respect for each other after the fight that there were no hard feelings, and when Rob asked him on my behalf, whether he would be prepared to spar, he had no hesitation. Jean rang me up before we started sparring and said he would only do so on one condition, that he would get another chance to fight me. He said it only half-jokingly but, knowing Jean, he will want it.

Jean was in training for his shot at the world light-heavyweight title and had just beaten Pablo Nievas in a warm-up clash at the start of April. Jean was to get his shot at the WBC version of the world light-heavyweight title two months after I fought Taylor and I was delighted when he beat Adrian Diaconu to win the belt. It couldn't have happened to a better bloke than Jean and, even though we belted the crap out of each other for twelve rounds, we became good friends and still speak to each other on the phone on a regular basis.

Everything was going fine, apart from my sore ankle, until four days before the fight when I woke up in the middle of the night with an eye that felt like it was on fire. The pain was searing and it felt like something was burning in there.

Somehow I had picked up an infection in my eyeball and it had progressed into an ulcer. I can't really explain how unpleasant it was, except to say I'm used to pain and the feeling from the ulcer in the eye was horrific. It had come about because I'd picked up a small tear in my cornea in sparring. I'd originally thought nothing of it, but I think because of the air conditioning in the hotel rooms, which made for a very dry atmosphere, I gradually began to notice there was a burning sensation in my left eye. I went to bed hoping it would be gone by morning but the pain was so great that midway through the night I got up to look in the mirror. My eye was half-closed and my eyeball was beetroot red.

I couldn't believe it. Four nights before the fight and in the middle of the night, I had to ring the hotel medic and said I could not stand it any more. The pain was giving me a headache, and as I hadn't slept properly for a couple of nights I was feeling pissed off and tired as well. It was even worse if I shut my eye as the sore bit would touch skin. Even now when I think about it I feel sick, because the pain was that bad.

The medic cleaned it out with some sterile water and said in quite simple terms, 'You need to go to hospital.' There was nothing she could do with just some cheap cream. I went to hospital with Mick in an ambulance and landed at about 3.30 a.m. I was told the eye specialist wouldn't be in until nine, so I could either go back to the hotel or stick around in the waiting room. I decided I had no choice, as I couldn't sleep anyway. At least it was quite a nice hospital. I eventually saw the eye specialist, who gave me some anti-inflammatory eye drops and antibiotic drugs to ease the inflammation. As you know, I am totally against antibiotics, but four days before a fight I had no choice but to take them, and also there was the rather large fact that I was in agony.

The specialist was told I would be fighting in four days and he said the eye might have cleared up by then, but on the other hand it might not. The cream starting soothing straight away, but as I went back to the hotel it began to wear off. I wasn't allowed to put any more on so I endured another horrible night in bed, not sleeping a wink. The eye was filled up with all kinds of gunge and I looked a right case, but slowly it started to heal. Three nights before the fight it was getting better and two nights before I at last got a decent night's kip.

That night, a day before the weigh-in, I got a call in my hotel room. It was from a WBC official, who said, 'Mr Froch, I gather you have a corneal ulcer in your eye. The fight won't go ahead unless you make an appointment tomorrow to see an eye doctor. I will give you his name and unless he passes you, the fight won't go ahead.' I tried to bluff him by saying I didn't know what he was on about, but he said he had my medical notes in front of him, so there was no point in telling porkies.

Just before the weigh-in I had a look at my eye and it seemed OK. It appeared to have healed, but I still couldn't be sure the doctor would OK me. Although it was all a major pain in the backside, at least it took my mind off the fight somewhat. In the days leading up to taking on Taylor, I didn't really spend a minute thinking about him because the fight was in real jeopardy. What was the point in worrying about something that might not even go ahead? In the last three or four days before any fight you don't really do anything anyway: you just sit around waiting for fight time. So, in a way, the eye was a good distraction because one minute I was in agony in my bedroom and the next minute I was at the weigh-in, then I just remember walking into the ring.

The doctor examined me before the weigh-in and thankfully he said he could see where it had healed. I was lucky in that eyes do tend to heal really quickly, much faster than other parts of the body. I suppose it is for obvious reasons, as we all need our eyesight, but the doctor wasn't totally convinced. He made no bones about it and said the fight would have been off if my eye hadn't healed up. Eventually, after he took another good long look at it, he passed me to take on Taylor. The fight was on.

Rachael came out a day before the fight, along with my mum, my other brother Lee and some of my mates from back in Nottingham. Even with their support, there was no mistaking the fact they were going to be in a very small minority at the fight, with 99 per cent of the crowd backing Taylor.

In the hours and minutes leading up to the fight I didn't want to see Rachael or my mum. I am not a big one for hanging around with a big crowd before boxing, so there were maybe only half a dozen mates in the dressing room before the fight. I could hardly have allowed too many people into my dressing room anyway as it was tiny, so small that you could hardly swing a cat in it. I don't mind seeing my dad and brothers, because they are blokes. Don't ask me why, but I don't mind male company before a fight, just not female. Rachael and my mum bring about the softer side of me and I don't want my emotions messed with just before a big fight.

The preceding fight, Allan Green versus Carlos De Leon, finished really quickly with Green sparking out De Leon in the second round. So when the officials came in to tell me six minutes and you're out there, I was nowhere near ready. It usually takes me twenty minutes just to lace my boots up and I hadn't even started doing them. I am a bit fidgety before a fight. I'll do my boots up, then take them off because they're not tight enough, then put my box on, then take it off. Next it might be my gum shield which I'm not happy with. There is definitely some obsessive compulsive disorder going on!

I like everything to feel right and I like taking my time, so when they said you've only got six minutes before you start your ring walk, it was all a bit of a mad rush. I wasn't happy but the officials didn't look as though they were ready to discuss matters and, in fairness, their only job is to get me in the ring when the TV bosses say so. There was no arguing.

My right glove was very tight and didn't really feel right, probably because of the operation I'd had on it. If I had kicked up a fuss and said I'm not ready, there's no way Rob would have allowed me to leave the dressing room, but I was resigned to the fact the fight was about to start. I hit the pads for about a minute and we were off. I got put into a lift and the second the doors opened we were in the main arena. It was almost as if the lift had been purpose built to take you straight to the auditorium. The doors opened with a whoosh, a bit like those ones on the Starship Enterprise in *Star Trek*, and we were there.

I had obviously got used to fighting in Nottingham too much because I got the most hostile reception I've ever encountered in my life. The ring walk began with a lot of booing and jeering, then some fat American blokes, each with a can of Budweiser in their hands and one of them in particular wearing a big pair of glasses, were shouting, 'You fucking English bastard!' I tried to stay cool, but I remember thinking I could stretch out to my right and clock this one bespectacled tub of lard with a little snaky right-hander, while pretending that I was just stretching my arm out. I was close to back-handing him, but just as I was about to do it I thought it might not look too clever on TV if I was banjoing some fat Yank just seconds before getting in the ring.

I controlled myself, but getting rushed into the ring so quickly meant I wasn't properly focused on the job. My concentration got worse because when I got into the ring itself I tried to face the camera to show off one of my sponsors' logo, namely Nottingham City Council. The big screen in the auditorium showed exactly the same picture as the one the punters were seeing at home, so I swivelled around to see if the camera had got the logo. I did that two or three times, which just goes to show how unprepared I was for the fight. Rob was quietly talking to me but I wasn't really listening. I was glazed. My mind just wasn't on the job and it wasn't until the MC announced Jermain Taylor's name that it kicked in the fight was about to start.

Taylor did his trademark imitation of a bull about to charge when his name came booming out. I remembered watching him doing the same thing when he fought Bernard Hopkins. I thought 'Fucking hell, I'm in a fight here.' I had watched Taylor for many years and, I'll be honest, I thought he was a brilliant boxer. He had no obvious weaknesses, respectful punching power, was brave and could take a shot. He had question marks over his stamina but when he beat Hopkins twice I was convinced, along with plenty of others in the sport, that he would rule the roost for many years to come. It wasn't just that he beat Hopkins to win the unified world middleweight crown, it was the dazzling hand speed which really suggested that Taylor could be the new king of the hill. He had also beaten good names like William Joppy, Ronald 'Winky' Wright and Cory Spinks.

Taylor was abandoned by his father when he was a youngster, won bronze at the Sydney Olympics in 2000 and was a class act, no doubt about it. But his world came crashing down when he was stopped by fellow American Kelly Pavlik in seven rounds in 2007, losing his perfect record in the process. Although Taylor lost the re-match it was a close decision which could have gone either way. Despite those two defeats Taylor bounced back well by easily out-pointing Jeff Lacy five months before he faced me so I didn't think for one second he was a busted flush. On the contrary, I felt he was even more determined now to show he was back and had got the Pavlik defeats out of his system. Although you can never read too much into the pre-fight press conferences, certainly he looked keen as mustard to get back to winning ways and to prove he was the best out there in the super-middleweight division, having claimed he could no longer get down to middleweight.

When the MC said, 'And from Little Rock, Arkansas, the former undisputed middleweight champion of the world, Jermain "Bad Intentions" Taylor!' a slight shiver went through my spine. I knew I was up against the best fighter I had ever been in a ring with. I thought, 'Bollocks, I'm fighting a proper fighter in Jermain Taylor.' Nottingham and the Phoenix gym felt a long way away as we got down to business.

I didn't feel comfortable at first and, although Taylor was also very cautious, he did the unthinkable. Not once as an amateur or professional had I ever tasted the canvas, but three rounds in I finally knew what it felt like to be on the seat of my pants, where I had sent so many fighters over the years. Taylor was clever and really knew how to fight. He caught me with two decent little shots which I felt, but that was only the start of it. I decided to try and fight fire with fire, so I wound up a right hand. But mine fell short and as I was transferring my body weight, he hit me flush on the side of the head. It was a fantastic shot and, although I had been more hurt while standing on my feet, certainly against Robin Reid, I lost my balance and went down.

I know it might sound like I am blowing my own trumpet, but I wasn't badly hurt. Shocked, yes. Stunned, yes, but I wasn't out of it and felt I was in full control of my senses at all times. My lack of balance at throwing a shot and his perfect timing meant I went to the floor, but I knew I was fine. I sat down, looked over to Rob, looked at the ref and took my full eight count like a man taking his medicine. I didn't get up straight away because I was wondering if I was going to go all Bambi-legged when I stood up, but at the count of eight I got up and I was fine: everything worked properly.

It was a weird knock down. I am not going to say it was just a balance thing, because there was definitely a momentary flash, maybe a second, when I didn't quite know where I was, but there was no point where I lost consciousness. At least not for anything other than a split second. It was close to the end of the third round, so when I went back to my corner I was furious with myself and told Rob, 'I had him there and just lost concentration for a second.' Rob stayed cool and told me not to get caught by any more stupid shots like that. Instead of a tight guard, I had opened up with a big looping shot and got caught. His advice was to stay in my classic boxing 'unit' with my defence tight, not to go too wild and open myself up to shots like that again. The simple fact is, good fighters see those big shots coming from a mile off. I had to stay far more compact and not give Taylor another chance of whamming home another one, which he undoubtedly would do with those fast hands of his.

I got myself back together and weathered something of a storm in the fourth round as Taylor went for the kill. I had recovered from the crisis though and survived my first knock down. My game plan at this stage was to get to the half way stage and then really start to burn on the gas. I got him on to the end of my jab, which I feel is one of my strongest weapons and began, very slowly, to crank it up.

It was a strange fight and I can understand why many people at ringside had difficulty scoring it. My take on it is this: I hit Taylor with more shots per round from about the fifth onwards, but he always whacked me with a few eye-catching punches, usually towards the end of a round, which just showed how savvy he was as that is always likely to catch a judge's eye. Taylor finished round ten very strongly, but in general I felt I was getting the better of him in every round, simply because I was out-working him and the after-fight statistics backed me up on that.

It was a cracking boxing lesson between the pair of us. He hit me with some great shots, but over the course of the fight I felt I hit him with more. That's the way I read it. Having said that, it was a desperately difficult fight to judge and I can understand a little bit why there were such differing opinions from the press and judges. After the finish I discovered two judges had me down by four, whereas the third judge had me up by four! I think all three were wrong. It was very close but, as I say, I thought I was taking all the later rounds because Taylor just could not live with my work-rate. He stopped working as hard as me as the fight went past the half way mark and I caught up with him.

Anyway, the facts are I would have lost had I not flattened Taylor in what has been described to me by many fight fans as one of the best finishes ever in the history of the sport. As you can imagine, I've watched the ending over and over again and it still gives me goose pimples just thinking about it now! If it was unbelievable to watch, imagine what it was like to have been in the ring. I watched it for myself for the first time on YouTube the day after the fight in the hotel lobby and could barely believe my eyes.

In rounds ten and eleven, I could tell Taylor was tiring. It was clear he was starting to feel the pace, even though he always gave me a couple of digs right at the end of the round just to try and nick it from the judges. Before the start of the twelfth and final round Rob was really calm, just telling me it was close, so if I saw a gap I had to take him apart. I saw the gap all right. Midway through the round, a combination caught Taylor and his legs gave a little shuffle. He was going. For what seemed like an age I followed him around the ring, trying to finish him off. He went down once and I thought it was all over. How he got up I'll never know. But Taylor is as brave and proud as they come. Eventually with just seconds remaining I got him into a corner and blasted away. This time he couldn't stop me. He took a few clean, powerful punches flush on the chin and the referee, Mike Ortega, quite rightly, waved it off. Taylor was defenceless and any more shots could have caused some serious damage.

The next few seconds are a blur because I went bonkers, totally bonkers. I looked over into the ringside seats and all my friends and family were there, many of them in tears. It dawned on me later how close I had come to losing my unbeaten record as I discovered two of the three judges had me down, though at the time I couldn't care less. I had stopped Taylor with just fourteen seconds left on the clock and won the fight.

I got back to my dressing room and the place erupted. Everywhere I looked people were hugging and kissing each other. It was an incredibly special feeling and there was Rachael, crying her eyes out. Straight after the fight I went into a restaurant and bar called the Lion's Den. I tried to eat something, but I am not sure if anything really went down.

Rachael and all my entourage were there as we discussed the fight, barely able to believe what had just happened. After a while my brothers went off to the casino with their partners. I went back to my hotel room, even though I don't think

I slept a wink as I was full of adrenalin. I dozed off for an hour and a half at 7 a.m. and woke up feeling sore and tired.

My eye was killing me as I had got a thumb in it, but my pride at having beaten Taylor meant I didn't really feel a thing. We left the day after the fight and on the flight back I lent my brother Lee my first-class ticket, while I sat in economy. Half way through I thought, I'm not having this. So I sat down behind him in the empty first-class seating section and pretended to be asleep. A stewardess clocked the fact that there was one too many people in the first-class seats, so knowing I had a ticket she woke my brother up and said he had to go back to the cheaper seats. Under my breath I laughed my nuts off as my brother started complaining, but I kept my eyes closed and Lee didn't have the balls to wake me up! Thankfully Rachael's only little so she didn't mind being in economy. That's what she told me anyway!

I returned through customs with my belt wrapped over my shoulder and drove back to Nottingham. Just as Joe Calzaghe turned into a superstar overnight when he beat Jeff Lacy in Manchester, so the same seemed to have happened to me: I couldn't pick up a newspaper without seeing my face on the back page. The fight had clearly made an impression. The press were calling it one of the greatest fights in the sport's history.

Taylor took his defeat very gracefully, which was a mark of the man, and I could barely believe some of the plaudits that came my way. I think a lot of fight fans really started to believe in me after that victory. They had all heard of Taylor and I had stopped him. Unbelievably, Taylor was knocked out by Arthur Abraham a few months later in the first round of the Showtime TV-backed 'Super Six World Boxing Classic'. He then announced his retirement. Whether Jermain decides to return to boxing is entirely up to him, but he was a great opponent and a fantastic bloke. His defeat to me and Abraham just goes to show how things can change in sport in the flick of an eye. I can only give credit to Abraham for beating him, but I still think I took on and beat the best Jermain Taylor had to offer. Whether he was still the same fighter after I had beaten him I don't know.

I put the key in and opened my front door back in Nottingham. I then spent the week painting my skirting boards and generally redecorating. I know, don't ask.

CHAPTER 10

During my career, I've fought on the BBC, Sky, ITV and Eurosport, so I've got a fairly decent viewpoint from which to judge the various television networks and the way they treat boxing. Why do the so-called terrestrials not stick with boxing? To be perfectly honest, I haven't a clue. It beats me. Whenever the sport is shown on BBC or ITV, it gets great viewing figures and turns fighters into household names. Was there anyone better known in the country than Frank Bruno when he was boxing, or Barry McGuigan? Sir Henry Cooper didn't even win a world title but by all accounts he was pretty much the most famous sportsman in the land when he was fighting and he won BBC Sports Personality of the Year twice.

When I started boxing, the likes of Nigel Benn, Chris Eubank, Naseem Hamed and Steve Collins were right up there with footballers when it came to fame. So what exactly has boxing done wrong that made the terrestrial channels decide to walk away? They cannot use viewing figures as an excuse as I got fantastic numbers whenever I boxed, as did everyone else in the sport.

The budget that TV executives could use on boxing is going elsewhere. Not into other sports, but these garbage game shows and reality programmes that you see all over the TV schedules. It is such a shame. Of course, boxing must take its fair share of blame, some of boxing's budget must have been lost when TV started showing crap fights, and people stopped watching.

As everyone knows in boxing, the best don't often fight the best: just look at my proposed bout with Joe Calzaghe, which never came off. At least in football, the best teams play each other in the Champions League. In cricket, England regularly play the Australians for the Ashes. There is the Rugby World Cup and in athletics the pinnacle has always been the Olympics. In boxing, though, all kinds of things can go wrong and you can hardly blame the public for getting the hump about it all. Calzaghe against me would have broken all kinds of ticket sales records. I am sure ten million people would have switched on to it as it would have been all over the papers, TV and radio for weeks. It didn't happen because one side – his – preferred to relinquish the title rather than fight. The public, used to seeing the best against the best in other sports, must get cheesed off with it all.

Boxing could do itself a lot of favours, but the main reason why the BBC and ITV have pulled out is because they have taken a conscious decision to remove it. The TV executives who I met just did not have the desired level of knowledge about the sport, which is why they let Audley

Harrison get away with cherry-picking crap opponents. There was simply not enough expertise or understanding within the BBC to stop it happening. The Beeb got their fingers burnt by a fighter who had too much, too soon, following his Olympics success, and the BBC now treat the sport with suspicion – so much so, that it is no longer covered in any meaningful way. Other than the Olympics every four years, there is no boxing on the BBC.

Had the BBC continued in the sport, they would have ended up with both myself and David Haye, as we were regularly on their channel a few years ago. They would have had my story from the end of my amateur career and the day I turned pro as well as David's rise to fame. David is now a superstar, but boxes on another channel, and I can only imagine the BBC must be kicking themselves. I was live on the BBC from my debut against Birmingham's Michael Pinnock in 2002 all the way through to beating Damon Hague inside a round for the British title. BBC viewers saw some cracking fights in those fourteen bouts.

After that, the deal with the BBC ended and I boxed on Eurosport and HBO Latino for Henry Porras, then did a one-off with ITV for the terrible Matthew Barney fight in 2005. Later that year Mick Hennessy signed a deal with Sky and I stayed with the satellite station for six fights, up to and including Robin Reid in November 2007.

Mick then agreed a deal with ITV and my first fight on ITV1 was against Albert Rybacki, after Denis Inkin pulled out for a second time. My world title win with Jean Pascal was on ITV1 at 10 p.m. and pulled in about three million viewers, which I gather the TV bosses were delighted with.

Then the backside fell out of the advertising market and ITV said they could not afford to show my first title defence against Jermain Taylor live. It was delayed and put on ITV1 on Sunday evening. Again, I was told the TV executives were pleased as punch when it pulled in an audience of two million. Andre Dirrell was live on Primetime TV, a new pay-per-view channel, and a week after the fight, nearly two million people watched it on ITV1.

I know I am bound to be biased, but boxing needs TV coverage and for that matter so do all sports. Boxing is no different to golf, rugby, cricket, tennis, you name it: we are all fighting against the giant of football. While football can play to a different set of broadcasting rules because it is so big and popular, boxing, like all the other sports, has to fight for the scraps.

What has happened to boxing on TV is such a shame. We are now at the stage where only Sky really cover boxing, though I should add they do it very well. They have also stayed with the sport from day one, which again tells you they have real expertise in the field. Out of all the TV companies, Sky has been the only one to remain loyal to boxing.

When I moved to ITV from Sky in 2008, it was simply to do with numbers. I had the option of fighting in front of an armchair audience of millions and the alternative was maybe, say 80,000. Mick Hennessy chose to go with ITV. The audience figures we were getting, not just for my fights but also for the likes of Darren Barker and John Murray, were fantastic and everyone at ITV said so. Just before ITV pulled the plug in 2009, Darren fought on ITV4 and got an astonishing audience of 600,000, which surely underlines the point I am making.

I never heard one instance of an ITV executive saying they were disappointed with the figures they were getting. Put simply, if boxing is on terrestrial TV and the fights are good, the size of the audience will be impressive. That is just a fact. But because of the collapse in advertising revenues, ITV decided it wanted to pull out of the fight game and they did exactly that, after just over a year.

Television coverage isn't the only thing wrong with boxing. Here's a simple one for a start: you get more chancers and bullshitters in boxing than any other sport I know. It really is the last remaining stronghold of the 'wild west'. There are rules in boxing, but not many when it comes to what happens outside the ring. For a sport that prides itself on the values of sportsmanship, the fact that so many things are so blatantly wrong, is sad. To give you one example: how many times has one fighter lost only to see his ranking go up with a different governing body, then another fighter wins and his goes down? It happens all the time. It happens so often there is no point in me even listing a few examples.

I'm not a know-it-all, but without a doubt one of the first things I would bring back to boxing would be fifteen-round contests. I just don't think twelve rounds is enough to make it a proper test between two warriors. I think fifteen rounds would separate the men from the boys. If you can do fifteen rounds it would also prove that you are an athlete as well as a fighter. I just don't think thirty-six minutes is enough of a test.

Over fifteen rounds, the real men would take over. Fighters I consider 'pretenders' – those who 'pretend' they are athletes – wouldn't be able to go the distance. They can get away with their non-combative styles all night long over twelve rounds but wouldn't last the full fifteen. As far as I'm concerned, the likes of these fighters are frauds. They don't want to get hurt in a sport that is all about giving it out and taking it in return.

The confusion that surrounds boxing over the stack of different world title belts has gone beyond a joke. Not only do we have the so-called 'big four' – the WBC, WBA, IBF and WBO – we also have loads of other ones like the WBF and WBU. I am expecting KFC any day soon! To be honest, I don't pay the slightest regard for any of them other than three of the four main belts: WBC, WBA and IBF. I love boxing and I love watching and reading about boxing, but even I couldn't tell you who half the fighters are who own some of these belts. The amount of belts at stake in all the different weight categories means there is total confusion amongst the public, who have given up trying to work it out themselves.

Why there cannot just be a single statutory body running boxing, I don't know. All the other leading sports have one: they have got it in football with FIFA, and likewise for Formula One, cricket and rugby. There has been a pretty decent growth in MMA – Mixed Martial Arts – but I believe that is now suffering too because there are so many different titles and belts at stake. If only there was a statutory body in boxing, then we certainly wouldn't have all these nonsense belts.

I suppose the real reason why so many fighters avoid each other is the way boxing is governed on a day-to-day basis, not by the authorities but by the promoters. To get one fighter taking on another, there has to be agreement between rival promoters, and as any fight fan will tell you, that often doesn't happen. Promoters, by their very nature, are always trying to out-do each other. TV finds it hard to back boxing and that's one of the reasons why. The different TV networks often don't work together and neither do the promoters, and with too many rivals fighting against each other, the result is that boxers avoid each other. Just look at the fiasco surrounding the two best pound-for-pound fighters in the world today, Manny Pacquiao and Floyd Mayweather Jr. Everyone in the world wants to see the fight, but so far it hasn't been made. That's the business I am in.

My boxing hero in my teens was definitely Naz, but as a little kid I used to love sitting around the TV and watching four of the greatest fighters ever to lace a glove take each other on. Even now, fight fans talk of the match-ups between Sugar Ray Leonard, Marvin Hagler, Thomas Hearns and Roberto Duran. The whole country used to stop to watch them fight each other. I only wish it would be like that again, with the best boxers facing each other.

Which leads me on to the Super Six World Boxing Classic, which involved the best twelve-stone fighters in the world. It was an attempt by Showtime television in America to try and get the best fighting the best, with one recognised winner. In a sense, Showtime TV in America was great for my career. If it wasn't for my fantastic win against Taylor, which ultimately earned me a place in Showtime's Super Six, I don't know where I would be. I find that both sad and astonishing and, even though I am grateful to Showtime, I am not kidding myself. The reason I was made an offer was because I had the WBC belt and they wanted it. If I hadn't won the WBC against Jean Pascal I am sure they would not have wanted anything to do with me.

After beating Jermain Taylor in my first world title defence, Mick was approached by Showtime's boss, Ken Hershman, to see if we would be interested in a tournament. Financially backed by the American TV giants, it would pit the best six super middleweights against each other. We were told there would be three Americans and three Europeans in it, with a round robin in the earlier 'group' stages, leading to a semi-final and then final, sometime in 2011.

The concept of the Super Six was very good and my immediate thoughts were to go for it. I liked the idea and I liked the fact other big-name fighters were involved, including Taylor. The then-WBA champion Mikkel Kessler and Arthur Abraham were signed up for it and so joining it seemed an easy decision. I felt if I didn't sign up, with the demise of ITV's interest in boxing, I would be left on the outside looking in. Crazy, really, but I was a British world champion needing an American TV company to back me.

The Super Six was good for boxing because you could not hide: although it had flaws, the best fought the best. The fact the tournament started in 2009 and ended in 2011 was one problem as that was, by anyone's reasoning, too long. The round robin group stage I quite liked, as it gave everyone a chance of making the semis, even if they lost a fight. At least Showtime were trying to show some initiative and to get the best fighters taking on each other: fair play to them for that. I am not a massive fan of the way boxing has been treated by TV, but here was one company at least that was prepared to go out on a limb and try and improve things.

Super Six was a very lucrative TV deal and a chance to get the best fights out there, so it seemed a no-brainer. I did what I had to do to earn a living and, with Showtime's backing, I knew the tournament would be professionally run and well marketed. With a potentially massive fight with Joe Calzaghe no longer in the picture, it just made sense to sign up for it.

A few boxing fans at the time of Super Six were saying Lucian Bute should have been involved, but Lucian Bute was asked and he wasn't interested. Even without him, you still had me, Kessler and Abraham from Europe and Andre Ward, Andre Dirrell and Jermain Taylor from America. That's a very impressive line-up.

When I signed up for Super Six, I was told I would get either Ward or Dirrell first up, on home soil in Nottingham. That suited me down to the ground. Showtime decided it was to be Dirrell and I was very happy. I knew Dirrell was a decent level fighter: he was ranked number two with the WBC when the fight was made and was a former Olympic bronze medallist. Dirrell was also unbeaten and unbeaten boxers are always dangerous because they don't know how to lose. Pascal was also undefeated when I boxed him and he was as tough as old boots.

One aspect of the build-up to the Dirrell fight that was very different was the fact that it would be the first time I would train at home in Nottingham full time. Throughout the whole of my early career I had split myself between Nottingham and London, where Rob was based. For Dirrell I trained lock, stock and barrel at the Liberty's gym, just around the corner from the arena where the fight was to take place. Training in Nottingham was fantastic. I had my home comforts and I had Rachael near to me.

The launch of the Super Six was held in New York. I got on really well with some of the boxers, in particular Kessler, but Dirrell always seemed a bit over-aggressive towards me, as if he thought it would wind me up. I spoke to Rob about him and Rob assured me that Dirrell was his favourite pick out of all the other fighters and that I couldn't fail to beat him. It was only afterwards that Rob told me Dirrell would have been his last choice out of all the others! And now, looking back on the fight, I can see why.

For once, I suffered no injuries in the build-up at all. Unbelievably, nothing went wrong. I watched Dirrell on video and he had fast hands, no doubt about it. He was decent but I didn't think he could take a shot. In one of the fights I watched, Dirrell got dropped from a straightforward shot and recovered to win, but in the process had stunk the gaff out. I thought he was just a bit of a better version of Matthew Barney: faster of foot and speedier of hand, but still a Barney. OK, maybe he had a few more skills but there was no heart and he seemed like someone who didn't really want to fight. Before we met in the ring I had the evidence on video that

Dirrell was going to run like Usain Bolt. When I started getting to him in the later rounds, I thought from what I'd watched that he would crumble.

Because Showtime was beaming the fight back live to America, it was 2.30 a.m. when my ring music piped up. I walked out into the arena, which was packed to the rafters with 10,000 fans. I was absolutely gobsmacked by the response I had got from my fans, especially at that time in the morning when we should all have been in our beds getting some shuteye. I have boxed at the arena fourteen times and it was easily the busiest it has ever been for one of my fights. Even now it sends goose pimples all over me to think that all those thousands spent hundreds of their hard-earned weekly wedge to come and watch me in the middle of the night. Believe me, it makes me incredibly humble and thankful.

It was a wonderful welcome to the big time, and I felt I had really arrived when I saw the arena full. Maybe it was the Taylor fight which turned me into a marquee fighter but, whatever it was, I was hugely grateful because fighting in front of massive audiences gives you an enormous buzz. I've fought in front of a few hundred in Dagenham, so to box before 10,000 people was a new experience for me and one I was relishing. Froch–Dirrell, or maybe more correctly the concept of the Super Six, had caught the imagination of the public.

If only the fight had lived up to the expectations. In rounds one and two I thought Dirrell was being very cagey and would stay out of range. In the fourth and fifth I began to catch up with him and was roughing him up, but Dirrell then decided he didn't want anything to do with a toe-to-toe clash. Dirrell was better at running and holding than I thought because he did not stand and fight throughout the whole night. I honestly don't know if he can take a shot because he didn't really take any power punches from me all night: I could never catch up with him.

I had to do all the hard work in chasing him around the ring all night, whereas he would use his lightning-quick speed to throw a couple of shots before getting on his bike again or grabbing hold of me. It was safety-first boxing. If I ever closed the gap up enough to get near to him, which is what I tried to do throughout the fight, he would hold. It was frustrating and as the fight wore on he kept doing it. One shot and grab, one shot and grab. We are there to entertain and yet I felt that Dirrell just wanted to win the fight by throwing a punch, then holding, or running. It ruined the night for me.

At the end of round seven I looked up and watched the ring card girl, something I had never done before in my career. I stared at her until she turned towards my corner and I could see she was holding the card up for round eight. I thought I can't go through another five more rounds of this. I was bored and dejected because there was nothing I could do about it. Towards the end of the fight this pace seemed to be getting to him. If the fight had lasted fifteen rounds there would have been no way he could have kept it up and I would have caught him. He was quicker than me and had very, very fast hands. Undoubtedly the fastest I have ever faced in a fight.

The whole arena knew what was happening. Dirrell wasn't interested in boxing, he was only interested in self-preservation. It was a dull fight and I had never been involved in a dull fight, with the possible exception of Barney, who was exactly the same. Dirrell pulled away from shots all the time and I couldn't get him with my hurtful big shots. Barney spent the whole of his career not really getting whacked and Dirrell was the same.

Not before time, Dirrell got a point deducted from the ref in the tenth round for persistent holding. Afterwards I asked the official why it had taken him so long to start punishing him, but he just shrugged his shoulders. I shipped a few blows in the tenth and eleventh rounds, but although Dirrell was fast, he couldn't really bang and none of his shots caused me any damage whatsoever.

At last the fight ended and my corner told me I had got the fight in the can pretty comfortably. But before the announcement came, Rob told me it was a split decision. It was then that I started to worry. Surely the judges wouldn't take my title away and give it to such a negative non-combatant as Dirrell? I knew it was fairly close because I hadn't landed much, but I didn't have a mark on my face. Sure enough, the official result came over the tannoy. The MC announced a split decision and Dirrell got down on one knee and crossed himself. He tried to drag me down with him and I told Dirrell in no uncertain terms to fuck right off.

To my eternal shame I decided to copy Dirrell and I got down on bended knee as they announced the results. The reason for this was I was thinking about Ken Hershman, the boss of Showtime, and I didn't want it to look bad. I didn't want it to seem as if I wasn't getting involved with the whole drama of the announcement of the results. Even to this day

I am annoyed and embarrassed I did. I should have stood there like a man and taken the judges' scorecards standing up. Dirrell could have stayed on one knee for the rest of the night as far as I was concerned.

The announcer called out the scores: 'Judge Alejandro Rochin Mapula makes it 114–113 in favour of Andre "The Matrix" Dirrell. Judge Massimo Barrovecchio has it 115–112 for Carl "Cobra" Froch. And judge Daniel Van de Wiele has it 115–112 in favour of ... and still the WBC world super-middleweight champion ... Carl "Cobra" Froch.'

I pointed to the roof. It was the most frustrating performance I have ever delivered in my life. Watching it back now, I think I could have done a few things differently. I should have tried to cut the corners in the ring a bit more and I should have gone for him in the later rounds because I wasn't getting hurt in there. I landed a few single shots, but never followed it up with any combinations. So many times I missed his whiskers by an inch. But on the night I was just so angry because it takes two to tango in a boxing ring. Really limited boxers whom I had fought earlier in my career like Dale Westerman or Paul Bonson at least came to fight. They had hearts and guts and they wanted to get stuck into me. I thought that Dirrell had been cowardly and, in my book, that Dirrell fight was just not boxing.

Dirrell gave me some stick in the papers and on the internet, saying I was the worst fighter in the Super Six. Well if I was the worst and I beat Dirrell and outclassed Arthur Abraham, then what did that make him? He convinced himself he won the fight even though I didn't hear his promoter Gary Shaw complain afterwards, and during the fight I heard his corner saying he needed a knock-out in the last round to win. That doesn't sound like someone convinced he had just won. In the post-fight press conference Dirrell said I had been given a home-cooked meal decision, but everyone I spoke to says he stunk the place out, not me. I was in there ready to trade and to go toe to toe, but Dirrell just didn't want to know.

CHAPTER 11

In late 2009 Rob had got a new job with the British Olympic Association, and became responsible for both the male and female teams in the run-up to the Olympics in London in 2012. It was a fantastic opportunity for Rob and, as he is such a brilliant coach, I don't think the youngsters could have been in better hands. It meant changes to our training programme for the Mikkel Kessler fight.

Rob based himself for five days a week at the English Institute for Sport in Sheffield, about an hour up the road from me in Nottingham. To all intents and purposes that made it pretty much perfect for me, as I didn't have to travel very far. I could either drive up to Sheffield – and the facilities at the institute were first-class – or I could stay a few nights a week at the Hellaby Hall Hotel near Rotherham, where they looked after me fantastically, in particular the manager Tom, a real boxing fan. Nothing was too much trouble for them, for which I was hugely grateful. Training started well, although I took a week out to take part in the

BBCs 'Sport Relief' programme, doing a dance routine with 2008 Olympic medallist Tony Jeffries and former world champions Johnny Nelson and Duke McKenzie. It's fair to say none of us were exactly John Travolta. It was fun and for a very worthy cause but I probably should not have done it as it basically meant a whole week out of training, even if it was at the very start of my ten-week programme.

Going back into training for Kessler was a different feeling this time and for a good reason: Rachael and I were having a baby.

When Rachael, the girl of my dreams, first mentioned the name Rocco I wasn't so sure, but now it sits well with me. I love it. It sounds right. Rocco Froch.

We found out Rachael was pregnant in November 2009, shortly before going to Cuba for my brother Lee's wedding. We didn't tell any of our family in Cuba because Rachael and I both felt we were there for Lee's wedding, not for us to steal their thunder by announcing we were having a baby. Mind you, it was hard sometimes not to blurt it out.

Shortly after coming back to Nottingham we both told our immediate family and friends and when Rachael had a twenty-week scan we were offered the chance to know the sex of our baby. We both wanted to know and the nurse revealed we were having a boy. Knowing that I was about to become a father was the best thing that had ever happened to me and the fact that I am with such a wonderful woman makes it even more incredible. As a former Miss Maxim UK she is beautiful to look at, but more importantly, she is a lovely person as well. I'll stop now before I get too sickly!

How we kept it quiet from the media in the run-up to Kessler I will never know. We only told a few family and friends and thankfully they all kept it a secret. We wanted to keep it out of the press because Rachael and I both preferred it that way as we value our privacy. It was only on the night when Rachael turned up at the fight at ringside that it was pretty obvious to the press she was pregnant. The plan was for me to announce the forthcoming birth of our son in the post-fight interview as part of my celebrations. Well, we certainly weren't celebrating after the fight, but Peter Schmeichel, who did the interview in the ring asked about Rachael and our then-unborn son Rocco and it got a great reception from the Danish crowd.

The build-up to Kessler was far from perfect. Eight days before facing the 'Viking Warrior' I was getting stuck into some heavy sparring with George Groves. We were giving each other a bit of stick when George landed a shot on to my ear. Straight away I knew what had happened as I had perforated my eardrum in the build-up to the Pascal fight. The ear had 'popped' again. We stopped the spar and I got a doctor to look at it. He confirmed that I had suffered a 50 per cent perforation of my eardrum.

George also hit me in the eye. I have got a recurring corneal erosion. It's a bit technical, but in layman's terms it means the skin over the eyeball itself can tear at any time. It has happened quite a few times now, one of those times was just before I fought Jermain Taylor in America. It happened again before Kessler. It burns and it's horribly uncomfortable, but again, it's just one of those things.

The lack of quality sparring before leaving to fight Kessler was a concern to me. Tony 'Jaffa' Jeffries was good, except he got a cut early on which meant we couldn't spar any longer. In terms of competitive sparring, I didn't do anywhere near enough and that's wholly my fault. I did a couple of rounds with the amateurs up at Sheffield, but with the best will in the world I had it my own way in the ring with them. They are amateurs, very talented amateurs, but still amateurs. You need sparring which is intense and which stretches you. It was hard for me to get myself in top shape in sparring because I just didn't have the right quality of opposition in front of me. It is difficult to get fighters in with me these days because so few can hack the pace and my reputation for still being a bit 'no-holds-barred' means most of my invitations to spar are turned down. It is easy to get a fighter to come in for one day and do an eight-rounder, but then you want them to come back a few more times. That didn't happen because once they had tasted sparring with me they didn't want to come back for more.

I needed to spar Monday, Wednesday and Friday for five weeks against two hard bastards and I didn't have anyone who fitted the bill. I didn't even have one. Rob and I did try, but with no success. Not only did I feel I was not right physically, but also mentally as well. I record in minute detail all of my training programmes in my diary and the sparring just wasn't there, which meant I felt under-cooked.

With all these things taken into account I could have pulled out. I should have pulled out. But I pride myself on the fact that before the Abraham bout I had never ever pulled out of a fight as a pro in my career and I've had stacks of injuries. The fact is, I just feel that as a boxer you would have to wait a very long time to fight if you only ever went into the ring at 100 per cent. Therefore, I shrugged it off and said I would still go to Denmark to defend my crown. I felt, even with these disadvantages, that I was the best super middleweight in the world and I would come through.

The day at last began to loom and the plan was to fly out to Denmark on the Saturday before the fight. That plan went pear-shaped from the word go as there were no flights out of England at all on the Saturday due to a volcano in Iceland spewing up ash all over the country. The no-fly situation carried on for days and by Tuesday I was of the opinion that the fight was not going to happen. Showtime TV, who were in charge of the Super Six and called the shots, started talking about another date six weeks down the line. Even though I wanted to fight Kessler at the first possible opportunity, in the week leading up to the bout I honestly thought the fight would be delayed. I even hosted a barbecue at my house with friends and family on the Monday before the bout as I was so convinced it was off. That again was a mistake and again it was my fault.

The German promoters Sauerland came up with the idea of sending a private jet and, although I agreed to it, I wasn't 100 per cent happy to do so. One thing I wasn't going to do was catch a ferry and drive to Denmark. That idea was mooted by Sauerland and that was just a non-starter as far as I was concerned. It wasn't going to happen. There was no way on this planet that I was going to drive ten hours, or whatever it took, to get to Herning, with a cross-Channel ferry thrown in between. I think even Sauerland realised that was not fair on me. I just said I wouldn't even discuss it.

I was supposed to fly on the Tuesday before the fight, but there were several contractual problems with Sauerland, so I eventually flew out on Wednesday morning. I wanted the contracts with Sauerland over who got what proportions of the Herning gate money sorted eight weeks before the fight. In fact, I eventually signed the contract when I landed in Denmark. To be discussing money so near to the fight was far from ideal.

It was a horrible, horrible flight. Strong winds meant our little plane was bumping up and down all over the place. Rob was convinced we were going to crash, while Rachael and I weren't exactly enjoying it either. It was, not to put too fine a point on it, bloody horrific. I don't particularly like flying anyway, but the fact we were in this tiny little plane being buffeted by high winds made it even worse.

I wanted Rachael to be with me even though she was heavily pregnant, but obviously I was concerned about her as any partner would be. Looking back on it now, I was naturally worried about her, which again I don't think was ideal preparation for going into such a massive fight in someone else's backyard.

At the time I didn't think flying for an hour and a half on the Wednesday before the fight would be a problem. In hindsight I was wrong. Anyone who has ever travelled will know the score. You spend a small amount of time in the air and hours hanging around at airports. We got up and went to the airport and waited. We got the flight, then I agreed to drive a fast car around a race track near the airport so that Viasat, the TV company showing the fight in Germany, could get some good footage of me. It was a bad idea and I should have refused. It got my adrenalin going and by the end of the drive I was all hyped up. And all this just a few days before facing Kessler.

By the time we drove from the race track near the airport and got to the press conference in Herning I felt like I had been travelling for days. Then after the press conference we had to drive about half an hour to our base in the small town of Silkeborg. Again, hindsight is a wonderful thing. I shouldn't have done it. I had spent just about all day on Wednesday travelling. It was too close to the fight to be doing that and with that and my perforated eardrum I should have pulled out of the fight. I feel daft now that I didn't but there you have it. I got to Denmark and thought I just have to get on with it and beat Kessler.

The 10,000 sell-out crowd in Herning were right behind their man, as they should be, but after a cautious start from both of us in the fourth and fifth rounds I started to get through. In the fourth he went down and the referee indicated a slip. I don't know. I certainly threw a punch which I think caught Kessler on the arm, so is that a knock down or not? In Nottingham it would have been, in Herning it wasn't. That's the way boxing works.

I hit Kessler with a peach of a right hand in the fifth and thought for a moment he was going to go down. I should have jumped on him and tried to finish the fight there and then, but instead, maybe because I was feeling tired, I stood back. I had the win in the palm of my hand and I didn't finish him off. The first time I have ever done that as a pro. I wasn't as mentally switched on as I should have been. I have no excuse. There are reasons why I lost, but no excuses. I had him in trouble and it was me that didn't try to finish Kessler off, no one else.

It is hard to say I was beaten by the better man because I felt I won it. Kessler did enough on the night to keep me off him and to fight his kind of fight. He kept me out of range of my right hand and he did enough to get the verdict – in Denmark. I am guilty of not throwing more shots, but you can't say if I was better prepared and conditioned I would have got the stoppage, because you never know what will happen in a ring. All I know for certain is that I rocked him in the fifth and I didn't take advantage of that when I should have done.

I walked into a few shots of his later in the fight when Kessler regrouped brilliantly. I have to say this: Kessler is every bit as good as I expected him to be. He is a great fighter, simple as that. It is all right saying I should have jumped on him, but I have been there myself. Fighters have had me in trouble and I have knocked them out as they have gone for the kill. Robin Reid had me in a bit of bother and I stopped him almost straight away. So to say I would have beaten Kessler if I had gone for him in the fifth is not that simple. He could have caught me with a KO shot as I tried to finish him off. That happens all the time in boxing. It is so easy to say ifs, buts and maybes. What happened did happen. You can look back on a fight and say I should have done this, I should have done that, but the fact is I didn't. All the experts at ringside said I should have polished

Kessler off in the fifth, but they are not in the ring fighting a bloke who is one hell of a fighter.

During the fight I never felt in real trouble and I slipped a lot of his punches. It wasn't easy in there as Kessler loves a tear-up as much as me, but his movement on his feet was very predictable and crude. He tends to use his jab then his right hand, although the right has got some power behind it. He throws the odd hook, but everything else is pretty straightforward. I'd love to spar with Kessler because I think I would run rings around him. He is the sort of fighter I would play with in sparring because I would get used to how he fights very quickly, but in the ring, in a proper fight, he is a handful.

He was there to be beat and by my standards I should have done that. He was beatable and that is what is more frustrating than anything I have ever known in a ring. By rounds six and seven I was more tired than I have ever been in my life and whether that was due to the lack of intense sparring I don't know. It could have been something to do with getting to Denmark so late, but I felt there was lead in my boots and in my arms, which was so strange because usually I finish a fight much stronger than that.

He hit me with a couple of good body shots in the later rounds which took the wind out of me a little and he was very strong as he could take a punch as well. In the ninth he tagged me with a quick shot which caught me on the bridge of my nose and caused a cut, but all in all, I felt I handled what he dished out pretty well. Kessler was a formidable fighter and I could see why, over the years, he had mixed it with the best and so often had come out on top. It was a below-par performance for me and yet I think it was good enough to retain my title.

We both fought our hearts out and I punched myself to a standstill in a gripping last round. Some press reports and fight fans even commented that it remains one of the best rounds of boxing they have ever seen and I wouldn't argue with that. I can gripe about my preparation as much as I want but it won't change the outcome of the fight. In Denmark, what I did wasn't enough. In Nottingham, I think it would have been. I have watched the fight on video and I think I won a close one. You have to remember I was the champion, which meant Kessler had to take my title away and I just don't think he did that. He got the nod on his home turf and why is boxing like that? If that is the case, as champion, I shouldn't have been in Denmark in the first place.

As the judges' scorecards were about to be announced one of Kessler's corner men came over and I heard him say something derogatory to me. I asked him to repeat it and he just said 'I meant bad luck,' with a smirk. I was tempted to flatten him there and then, the little weasel, but thought that might not go down too well, especially as I had clearly not got the verdict.

The truth of the matter was I needed to knock Kessler out to win in Denmark. That is disgraceful. To think that a champion has to KO another fighter in order to keep his title is wrong, wrong, wrong. That was the position the Super Six had put me in. I could be bitter, but what's the point? I had a contract with the Super Six which was not in my favour. When I signed it I got the contract on the Monday and flew to America two days later. I handed the contract over on

Friday, so I had less than five days to go through it. Basically, I was a world champion, but was signed up to make a defence in Denmark, where my opponent is a national hero. I might add Kessler was WBA champion going into the Super Six tournament and guess where he fought? In Oakland, California, where Andre Ward is from. How does that work then? The world champions have to fight abroad and yet Ward, who was not a world champion going into Super Six, gets the chance to fight on his doorstep.

If I had realised my second fight in Super Six would have been against Kessler in Denmark, with the show being promoted by Sauerland, Kessler's promoters, I would have never have signed it.

The champions should be the ones who get the advantage and it is up to everyone else to take the title off you. Champions should be the ones fighting in their backyard, where they are more comfortable and the challenger has to rip the belt away. In fact, of my three defences, having beaten Pascal to the title, only one of them, against Andre Dirrell, was at home. Taylor and Kessler were both in their country.

I missed that clause in the contract and I suffered for it, but then Kessler suffered for it as well when he travelled to California. My best interests, as a fighter and as a defending champion, were not served by me going to Denmark. Before going to Denmark I said to Mick I didn't really want to go through with the fight, but I was assured the judges would be fair. After the fight Mick and I had a few harsh words because he told me he thought I had to knock Kessler out to win. I said I thought that before the fight that wasn't his opinion, but he disagreed. I felt to have to do that it was a bit insulting, especially as Kessler had never been knocked out as a pro and doing exactly that in Denmark was always going to be a tall order. Anyway, me and Mick fundamentally disagreed on what was said between us before the fight.

I went to Denmark convinced I was going to win, but I also went there because I was told my next fight in the Super Six would be at home to Arthur Abraham. After the fight Sauerland started protesting that there was nothing in writing to say Abraham had to come to England. Surprise, surprise, Sauerland wanted the fight in Germany. I know what would have happened had I gone to Berlin. Unless I had knocked Abraham out, there would have been no way to be sure of the decision. One judge in Berlin gave Nikolai Valuev a draw against David Haye in their 2009 bout. I can't possibly fathom how is that possible when Valuev didn't land a clean punch on David all night?

After the fight, I looked at Kessler and he looked at me at the post-fight press conference. He looked properly banged up. I had a small cut above my left eye, a cut on my nose and a slightly swollen eye socket, but the one side of his face was hanging off. I had made a mess of his face. He looked much more like the one who had taken a real beating than me and the post-fight pictures prove that. It looked for all the world like I had hit him with more shots than he hit me and I still believe that to this day. By the look of him, there was only one winner.

Was it a robbery? It wasn't a total rip-off because quite a few pundits at ringside gave him the nod and quite a few said I had won it. Two of the three Showtime TV pundits doing it for television had me winning. I asked the BBC crew and the three of them made the score me one, Kessler one and Richie Woodhall, who knows the fight game inside out, made it a draw.

Looking back it was my fourth straight tough fight, following Pascal, Taylor and Dirrell. The Dirrell fight didn't take much out of me at all, so I can't say I was weary going into the Kessler showdown, but I am of the opinion that everything that could have gone against me, did go against me, including volcanic eruptions in Iceland!

I had nothing but the highest regard for Kessler – a great person out of the ring and a brilliant fighter in it – but now I had to regroup. Rob and I were determined to learn the lessons of what went wrong in Denmark and what needed to change. That's the job of a trainer and a fighter. We had to move forward and correct things that needed correcting. I certainly feel the sparring leading up to Kessler was not of a sufficient standard to have me 100 per cent on top of my game. And believe me, you have to be 100 per cent when you go in the ring with the likes of Mikkel Kessler. What did it feel like to come out of the ring second best? It was strange. I had got so used to winning it was a feeling which I hadn't experienced for so long, since my amateur days. I think adversity can make you stronger. Stacks of fighters over the years have been beaten and have recovered to become better fighters and I fully intended to be one of those. I didn't think I would ever be beaten in the ring, but the reality is that nearly all fighters suffer defeat in their careers, so why should I be different? I think I fought Kessler when he was at his absolute 100 per cent best in front of a partisan home crowd and I wasn't at my best. Maybe it is as simple as that.

Did it hurt? I'd be lying if I said it didn't. I was no longer an unbeaten world champion, but that defeat to Kessler made me even more determined to become the best in the twelve-stone business. There was unfinished business between me and Mikkel Kessler and I was desperate for a re-match.

The Kessler defeat for me was the start of a new chapter because next up was going to be Arthur Abraham. The way I looked at it was I had three fights and when I won all three I would be proclaimed as the best, the undisputed super middleweight in the world. I was very excited by that and it all would start with me beating Abraham. I had seen enough of Abraham to know he was a high-class fighter, short-ish and stocky, but he was essentially a middleweight in my book and had been outclassed by Dirrell for most of the fight in the Super Six, somebody I had already beaten.

I boxed Kessler on the Saturday night and by Wednesday I was doing a three-mile run around my area in Nottingham just to keep things ticking over. I wanted to get straight back in the gym because I knew I was good enough to do it and become the twelve-stone king of the division. I also felt I had at least another couple of years in my prime. I promised to learn from my mistakes and go out there and beat Abraham for me and my family. I was determined to prove that losing to Mikkel was not going to be the end of the 'Cobra' story, just the start of a new chapter. And as events turned out, I was absolutely right.

CHAPTER 12

Just as I take my job as a fighter seriously, so I take my role outside of the ring seriously as well.

I've done quite a lot of work around Nottingham dealing with what society deems 'problem' kids, some of whom haven't got much of an idea how to behave. I like to think I can communicate with them because of my background, having grown up in an old-fashioned working-class area of Nottingham. I like decent, well-made clothes, I have never worn bling and I don't try to pretend to be something I am not. I was brought up in a pretty tough part of the world, but it was no better and no worse than thousands of places in Britain.

Nottingham has developed a terrible reputation in the media for its gun crime. The city has been dubbed 'Shottingham', but growing up in Gedling and Carlton, I never saw the gun side of crime at all. 'Twocking', or taking a car without consent, was quite a big thing and there was a bit of small-time drug dealing going on, mainly in cannabis, but I certainly never saw a gun. Years ago, I was asked to take part in a council-backed gun amnesty week and I had no hesitation in saying yes. I told the organisers I would love to help out because I know how kids of a certain age group can find themselves under pressure. I don't want kids in Nottingham, or anywhere for that matter, to be involved in guns. I don't want to see kids involved in drugs, which can lead to petty crime, which can in turn lead to something bigger.

I didn't do particularly well at school so I sat down with these kids and told them it straight: about how important it was that they get good grades, otherwise life could pass them by. The levels of violence out there can be frightening but the one thing that hasn't changed is this: the kids are the same as they have always been. There are probably more dysfunctional families knocking around these days compared to when I was a youngster, but kids haven't suddenly become bad.

I've done countless visits to schools and youth clubs in and around Nottingham and I don't do it to boost my ego: I do it because I genuinely care. I know I was one of the lucky ones. I latched myself on to a sport I was good at and my life has benefited from it. I hope some of them listened. If I can be any kind of role model to the kids around my hometown then that's fantastic and if it stops some kids from messing up their lives, even better. I used to look up to people who had achieved things and there is no harm in that.

At this point in my career I'd been fairly well known in Gedling and the rest of Nottingham for a while, but my profile changed dramatically when I became a world champion on that day in December 2008. Before the Pascal fight I could go shopping in relative peace and quite, but not any longer. I started to become a household name, especially in Nottingham, which despite its size as one of Britain's larger cities is still a pretty closed world where everyone knows everyone else.

In Gedling and Carlton, I used to get the odd wave and horn sounded, but it seems wherever I go now I am approached for an autograph and a photograph. People ask me if it bothers me and I just tell them the absolute truth: not at all. As long as people are polite and ask in the right way then I've got no problem with signing anything. Though I went down to my local DIY store once and came back about an hour later because every time I tried to get out of there and pay for my goods, someone else spotted me and asked for a photo or an autograph. The way I look at it is a pretty simple one, I was a kid once and even as an adult I queued for Naseem Hamed's autograph. As a big snooker fan I love to watch Ronnie O'Sullivan at the table. We all have heroes, don't we?

I like the fact that I have a decent reputation in my hometown. It makes me feel good. You don't want to be regarded as a great fighter with a terrible personality and I'm very down to earth. I've been very grounded since I was an amateur and the same was true when I turned pro. I'm not too big for my boots and if I ever got that way, Rob and my family would soon tell me. I pop into the Phoenix gym on a pretty regular basis and the local snooker club and nobody pays much attention to me. I just fit in. They just leave me alone because I am part of the furniture and I like it that way.

I don't give it 'the big I am'. If people want an autograph or a photograph I'm here to accommodate them. Though there have been one or two occasions when people have been rude. I recall once being in the middle of taking a mouthful while out having a meal and just being told, 'sign here'. That sort of thing won't get you anywhere with me. I like to think though that I am a people's champion, someone who will never get too cocky, no matter what happens.

Becoming a successful boxer has its upside as well. I can get into decent restaurants now! I've got to know some of the Nottingham Forest players pretty well. I first went to a game at the City Ground when I was eleven years old as a family friend took me. To be perfectly honest, I didn't like it. I stood on the old terracing at the Trent End and froze my nuts off for two hours. I think I was just a bit too young. Nowadays I am a massive fan. I need to know the Forest score if they are playing away from home and I go to as many matches as I can. I've been lucky enough to have been invited on many occasions to go on to the pitch by the club and for that I will be forever grateful. They're my club and always will be. I just wish I had been around when Forest were the best team in Europe and had arguably the greatest manager of all time. If Naz was my boxing hero, Brian Clough is certainly everyone's hero who has ever been to the City Ground.

As for boxing itself, I wouldn't say I'm an anorak about it. Not compared to boxing fans who know every boxer in every weight division and every champion. I watch my own super-middleweight weight division and I like to think I know the runners and riders at twelve stone, but other than that I'm not a mad boxing obsessive. It's only the top, world-level fights that I watch without fail. I'm a big mate of David Haye from our days as amateurs and I love watching the 'Hayemaker': a fantastic technical fighter and a great bloke, and still the same David Haye he always was, back when we were amateur kids.

I am careful with my money, no doubt about that. When I was 21, I got a lucky break as I met a friend when I was working at NTL called Avtar Singh. We have lost touch nowadays but he was good for me. Avtar was my office buddy and he badgered me for months about getting a mortgage. Avtar reckoned it was important to get a good credit rating, so I applied for a few credit cards and got them.

I had a full-time job at NTL earning about £15,000 a year and was also boxing as an amateur. Thanks to Avtar I bought my first house in Gedling, for the princely sum of £33,000. I secured a mortgage for it and was on my way. Funnily enough, when my mum first moved down to Nottingham from Newcastle the first house she and her parents lived in was on the same street. Anyway, after buying my first house Carl Froch the property tycoon had started!

It was a cracking house with loads of space, although it is fair to say it was a bit dilapidated. I went around to look at it and my dad did it up for me and made it decent.

My elder brother Lee moved in and helped towards the

bills and I was away. I got my second house nearby when I signed to become a pro at the age of 24. A fair proportion of the signing-on fee went on the house in Sneinton in Nottingham, and I now have a few properties in Nottingham as well as a house in north London where I used to live. I'm into double figures for properties and, although it can be a real pain at times dealing with tenants, getting into it was a great decision. Thank you, Avtar!

Buying properties and doing them up to rent them is a fantastic way of looking after your financial future and thankfully I have got both my brothers helping me. My younger brother Wayne is an engineer by trade and he studied it at college for several years. He wanted to go into sheet metal work as a welder but the jobs just weren't there any longer in that industry. It was a dying trade, so he is now a plasterer and builder. My elder brother Lee is also a plasterer by trade and owns his own business. He is pretty good at bathrooms and, although his tiling is good, it isn't a patch on mine!

I have had good and bad tenants. I've had alcoholics, drug users and blokes who never paid their rent. It was a lot of hassle in the early days, especially with some tenants who simply couldn't pay their rent, but my little brother works with me now and looks after my properties very professionally.

People ask me why I went into renting properties and why I am still doing it now. I can only answer this way: I have always been pretty savvy about money. I like to have cash in my pocket and the real reason is because I tasted what it was like once to be really skint. Not having money is an experience I don't wish to repeat.

When I was 21 and I moved into my first house, my brother Lee was helping out where he could and putting some food in the fridge but to all intents and purposes I was flat broke. I was on about £800 a month when I quit my job at NTL and got category 'C' lottery funding as an amateur fighter. The funding meant I was then only taking home about £600 a month. My mortgage was about £300, then there were bills like council tax, heating and lighting and running a car. You don't need to be a maths genius to realise I didn't exactly have a lot of dough. Even though I was boxing for England I was completely broke. The fridge was usually down to a piece of cheese and maybe half a pint of milk and going out for a meal was a non-starter. I could barely afford to put petrol in my car. I could have asked my mum for some cash, but I was reluctant to do so even though I know she would have given it me. I didn't want to put a burden on her, so often I just went without.

I struggled on about £100 a month to live on. How I got by I will never know but being that flat broke was a horrible feeling and not something I would ever want to repeat. I am not a flash bloke by any stretch of the imagination but I don't like to worry about whether my cash card works in the bank and thankfully those days are long gone. They always say it is a massive motivation to make money by having a period where you didn't have any, and in my case that is so true. Not having money makes you aware of the value of a pound coin. However much I earn, I will never lose the concept of the value of money. Being without it was a very valuable lesson to me.

Theo Paphitis on TV's *Dragons' Den* said that when you are down to your last quid you know what money means and he was dead right.

I'll certainly introduce our son Rocco to boxing, and Natalia too if she's interested; after all, it has helped turn me from a naïve young boy into a man. But I will also of course introduce my kids to other sports as well. I think taking part in sport, as a kid, is so important. It brings together all communities and all countries. It is an international language. I can't for the life of me work out these educational busybodies who seem to think sport, because it involves winning and losing, can be bad for children. Surely that's what life is all about, learning to deal with the good and the bad. As far as I am concerned it is more important than religion, certainly it is to me. Sport, of any kind, is such a binding part of society and the world wouldn't get along anything like as well as it does if it wasn't for sporting contests between all nations. The world stops for the Olympics, for big boxing match-ups and the football World Cup.

Hopefully Rocco will be into all sports, although I wouldn't particularly want him to box as I think there are easier ways to make a living. But if that was what he chose to do I certainly wouldn't try and stop him. Boxing has been very good to me and I have reaped the benefit by becoming the best in the world. I love the sport, but the reality of it is that only a tiny fraction of the fighters who go into it make any real money out of boxing. But if that was his decision I would teach him everything I know.

CHAPTER 13

Straight after losing my unbeaten record against Kessler it was back home to Nottingham for the final weeks of Rachael's pregnancy. As the days slipped by it got closer and closer until on the morning of 23 June she woke me up at 2.45 a.m. as her waters broke. We dashed over to Nottingham City Hospital, where I was born 33 years earlier, and went into our own birthing room. That was when the fun started.

Rachael was in a whole world of pain and she had the usual painkillers, but nothing seemed to be shifting for hour after hour. I watched England versus the USA in the first match of the World Cup, which almost sent me to sleep, but by the evening and late into the night there was still nothing! She was dilated, but nowhere near enough, so the doctors said she would have to be induced to move things along as Rocco was the wrong way round, back-to-back with Rachael, which meant he was wedged in the birth canal and he couldn't pop out, poor little Rocco. So it was either speed things up or Rachael would need a C-section, which she really didn't want.

She had an injection to ease the pain and shortly afterwards it started to kick in. I held Rachael's hand until Rocco arrived at 7.44 a.m. on 24 June. Jeez, it was hard work! I didn't cry but I certainly felt very emotional and it was all incredibly moving. The whole thing was a barbaric yet wonderful experience and Rachael was absolutely brilliant throughout. Believe me, boxing is a lot easier than having a baby!

Our friends and family came over to the hospital to see little Rocco and I was the happiest bloke in the world. I held Rocco in my arms and was now a dad. Rachael stayed in overnight, just in case there were any problems, and I went back home at about 11 p.m., flopped into bed and fell asleep straight away. Early the next day I drove back to the hospital and picked up Rachael and my new son, Rocco. When we got back home we videoed the whole event, with Rachael walking through our front door with our son, coming into his home for the first time. You can only imagine how proud I was to be a father and with such a perfect little boy. Words can't do justice to sum up how I was feeling.

I had to pull out for the Abraham fight which was initially set to take place in Monaco on 2 October. It was the first time in my professional career I have had to do a no-show and I wasn't proud of it, especially as a lot of people had paid for flights and accommodation in not exactly the cheapest country in the world. I also lost a lot of money on flights for myself and my family, but I definitely did the right thing. The lesson I learned flying over to Denmark taught me never to go into a fight unless I was one hundred per cent mentally happy and close to being in my best shape.

Two weeks before the original fight date I was asked to go to a press conference in Monaco, towards the end of my final preparations. And I must confess, I couldn't really see the point in it. My back was really bad and I had a choice to go to the pre-fight press conference or pull out. I really had no choice. The press conference would have been pointless. I have had a sore lower back for most of my career, but this was beyond sore and not getting any better and this time I felt I had to be in the ring absolutely nailed-on 100 per cent against Abraham. I could not afford to be anything less than that. I was certainly less than 100 per cent against Kessler and look where it got me. My back was killing me and it was hindering my sparring so I decided, on this occasion, I would look after number one.

Hindsight tells me it was the right thing to do. I was in a now or never situation because if I had lost to Abraham I would probably have retired, even though with Andre Dirrell pulling out of the Super Six I was already through to the semi-finals even if I had been beaten by Abraham. I just felt I couldn't take on Abraham at 90 per cent because I believed he was just too good to take that risk. I couldn't afford to lose another fight. One loss was bad enough. I'm not sure if I would have carried on after two defeats. Thankfully, it didn't turn out that way.

I didn't feel good about pulling out of the Monaco date though, in fact I was very upset because I'm proud of the fact I have always been in the ring when a fight has been made, unlike some serial pull-outs. It was a shame, but there you go. On the weekend when the fight was supposed to have taken place my best pal Adam Fukes rang me and said he was sitting in the hotel lounge in Monaco with a load of Cobra fans and could he have a word. I said sure, so they put me on the loudspeaker in the hotel. I spent a good hour on the phone answering loads of questions to supporters who had paid to go out there. I think I apologised a few times because I felt so bad, but at least I could explain myself to them. That, at least, made it a little bit easier to take. The supporters all said they would be following me to Finland, which again, made me feel a bit better.

The injury gave me an extra five weeks, which meant I rested my back so that the muscle strain cleared up, then I got in some more high-class sparring. Edwin Rodriguez and Adam Trupish were my main sparring partners in Sheffield, as I carried on training alongside the Olympic prospects who are all under Rob McCracken's tutelage at the English Institute for Sport.

I stayed again at the Hellaby Hall Hotel near Rotherham. Tom the manager and his staff played a big part in my victory over Arthur Abraham because the hotel, just fifteen minutes from the gym in Sheffield, is tucked away in a nice, quiet corner. I could go there after training and really relax, although I really missed Rachael and little Rocco, but the day job had to come first. I could sleep very well at the hotel and getting rest is just as important in training as the training itself.

The training camp went excellently and I felt in really great shape. I don't know, maybe I pushed myself just that little 1 per cent extra more because I was now a challenger and not a champion. I know that I was in fantastic nick. All I could see was Kessler standing there opposite me in the ring in Herning with the belt around his waist and his promoter Kalle Sauerland grinning from ear to ear like a Cheshire cat.

Monaco was rescheduled for 27 November in Helsinki. I had been to Finland a couple of times before for amateur tournaments and so I knew the country pretty well. I had no problem with going to Helsinki as I was convinced I would get a fair shake there, unlike if it was held in Germany, where Abraham now resides. I was happy with it. Finland was as neutral as it gets. It is also a beautiful country, even in the dead of winter, covered in stunning snow-capped forests.

Mind you, I put my foot in it in spectacular fashion a couple of weeks before the fight by making a light-hearted joke which caused no end of a stink. A press conference had been arranged a couple of weeks before the bout and I landed in Helsinki. As I checked in I told the hotel manager that this sort of weather for six months must be depressing and it's no wonder people chuck themselves off buildings. It was a tongue-in-cheek comment based on the conversation I had had with the taxi driver on the way to the hotel, who said one of his relatives had killed himself in Finland because it was so cold and dark in winter. We were just chatting, so when I got out of the cab I was greeted at the hotel by the manager and I said the first thing that was fresh in my mind, which was 'It's cold and dark here, the sort of place where you would chuck yourself off a building.' It went down like a lead balloon. It had all been filmed for Showtime, for their 'Fight Camp 360' programme. The programme didn't do me any favours as it showed me landing in Finland saying basically how depressing it was, then cut straight to Abraham telling the world that Helsinki was one of his favourite places. If it had been designed to get the Finns against me I think it worked. The comment was splashed all over their papers with me saying people in Finland all toss themselves off buildings.

At the press conference I decided to try and hit back. I went up to one of the receptionists at the hotel and asked what the Finnish was for 'It is a pleasure to be out here in a beautiful country, with such friendly people.' It took about forty-five minutes to learn it parrot fashion. I said it in the conference when I was introduced and got a round of applause from the locals. Kalle Sauerland went red and Abraham just looked around with a face which said 'Why is he getting a round of applause?'

The Finnish newspaper boys asked me about my comment and I just explained it was a light-hearted joke and everyone is making a big deal about nothing. I told them I had been to Finland twice before, to Tampere and Helsinki for amateur competitions, and I think that went down well because I said how much I enjoyed it. I didn't apologise for my comment, but I did try and justify it and said it came into my mind because of the conversation I had been having with the cab driver. That seemed to be that. I started to get a little annoyed because I thought if the Finnish people want to go against me because of a throwaway comment, let them. They can boo me all they like because once the fight starts they will be silenced.

I thought Arthur Abraham looked nervous. The fight was getting close and he never looked at me directly in the eyes. He had a little smirk on his face, but I thought it was a nervous smile. He didn't have much to say either. There was just something about him though which didn't look convincing. I said to Rob, 'We have got this one beaten before it even starts.' I was that confident. It was dawning on him he was facing me and he didn't seem to like it.

I landed back in Nottingham then went back to Finland a few weeks later. I felt great all week. I walked into the public workout a few days before the fight itself and I felt in top condition. Whenever I actually see a fight venue I often feel a bit tight and apprehensive, but not on this occasion. I just felt relaxed. I had a few pre-fight nerves, the usual, but I felt happy. I felt calm and in control. Rob told me to remember that feeling and let it relax me. The sparring and training had all gone perfectly and I was absolutely 100 per cent. I felt nothing could go wrong. As it happened, it didn't.

Everything that had gone wrong before Kessler had gone right on this occasion. Maybe I hadn't pushed myself quite as much as I had to for Kessler because I was the champ. That is only human nature I suppose. This time I felt ready. This was going to be me at my very best.

In the build-up to the Abraham fight I was conscious of the fact that everyone I spoke to warned me about his big right hand. Everywhere I went I was told to watch out for it. I was the underdog with the bookies, which made me laugh because what do they know? Most of the press boys wrote me off as well. In my view the bookies know about as much as the British press about boxing.

Many of the press boys don't have the required level of knowledge about the sport, simple as that. A lot of them don't spend enough time immersed in boxing. TV does not give it the full coverage it deserves, except on Sky, and some of the newspaper writers have a complete lack of knowledge. I don't think you have to be an ex-fighter or ex-trainer to understand boxing and write about it, but I definitely think it helps. When Boris Becker or John McEnroe talk about Roger Federer doing this or that, at least they are talking about something they know about. You listen to them because they are educated about tennis. I read some stuff on boxing written by people I have never seen, who know nothing about it. They are entitled to their opinion, of course, but that doesn't make it right. In fact, I think boxing is pretty badly served by the media. The specialist boxing magazines are fine, but the sport never really gets as much coverage as it should. It is only when there is a big fight on that it makes the back page and that is a real shame. Boxing has been its own worst enemy over the years of course, but there is not a level of expertise out there amongst the media. A lot of them don't know what they are talking about, so it is pointless getting too narked about it.

The fact is though that the boxing writers in the nationals only go to the big fights and there might be only half a dozen a year, so that means in my book they are just not educated enough about the sport. They might have covered it for ten years, but that might only mean a few fights every year. It is not enough.

I like Jim Watt on Sky TV, he knows the sport inside out. Mind you, just to show boxing is all about opinions, Jim gave the Nikolai Valuev–David Haye fight to Valuev and by a couple of rounds. How he made that when Valuev didn't land a punch all night is beyond me, but at least Jim has been there, seen it and had the experience of many years in the ring. He might be occasionally wrong in my opinion, but he is very much entitled to that opinion. Jim also had Brian Magee down to do a number on me, and look what happened there.

Boxing is such a subjective sport. One person's aggressor is the thing that catches the eye, while another person looks for the defensive fighter who counter-punches brilliantly. It is very much a matter of opinion. You have to take people's opinions exactly as they are, just opinions. I know what happened to me after the Abraham fight in the press. I went from being a potentially finished fighter to being hailed as one of the greatest ever from this country. It happened overnight. After the Kessler fight I got some stick for being, in essence, a limited brawler. After Abraham I was reading articles saying I was great, legendary, outstanding and all the rest. All of a sudden I was the best thing since sliced bread. One minute I was considered average, the next I am the greatest. I don't believe the hype either way.

Although I do think I gave the best performance of my career, especially bearing in mind the quality of the opposition, but I am not, nor ever have been, an over-night sensation. I have worked at it for years and years and OK, so Abraham was me at my best, but for writers to say I had come from nowhere was as insulting as it was wrong. I hands down beat someone at the top of his game and one of the best fighters in the world.

In my eyes the win against Abraham was magnified much more because I had lost to Kessler. My defeat to Kessler was devastating at the time, but I benefited from it because I trained just that little bit harder and the press love a comeback story. Losing to Kessler and responding by beating Abraham was a great story for them.

I also think fate had a hand in it. Fate does exist. I believe in it. I am not remotely religious but I do believe in fate, or karma, or call it what you like. I lost that fight against Kessler for a reason, because I needed a bit of a kick up the backside. If you do bad things, it will come back to you and I believe the same is true if you do good things.

Finland at that time of the year, you will not be surprised to hear, was bloody cold. There was a blizzard going on when we landed, with snow flakes as big as a table-tennis ball. Then as the week progressed it got colder. By the end of the week the whole of Helsinki was just white. The snow never stopped coming. I looked outside my hotel window and it made you blink it was so white.

The press conference just before the fight was great for me. I told Kalle Sauerland that I was happy with the fight being in Finland as it would be a level playing field, which I didn't think I got in Denmark against Kessler. That made me feel good.

There was nothing personal against Kalle Sauerland or Arthur Abraham, I just felt I had his number and I was going to prove it. I also wanted to erase the memory of the last time

I fought in Finland, in the European Championships as an amateur when I lost to Stjepan Bozic, who is now a real name in the twelve-stone division. Although, in February 2011 Bozic complained of breaking his hand in a clash with Arthur Abraham and the fight had to be stopped. I boxed really crap that day. I jarred my arm in warming up and lost 7–6 on points with a performance I am not proud of. I let myself down.

At the start of the week the lake in front of my hotel was still a lake. By the end of the week it was frozen solid and the temperature went down to something like minus twenty degrees. People were fishing out on the ice, cutting a hole like an Eskimo and sitting there with a rod in their hands.

I trained at the hotel, the Hilton Strand in Helsinki, as they had a little gym there. Everything went fine. At the last press conference Kalle Sauerland pulled out a stuffed cobra and Arthur Abraham tried to laugh about it. Kalle cracked a weak joke about stuffing me in response to a previous comment I made that I was going to stuff Arthur like a chicken as he always comes into the ring in a feathered robe. I was in no mood really for jokes because I was so focused about what I needed to do. Rob and I chatted every night in our hotel rooms about how the fight was going to go and what I needed to do to win it. I concentrated on the fight from the minute I landed in Helsinki to the last second of round twelve and during the bout I knew I had to focus for every second, otherwise it could all go belly up.

In the changing rooms immediately before the fight I was sitting there with Rob and just a few friends. Rob and I were doing a bit of light pad work every now and again just to loosen up the muscles. I was sitting gathering my thoughts when an official walked in to say, 'Six minutes and you're on'! Then I would start my ring walk. The reality kicked in. I knew this was fight time, the place of no return.

I was just a touch nervous and apprehensive, but at the same time super, super confident. I had never had such a good training camp. It was dead quiet in my dressing room and you could have heard a pin drop. It was then that David Haye came out with a classic and said, 'I love this bit now, the period just before you are about to go out and beat the shit out of someone.' Cue laughter all round. He carried on, saying, 'I bet you feel really good, Carl, don't you?' I replied that actually I was a bit nervous but his confidence made me feel great and I remember saying to David, 'That is exactly right. I am going to beat the shit out of Abraham and I am going to come back into this dressing room in an hour with the world title belt wrapped around my waist.' The piss-taking banter on all sides started as I told David he could just sit back and watch the fight, whereas I was in it. But David's comment had the desired effect because I relaxed. I was joking and laughing inside my dressing room just minutes before the fight of my life. I was very much of the belief that if I lost I would probably walk away from boxing so not only was it one of the biggest nights of my life because it was for my old world title, it was also the fight where I would go one way, or the other, in terms of my future in the sport.

David's comment is typical of him. He has always been laid-back, even when we were amateurs together. He always used to handle the pressure brilliantly, by just saying he would take care of business. It is not arrogance, just ultra confidence in his own ability. People often ask me what he is like these days because of the success he has had in boxing and I always say David is the same now as when I first met him when we were barely shaving. He had an aura about him then and he has an aura about him now. Nothing has changed. David's a great bloke, a superb fighter and his presence was perfect in my dressing room before going into the ring. I might also add it was really decent of him even to come to Helsinki. OK, we are mates who go back a long way, but it was still a nice touch from him to take the time out to come and back me. Not all fighters I have known over the years would do that.

Six minutes later I began the ring walk. I glanced over to Abraham's corner, nothing more than that. The fight started. I landed three or four shots, then pulled away. Every time I did it, I could hear Rob shouting at me to hit and move, hit and move. All I did in the first round was jab, jab, throw, move, jab, jab, throw, move. That's all I did. I didn't stay in there to exchange for any extended length of time with Abraham. The old me, when I had him on the ropes, would have gone for it and tried to bang him out and punish him, but he would probably have caught me with something. The old me would have taken a few shots on the chin to get a few of mine through. On this occasion that wasn't going to happen. I had to get the job done.

I think if I had gone for it I would have stopped Abraham but I would have shipped a few myself and Rob wasn't prepared to take the risk. We weren't going to gamble on Abraham's power. I boxed to a plan which we both agreed with and as the fight progressed, because I was having so much success with it, I wasn't going to risk changing tactics. The plan had been devised four months before the fight, when I first went into the gym after the bout was announced. Rob and I sat down and chatted about the best way to beat Abraham and the high-risk strategy was not the one we both wanted to take. After being with Rob for so many years, whatever he says I do. If he thought this was the best way to beat Abraham, then that was the way it was going to be. I have complete faith in his judgement and he has never been wrong yet. I suppose in the past I haven't always listened to Rob during a fight, because it is hard to listen to advice when you are actually in the ring, but on this occasion I was 100 per cent focused and followed his advice to the letter.

Rob and I went through it in training for week after week. He would come towards me and threaten to throw his right hand and I would have to move anti-clockwise out of the way. It was quite boring and mundane at times but we stuck with it through my training and it worked on the night. It worked because we had practised it so many times it felt very natural to fight like that.

I jabbed and moved. I boxed in spurts. Three or four shots then move. Three or four shots then move. Don't stay in there. This was drilled into me for hour after hour. In training I always kept a nice tight guard, or stood very side on so the only thing to hit was the side of my shoulder. I executed all the training on the night perfectly.

At the end of the first round I felt great. Ditto the end of the second, third, fourth and fifth, although in the second round he did catch me with a ramrod jab which made me realise just how much power Abraham had at his disposal. It was his left hand as well, so I didn't want to think about what he had in his right fist! In fact, it was that jab which gave me a black eye. It was also a punch which made me realise I had to stick to the game plan. The fight seemed to be going so perfectly because Abraham had hardly laid a glove on me and I knew I had hit him with some pretty good shots as I heard him wince a few times. He looked confused. At the end of the sixth Rob just said, 'Keep fucking doing what you're doing because you're walking this fight.' I said to Rob, 'I reckon I can do him. I can get him out of here.' Rob's reply was unambiguous: 'No you fucking won't. Keep jabbing, keep moving.' He was putting a bit of fear into me because he kept saying, 'Just wait, Carl, this kid is going to open up. He's going to have a go, because he is losing by so much. You've got to be ready for it.' Except the bombardment never really came because I think Abraham just ran out of ideas and didn't know what to do.

I kept quite a lot in the tank in reserve. Instead of throwing three or four punches in a bunch I could have thrown seven or eight. My stamina has always been one of my strong points, but on this occasion I was bossing the fight so much, I thought I would just keep a little supply in reserve for when the onslaught came. As it happens, it never did. That's not because he lacked bottle or anything like that, Abraham is far too good a boxer for me to accuse him of that. The simple fact is that every time he wound himself up to come and

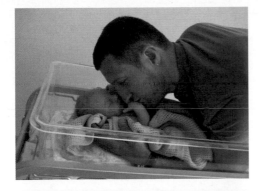

Rocco was born on 24 June 2010. Becoming a father is the best thing that has ever happened to me.

Rachael with my mum Carol and my stepdad Steve.

Fighting Arthur Abraham. I stuck to the game plan and fought a tight and controlled bout. Abraham couldn't find a way to get round me and land anything hurtful.

In training with Rob on the pads.

© ACTION IMAGES / ANDREW COULDRIDGE LIVEPIC

Wrapped up against the cold and snowflakes like tennis balls in Finland before the Abraham fight.

With the WBC Super Middleweight World Championship belt.

Celebrating with the belt after beating Abraham in one of the best fights of my career.

With Arthur Abraham after the fight.
A true gentleman and gracious in defeat.

A very happy Robert McCracken.

The punch that finished Groves.

With Kessler at the weigh-in. A true fighter, and someone I have massive respect for.

The aftermath of the punch. When I saw how awkwardly Groves was lying on the canvas I knew there was no chance he was getting up.

With Natalia a few days after the Kessler fight in May 2013.

Working out with Rocco in the garden.

My family.

have a go he walked straight into a stiff jab and usually a couple of body shots. Tactically it was about as good as it gets because he had no answer to the questions I was posing him. He just couldn't work out a way to get around me and to land anything hurtful.

As the fight wore on I could hear Rob, David Haye and Rachael all screaming at me. I could only really take advice from Rob and David, but it was great having Rachael's support and she certainly proved the old adage that Scousers are always seen and heard! Pals of mine watching the fight back home on Primetime TV said all they could hear was Rachael's Liverpudlian screams! And I can vouch for the fact she can certainly turn up the volume, but she was there supporting me and the fact that she was screaming and shouting shows her passion. People asked me when I got home if I could hear Rachael. Afterwards she asked me if I could hear her. How could I not hear her! Everyone in Finland heard Rachael.

The fight developed into the later rounds and I felt so good. My tank was nowhere near down and in fact, at the pace I was going, jab, jab, jab, bang, move, jab, jab, jab, bang, move, I could have done twenty rounds. I was as fresh as I was in round one. He was breathing a lot heavier than I was but then he was getting hit and I wasn't and also Abraham just kept throwing punches into fresh air. I know that the most knackering thing in boxing is hitting nothing. If you throw a punch and it lands on fresh air it takes the wind out of you as it uses up so much more energy. If a punch stops on someone's face or body there is less energy used. That is what happened to Abraham and why he tired so badly. He kept missing, time and time again, or more accurately I kept making him miss.

The rounds ticked by and followed a very similar rhythm. I would jab, jab, jab, punch and move and Abraham wouldn't get near me. He caught me with a shot which landed on the back of my head at the start of the twelfth round. It knocked my equilibrium a bit. It was a similar shot which sent me to the canvas for the first time in my career against Jermain Taylor, a punch to the back of the head. For some reason they do knock your balance off kilter. On this occasion I was never remotely hurt but it certainly made me temporarily unbalanced because of where the punch landed. I recovered quickly and for the rest of round twelve I hammered him. Afterwards Abraham's punch was highlighted on TV as evidence of how powerful he could be, but I think that missed the point. For eleven previous rounds I had battered the living crap out of him. The seconds ticked down in the last round and yet I remained calm because I kept going back to my game plan. After his initial success in round twelve Abraham didn't lay another glove on me. Should Abraham's corner have pulled him out? That's up to them I suppose, but in my opinion, towards the later rounds, it was pretty clear I was going to win. A fighter like Abraham is always dangerous so maybe they were hoping I would walk into one, but I did daft things like that when I was an amateur, not a seasoned pro.

The bell went and it was no contest. I knew I had won. There was hardly any point in the referee asking the judges what they thought because I knew, and Abraham knew, I had won by a landslide. Two of the judges gave me every round, while the other gave Abraham one to my eleven. How he worked that out I'll never know as I cannot fathom for the life of me where Abraham won a round.

It was different to the first time I won the world title. I didn't cherish the moment as much. The first time, against Jean Pascal, was extra special, probably because it was the first time I could call myself a legitimate world champion and with one of the most prestigious, oldest belts in the sport. I never really thought I lost to Kessler, so I still considered myself the best in the world. When they wrapped the belt around my waist in Helsinki I felt it was my belt anyway. It had only been temporarily taken off me. The fact that I had got back what I knew I owned meant it wasn't quite that special. Of course, I was elated with my performance, but when I hugged my mum, dad, Rachael, Wayne and Rob, it was definitely not with the same level of euphoria as the last time. I suppose 'satisfied' is the nearest emotion I can think of. I was satisfied with what happened in the ring, but I never thought for a minute I wasn't the best twelve-stone fighter in the world.

Maybe I wasn't as excited second time around because nothing ever is as exciting second time around. That is a shame, but a fact of life. I was delighted with the way I had stuck to my task and proved a few doubters wrong, but other than that, it was a feeling of justification more than anything. I had justified my faith in my ability. It was as near perfect as I have ever performed in the ring, especially when bearing in mind the quality of the opponent.

*

I did loads of interviews in the ring and then a drugs test, which took an hour for me to pee. I tried to find my 'Cobra' robe which I left at ringside but someone nicked it and I have never seen it to this day, so if anyone reading this ever travels to Finland and finds a bloke trying to flog a Cobra robe, then you know where it has come from. I saw Abraham in the drug-testing room after the fight and I have to take my hat off to him as he was dead friendly. We introduced each other to our friends and family and Abraham could not stop smiling. His face looked bad as it was swelling up, red and sore, but he was in very good spirits, bearing in mind he had just been stuffed. I took some snaps of us all in the dressing room and he was a proper gentleman. I suppose in hindsight I was surprised he took it so well, because if I had taken a battering like that I am not sure I would have been smiling about it, but there you go, each to their own I suppose. I felt a bit bad for him, but this is boxing so I couldn't really say I felt sorry for my opponent. Abraham had won enough fights himself to know the score.

We got back to the hotel at 4 a.m. and everything was closed. The bar was shut. The night porter brought out some beers for my family and friends and I had water and a couple of energy drinks which I had taken from the drug-testing room. My elder brother Lee didn't come out to Finland as it was his wedding anniversary but my mum Carol and my stepdad Steve, dad Frank and little brother Wayne were all there, as were loads of other friends and family. It wasn't really a party atmosphere though because it was so late and I think everyone felt tired once the adrenalin left their systems. I went to bed and got a couple of hours' kip. When I woke up I was looking forward to getting back to Nottingham to see my little boy Rocco, who had been looked after while Rachael and I were away by Wayne's partner Laura.

I've been asked since then whether the element of fear made me box the fight of my life. I wouldn't go so far as to say it was fear, because I've never been scared of anyone in the ring and that includes Arthur Abraham. Being scared doesn't come into my vocabulary. I suppose there was more a feeling of being threatened. Abraham stood between me and what I wanted. I also heard stacks of so-called experts saying Abraham's right hand could knock out a mule. A few weeks before the fight Andre Dirrell predicted Abraham would spark me out. I thought, 'Bloody hell, does he really hit that hard?' The fact Dirrell tipped Abraham to beat me was on my mind throughout the build-up to the fight, because the American had shared a ring with him as well. But again, it was not fear.

I would go in the ring with any other twelve-stone fighter in the world and back myself. I suppose my display was down to a combination of things. My training camp went perfectly, there were no volcanic ash clouds getting in the way and Abraham brought out the best in me. You don't have to be a boxing genius to realise that Abraham can properly dig, so to beat him in such emphatic style in every round made me feel very proud. I was a father and now a two-time world champion. Not a bad combination.

CHAPTER 14

I felt great after beating Arthur Abraham so emphatically. I was still in the Super Six tournament and I wasn't sure who I would be fighting in the semi-final for a place in the show-piece final. Mikkel Kessler was the one I wanted, but shortly after the Abraham fight in November, word got to me that Kessler was suffering an injury and, sure enough, shortly afterwards he announced his retirement due to a recurring eye problem. Thankfully it was short-lived and he was soon back fighting and made short work of Allan Green in one of his comeback fights.

I'd heard of Glen, or Glengoffe Johnson before his name cropped up as a possible opponent. He sparked out one of my all-time boxing heroes, Roy Jones Jr a few years earlier. It wasn't anything like the Jones of his prime but it meant that Johnson could clearly bang. Jones in his heyday was a perfect fighting machine. Now I reckon he is finished at the top level. Johnson had also just beaten Allan Green a few weeks prior to my victory over Abraham, again proof that Glen could punch.

I spoke to Rob and he told me all I needed to know about Glen Johnson. He was rough, tough and hard to stop. Bernard Hopkins was the only person who had halted him, in the latter rounds when they met as long ago as 1997. That was Hopkins in his absolute prime.

I was excited though because when Showtime told me after the New Year that they would like the semi-final to be between me and Johnson – now that Kessler had dropped out – they invited me to a show in Las Vegas for a press conference. And it wasn't just any old show, but Manny Pacquiao against Sugar Shane Mosley. It wasn't a great fight, but it was a great match-up between two legends of the sport so I still enjoyed the whole occasion. The last time I had been to Vegas was years before when I saw Naseem Hamed lose to Marco Antonio Barrera and it was a very disappointing fight.

At the press conference Showtime announced the other semi-final would be between Andre Ward and Arthur Abraham. I expected Ward to win, especially on home soil, which he did comfortably, beating Abraham by a wide points decision.

The press conference was the first time I had met Johnson in the flesh. He was a big lad. He had fought a lot at light-heavyweight and you could see why. Every bit of him was muscle. He didn't say a lot, but what he did say was very polite and respectful. In fact, I wasn't even convinced he could speak until he starting talking at the conference, as no one could get a word out of him. There was no trash-talking. Glen wasn't into that and neither was I, so we both said our piece, promised we were going to be victorious, shook hands and that was that. Glen had a stern, business-like approach to the whole thing. He had a strong Jamaican accent so I didn't understand too much of what he said anyway, although I am sure he would say the same thing about my Nottingham accent!

Glen also came across as confident and with his experience I knew I was in for a testing night, despite being convinced that I would win. I knew Glen would bring his 'A' game as this was his big chance, not just to become the world WBC super-middleweight champion, but also to get into the final of the Super Six. It was his opportunity to earn some big bucks and he wasn't getting any younger either; the 'Road Warrior' was already over 40 when we met in the ring. Mind you, he looked good for it.

Glen was a wise old fox, and I knew he'd train like a maniac to take my title, and Rob warned me he was absolutely no mug. I didn't think he was in my league in terms of skill, but he was still a proper opponent and one I had to respect. He was very much a come-forward fighter. What I mean by that is that Johnson mixed it up with the best and wouldn't take a step backwards. You didn't have to go searching for a fight with Glen Johnson. He came to you.

With his impressive record I expected Johnson to be very durable and incredibly strong. I had seen him fight quite a lot and was impressed. Not so much with his skills, but with his fighting heart. His nickname suited him perfectly as he was prepared to get on the road and fight anywhere against anyone. Joe Calzaghe was supposed to have fought him two or three times but the bout always fell through, so I had also heard Glen's name mentioned going back many years.

After the Abraham fight I split from my promoter and decided on a new course. I was determined to get back on Sky television and try to become a much bigger name. I felt I had suffered from a lack of exposure on Primetime TV and wanted to go back on Sky. I took the bull by the horns and spoke directly to Barney Francis, the head of sport at Sky, who was very excited about getting me back on his channel. It was Rob who first suggested Eddie Hearn as a possible new promoter, so I gave Eddie a ring. I thought about managing and promoting myself, but realistically that wasn't possible as there is so much organisation and paperwork that needs to be done for any boxer. So I arranged a meeting with Eddie and Rob in the canteen of the English Institute for Sport in Sheffield, where Rob trained all his Olympians and me. Rob said Eddie was a good bloke and that's all I needed to hear.

I suppose it is fair to say I got on well with Eddie from the first minute. He is an impressive person to look at and an impressive person to work with. We sat down, had a cuppa and talked things through. Straight away he said he would love to take me on board under the Matchroom promotional team.

Eddie was very honest. I could tell he wasn't exactly desperate for money, as he and his dad had been successful promoters for many years. There is a real aura about Eddie. It is an aura of success and I like that. In a few words, I'd describe Eddie as clear, precise, confident, tidy and someone who expresses himself calmly and with no hint of bullshit. He's a tall, good-looking bloke, who speaks well and dresses well. He looks after himself and keeps himself smart and trim. I have a lot of time for that because it tells me that here is a person who cares for himself, an important characteristic in my book. He had also been taught how to do things properly by his dad Barry, who is one of the best sports promoters out there, if not the best. Everything Barry touches turns to gold.

Eddie keeps in good shape, and I'm not being funny but if you're very overweight it is often the result of greed. So if you are greedy with yourself, you're surely more likely to be greedy towards others.

Eddie's well-spoken manner and professionalism meant I didn't have to look any further. In fact, after speaking to Rob before our canteen meeting, I knew I would sign with Eddie and had no interest or intention to go and see any other promoters. Eddie has a great relationship with Sky and that's what I wanted. We talked for an hour or so and it was pretty much agreed there and then. Eddie said he was absolutely certain he would get me back on Sky and I was convinced of this anyway through my previous conversations with Barney Francis.

We shook hands and a deal between us was done. I was delighted. I felt I was in the hands of a real professional. I would carry on training for the Johnson fight, splitting my time between Nottingham and Sheffield and Eddie would start the business of improving my profile and working as my promoter.

The Johnson fight was made for June in Atlantic City and I was ready. Three weeks before, I travelled over and made my base in New York, along with my kid brother Wayne and Rob. It was ten minutes' walk from Central Park, although it was only a small two-bedroom apartment, so poor Wayne got the sofa bed and me and Rob had the bedrooms.

Every day, I basically woke up, had a run, had breakfast, got a cab to the gym, finished training, got a cab back, relaxed and had an evening meal. It was pretty tedious, and New York at the time was very hot and humid. I didn't much like it and I counted down the days to the fight.

I considered training at the world famous Gleason's Gym in New York, but Rob said it would be like a bus station in there, far too busy to get down to proper work without any distractions. So instead we chose the Mendez gym and the famous Trinity gym, near Ground Zero, for training and sparring. Both of them were like an oven and it wasn't much nicer when you stepped outside either. Despite the heat, sparring went well with Peter 'Kid Chocolate' Quillin and Newton Kidd, known to everybody as Butch. They both tried to take my block off but it was good preparation for what I knew was coming from Johnson.

I liked jogging through Central Park every day, apart from very early on when I felt a twinge in my calf muscle which bothered me the whole time I was in America. It was one of those injuries which wasn't too serious, but at the same time it was always there nagging away.

I was losing a lot of water in the gym and dehydration was definitely a problem while I was in New York. It was so hot and the humidity was excessive. Every time I weighed myself after finishing training I would look at the scales and I would be down to 11 stone 10 lbs or 11 stone 11 lbs, well inside the super middleweight limit of 12 stone. My calf was still bothering me too, and I told Rob and Wayne I couldn't wait to get down to Atlantic City.

I'm not a massive one for sightseeing, but I'm still disappointed I saw hardly anything of New York as it is an amazing city. I took a quick look at Ground Zero, but hardly saw anything other than my apartment, the nearby restaurants and Central Park for my run. I had an offer from the promoters to go up the Empire State Building but I just didn't feel in the mood. I was there to work, not enjoy myself. At least Central Park was close by and that was one advantage of the small apartment we had. I'd like to go back there one day with Rachael for a proper holiday and take in all the sights, as I feel I didn't really see a thing during my two weeks there.

My lasting memory of New York was how long it would take to flag cabs down and the humidity. Thankfully five days before the fight I moved with Wayne and Rob down to Atlantic City. Being on the coast was much cooler, which made a pleasant change from the heat of the Big Apple, and it also meant fight night was getting near.

Mind you, I wasn't massively impressed with Atlantic City either. It really is a bit of a poor man's Las Vegas. Parts of Atlantic City are a ghost town and, although the boardwalk was nice enough, just a few blocks inland from there was pretty horrible. But we booked into Bally's, our hotel, and I was finally on the homeward straight to the fight with Johnson.

However, it was all very low key. I was in the semi-final of the biggest ever boxing tournament to find out the best super-middleweight in the world and there was hardly a soul to be seen in Atlantic City. At the start of the Super Six I was expecting the final and semi-final to be in Las Vegas or New York's Madison Square Garden. Instead I was in a near-deserted, run-down casino resort. I was massively disappointed as there was no real pre-fight vibe around the place, no feeling in the air that something special was about to happen. I also realised that, against Johnson, I was in a no-win situation. I was widely expected to succeed by all the pundits and so if I won I would get no particular praise and if I lost it would be a humiliating defeat.

I struggled to get up for the fight. I was being professional, as I had trained hard and not cut any corners – not that I would anyway – but the lack of drama at the venue in Atlantic City was a downer. I suppose I also knew I would win, which takes away a little of the nervous energy you need as a boxer to perform at your very best.

The Showtime cameras followed me everywhere for the 360° programme, but there was no real buzz around the casinos or on the boardwalk. There were a few fight posters up, but even these were very limited. You hardly knew the fight was going on at all.

I went down and had a look at the fight venue itself, which was a room just off the world famous Boardwalk Hall, holding around 2,500 – only a quarter of the size of the Capital FM Arena in Nottingham. That said it all. On fight night it was sold out, but it still didn't create much of an atmosphere.

Lots of my family were able to make it out for the fight. Wayne's girlfriend Laura, my elder brother Lee, Mum and my stepdad Steve, all flew over and enjoyed a few nights at a beach bar right next to the boardwalk.

Annoyingly my calf was still sore, and my ears had been bothering me every since we landed in the US. A day before the weigh-in, the Thursday before the fight, I finally got round to going to hospital where a doctor had a look and said there was excessive wax in my ear canal. I had them syringed with water and I'm sure my right ear got slightly perforated in the process as everything around me was echoing.

I was OK though, and after the weigh-in everything was set. I slept all right on Friday night and at last fight day had arrived. I'm an experienced pro nowadays so nothing really fazed me in the ring walk, or when we first swapped blows together in the ring. I remember thinking that all the water I had lost in New York meant I should be pretty cagey at the start and I was. I jabbed and moved for the first two rounds, with both of us taking our time to work out the opposition.

In round three, Johnson came forward with his guard up high and I decided to let go. I smashed him in the face with four shots, all of which connected. It went jab, straight right, jab, straight right. They were all on the button and it was then I realised just why nobody bar Hopkins had ever stopped Johnson. He grunted, shook his head, then just came barging straight back at me. 'OK, no problem,' I thought. I had just hit him with four good, heavy shots to the face and he hadn't done anything other than grunt! It was at that moment I knew this guy was tough. I always felt I was going in there with a proper light-heavyweight and now I'd had it proven to me.

Throughout the fight I was never worried or in trouble, although I'll be the first to admit he caught me with some decent right-hand shots which I should have avoided. He could certainly bang hard, but I've got a great chin and I just swallowed them up like a human Pacman. Early in the fight a double right-hand caught me and, if my right eardrum wasn't perforated before the fight, it certainly was then, as my hearing went funny. Having suffered perforated drums before, I knew exactly what it was and didn't panic. It was just part of the job.

As the fight wore on I started to get in some decent combinations, without ever really running away with the bout. I thought my performance was impressive, bearing in mind I was fighting abroad and had not had a great few weeks leading up to the fight. I never felt in any danger of getting knocked out. I did a professional job on Glen Johnson, even though I would accept he is a very decent operator who I have a lot of respect for. I made the decision from the third round onwards, when I caught him flush, that I wasn't going to risk trying too hard to knock him out. If you do that you can get caught cold yourself, particularly as Johnson had some serious power. I kept the pressure on and won by a wide points decision with two of the judges. The third judge, a Japanese bloke, made it a draw, which I thought had to be some sort of joke. Even Glen's trainers said I had won it hands down. I felt it was a very workmanlike display, although there was nothing edge-of-the-seat about it, like I feel there was when I beat Jean Pascal and Lucian Bute on my home soil.

I never sleep the night after a fight and this was no different, especially with the ringing sound in my right ear and my sore calf. I went with my family and friends to the hotel diner, which was open 24 hours a day. Before the fight I had been eyeballing the pizzas and cheesecakes, but this time I could dive into them myself. I really enjoyed having something substantial to eat and spending time with everyone, and was very pleased to have kept my title and made the Super Six final.

A few weeks later I decided to take Rachael to David Haye's heavyweight clash with Wladimir Klitschko in Hamburg. It promised to be a great night, but unfortunately David came up short. It was a frustrating night for David as he had previously broken his toe, which can seriously affect your ability to push off your feet and throw hurtful shots. He was also up against a man-mountain of a bloke in Klitschko, a proper heavyweight who was much bigger than David, with a much longer reach, as well as being on home soil. Klitschko is a strong, rangy fighter and, although David did well to close the range between him and his opponent to try and get to him on the inside, when he got him there his injury meant he couldn't throw any damaging blows. Klitschko's height, reach and strength advantage won the fight. He didn't get hit with anything too special, but in the end Klitschko was just too big for him. I hope David gets the chance to make amends against Wladimir Klitschko or his brother Vitali one day because he is a proud warrior who loves to fight.

After his fight with Klitschko and totally out of the blue, David invited Rachael, Rocco and me on holiday to a mansion he was renting in Jamaica. This was the chance of a lifetime and I agreed straight away. We packed our bags in the middle of August for two very special weeks in the Caribbean with David and his lovely family. I've known and liked David ever since we first boxed together at Crystal Palace back in the late 1990s as amateurs, and we all get along fantastically. He is in some ways very similar to me and we have a similar outlook on life. I'll always appreciate him asking me to come on holiday with him and the memories of that vacation will stay forever.

David came with his wife Natasha and his boy Cassius and daughter Sienna. Cassius Haye, Cassius Clay – great choice of name, David! Derron and Jane, David's mum and dad were there too. We all bonded and it was an amazing fortnight. Rapper Dizzee Rascal dropped in one day, which was lots of fun, and the laid-back Caribbean vibe soon kicked in.

The mansion was immaculate and everything was laid on. We had breakfast, lunch and dinner cooked for us and the days went by, chilling out by the pool. We barely stepped outside the complex. Lennox Lewis was in the mansion next to ours so we all got to spend some time with the former undisputed heavyweight champion. One day he drove us around the island, stopping off in Negril to buy some fresh snapper. We got back very late to play chess at his place. I played the game quite a bit at school and I think I know what I am doing, but Lennox is a seriously good player and, I have to admit, he beat me. Not easily mind you! It was the perfect way to wind down after the Johnson fight, but now came the big one.

When I beat Johnson I already knew it was going to be Andre Ward in the final as he had beaten Arthur Abraham in the other semi a few weeks previously. Ward's performance didn't hugely impress me, however, and left me thinking he hadn't really over-exerted himself. I'm not totally convinced Abraham really tried that hard either.

I didn't think much of the Ward–Abraham fight and I'd expected what happened. I wanted Ward to get hit with decent shots so that when we fought he would have been going into our meeting off the back of a tough fight, but that didn't happen. Andre Dirrell had beaten Abraham very convincingly, then I'd had a go and tore him to bits, so by the time he met Ward he was possibly less certain of himself. I've got a lot of respect for Abraham but I think he knew he couldn't win at super-middleweight against the very best fighters.

I actually started training for the Ward fight while on holiday with Rachael and Rocco in Jamaica. I did a few runs with Rachael and a bit of weight training with David Haye in the second week of our holiday in August just to get things moving again.

The fight date was set for late November in Atlantic City, but when I got back to Nottingham and had started proper training the news came through that Ward had suffered a cut in sparring. I was a bit dubious at first. I did question whether he was genuinely injured, as you hear lots of rumours and hearsay in boxing and I wasn't sure about Ward wanting to fight me in the final.

I was concerned, but Ward put a picture of himself on Twitter and it clearly showed he had a cut above his eye. That was proof enough for me. This is professional boxing and sometimes fighters do suffer from cuts in training or sparring. It is a fact of life and something I could do nothing about. As soon as I saw the picture I knew Ward wasn't trying to pull out and it was a genuine injury. I couldn't do anything about it, so why get hot under the collar? I accepted it had happened and moved on. I had a week or so off from heavy training, then got back on it.

The worst thing about the delay by a long chalk was the fact that so many of my supporters from Nottingham and around Britain had already paid for flights and often they are non-refundable. That was a massive shame and I felt really upset by that. It was probably the only reason why I was upset because I knew a lot of fans had saved up and spent a fair amount of money to come and watch me. The same thing happened when I had to pull out of the original Abraham date with an injury. Lots of supporters went out to Monaco the weekend I was supposed to be fighting, except I wasn't there! But I just had to accept that there was nothing I could to about the Ward delay.

I'd always thought I would fight Ward one day. I had watched his career for a long time. I think the first fight I recall seeing him in was when he beat Edison Miranda in 2009, a few months before he got the better of Mikkel Kessler. He was an Olympic champion and had earned a decent reputation.

I first met Andre Ward in Berlin when we did a Super Six European press conference before the tournament had even started. He seemed very professional, didn't say much and I barely got more than a few words out of him. He seemed very confident about himself, but you couldn't draw much of a conclusion from him as he said so little – a bit like Glen Johnson. He's not exactly flamboyant. I think that's one of the reasons why Ward hasn't become a superstar in America – he has a safety-first style and he needs to open up a bit if he is to get sporting fans to follow him in big numbers. What he does, he does very, very well, but for me he doesn't set the world alight with his style of fighting.

Once I found out the fight had been delayed, we decided to go to Center Parcs for a week. The three of us – Rachael, Rocco and me – had a fantastic time there in late August enjoying some unusually hot weather. All now seemed set for the Ward clash, which was now going to be in December.

Training in England went well and just like the Johnson bout I travelled over to New York about three weeks before fight night and settled down in Manhattan again. This time though it was wet and cold, which was preferable to the humidity I had endured in the summer. There was a bit of 'Groundhog Day' going on as we booked into a similar apartment, although a bigger one this time, and trained at the same gyms – the Mendez and mostly the Trinity. I even sparred with the same fighters, Butch and Kid Chocolate. It was the same in so many ways, just hard graft in the gym trying to be in the best shape possible for 17 December.

My brother Wayne didn't come out this time with me, but I met up with an old Loughborough University friend of mine called Sean Sweeney, who was living in New Jersey. He spent quite a few nights at the apartment with me and Rob and showed us some of the decent restaurants in New York, so it was good to have a bit of local knowledge. Sean is living the dream out there and has really landed on his feet, which is great as he is a top bloke.

If the summer was unpleasant in the high heat and humidity, the only difference this time was that we spent what seemed like hours flagging down cabs in the pissing rain. Mind you, I'd rather be soaked through to the skin than soaked due to humidity.

The build-up was fairly quiet, although I did plenty of press interviews in New York. It was the Super Six final and I should have been a lot more up for it, but the tournament seemed to have fizzled out a bit, as if people had begun to lose interest because it had gone on for so long. The final was in Atlantic City again, as opposed to one of the glitzy casinos in Vegas or Madison Square Garden. When I found out it was back in Atlantic City, I genuinely thought, what a load of shite this is. I just wanted the fight and the tournament to be over as soon as possible so that I could move on with Eddie and Rob to the next fight.

While I was sparring in New York with Kid Chocolate and Butch, both big, strong lads, I was angry and fired up. The last few days of sparring went really well and I felt switched on, my timing was good and I was ready for Ward. I was ready there and then for the battle.

I travelled down to Atlantic City and a few days before the fight Rachael and my family, as usual, all came out to support me. Two or three days before the bout I think I switched off mentally. I gave Rachael a cuddle when I met her and from that moment on, I didn't quite feel the same. A similar thing happened to me years earlier when I reached the semi-finals of the world amateur championships, becoming the first English boxer to win a medal at the worlds. I switched off when I got to the semis, with everyone patting me on the back and telling me how I had created history. The same thing happened here. I felt I had got to the final and I'd left my best game in New York.

Looking back on it, maybe having Rachael there might have affected me. She's the woman I love and naturally I miss her like mad when I've been away from her for a long time, so when I saw her after two and a half weeks of just talking on the phone, I focused on her. It was emotional seeing her. Having said that, she has been with me from the Taylor fight onwards and I didn't exactly do badly that night. In a perfect world, as I approach the last days before a fight, I should lock myself away from family and friends, but realistically that's not possible. They all want to wish you the best of luck and in Rachael's case she's the mother of my children, so obviously she will want to be there at ringside supporting her man. It's a tough one and perhaps there is no ideal answer.

I got to the venue, the world-famous Atlantic City Boardwalk Hall, but it was far from packed as so many of my British fight fans couldn't make it, which made the audience a lot smaller.

When the fight started, Ward sat on my chest and, instead of giving him a whack with my elbow or going over to him and putting it on him from the word go, I looked at the referee and thought, what's going on here? I was pissed off and feeling sorry for myself. At the highest level you have to be switched on from the first bell because as soon as the fight starts there is a rhythm that both boxers get into. Looking back, I had quite a bad attitude and I've given myself a load of stick about that ever since. It was the situation I was in and for some reason I just kept thinking to myself, you know what, I can't be arsed with this. That's a terrible thing to admit to as it was a unification world title fight, with my WBC crown on the table and Ward's WBA belt and it was the final of the Super Six, yet I could not be arsed. That showed in my performance. It wasn't a great night for boxing fans there in Atlantic City, or back home in England, or watching in the rest of America.

At one stage in the first round Ward backed up and I didn't go chasing him. I boxed behind my jab and was pretty cautious, as was he. Against Jean Pascal, he and I went for it from the first bell. That's much more my kind of fight. I remember a split second moment in that first round when he backed into his corner and instead of throwing four or five shots straight down the pipe, I let him ease himself into the fight and gain some confidence. That was a mistake from round one. It was hard then to turn the fight into a proper scrap. He closed the gap between us cleverly and leaned on me. I felt uncomfortable with his style of boxing, I'll make no bones about it. I was expecting it as I had seen him fight like that before, but I should have thrown some big shots much earlier than I did. Looking back on it now, it is a case of could have, should have, yet I didn't on the night. We will never know what would have happened if I had really gone for it.

Ward does what he has to do to win and fair play to him, he does it very well. It's not to everyone's liking, but there you go, we all box differently. Ward throws a few shots, gets out of range and is very, very difficult to hit. He then sits on your chest, closes the gap and speedily moves out of range.

He is brilliant at it. I've heard it said that Ward is a bigger version of Floyd Mayweather Jr, but Floyd takes a few more chances these days and lets his shots go. I think in his earlier days he was a lot more cautious, but he has become more aggressive in his later years. Oscar De La Hoya said of Ward that, unless he starts to engage and take a few chances, he will never be a superstar in America because people won't want to watch him.

I never really caught him clean throughout the fight. I was trying to chin him properly, but you have to do the quality boxing beforehand to open high-class fighters up. I didn't do enough of that. It was a horrible, frustrating night, with round after round of me getting more pissed off. I looked up at the ring card girl showing round eight and remember thinking, oh no, not another five rounds of this. That's a really bad attitude, but that's how I felt at the time.

In the last couple of rounds I caught him a few times and thought I had won them fairly convincingly, but although I was trying, it wasn't really coming off. I punch hard – just look at the finishing job I did on Taylor – so I never gave up the ghost or anything like that, but it was so frustrating being in there. He was tired and I thought he could go down, but he got on his bike even more, ducking and skipping out of range, and he did what he did to win the fight. I felt he was fading in the last couple of rounds and maybe I would have stopped him if I had stepped on the gas earlier, but we will never know. I didn't feel like I had caught him with too many great shots. Usually my hands really hurt after a fight, but on this occasion they didn't. I think when the bell went I knew that I feared the worst.

One of the judges, John Keane, had Ward winning by a lot, but the Canadian and American judge obviously saw something that they liked in me because they had it so close that if I had won another round they would both have made it a draw, and the fight would have ended as a majority draw if two of the three judges scored it that way. So it was close, according to those two judges. I think the Canadian and American looked at Ward and thought, I'm not sure if I like what I am seeing in this fight so let's give Froch some leeway because he was the more obvious aggressor throughout.

But, regardless, the judges came down for Ward and I was devastated, totally gutted. I had lost my world title and the chance to win *The Ring* magazine belt for the best 12-stone fighter in the world, which I have always wanted. He beat me when I wasn't in anything like the best frame of mind.

I'm not saying if we had a re-match I would beat him easily or anything stupid like that because that would obviously be ridiculous. We could fight again and he could beat me again, I'm not saying that wouldn't happen. But if I boxed the same way I did against Jean Pascal, or the way I came back against Jermaine Taylor when I refused to lose, or the destruction job I went on to do on Lucian Bute, then who knows? It could be different next time, if there is a next time. I think everyone who was there in Nottingham when I beat Bute would agree that the Carl Froch on that night would have stood a really good chance of getting the better of Andre Ward. Being focused properly on the night makes such a difference and in Nottingham I was properly up for it, but in Atlantic City I wasn't. Ward got off the hook as far as I am concerned and didn't face me at my best. It's not an excuse.

I'm only human and, yes, I do think about it from time to time when my head hits the pillow.

To this day I have never watched my clash with Ward. That's not just because I got beaten and it is sour grapes. I accept I lost but to me Ward is essentially a spoiler who doesn't like to stand in his opponent's range and trade shots. I lost a very close one to Kessler a few years previously and I have watched that loads of times. It was a great fight. I haven't seen the Ward bout and I've got no intention of doing so.

Moving forward, immediately after the fight I tried to look on the bright side and thought about how Eddie and Rob and I could go on from here. We were already thinking about Lucian Bute, or a re-match with Kessler, so there were still plenty of fights out there for me. I had proved I was a top-quality fighter against Ward, one of the best pound-for-pound fighters in the world. I hadn't disgraced myself in there, I had just lost a close one. I didn't get outclassed or knocked out, but it was a bad night in the office. I had lost, I'll accept that. I didn't get robbed. But I didn't do enough to beat him.

Some boxers when they lose blame anybody and everybody. That's not me. Rob gives every fight, every training session his heart and soul, so there was no blame attached there.

Blaming somebody else is always the easy way out. I'd changed my promotional outfit, but I was not in a million years going to change anything else. I was in there doing the fighting and I was in great physical shape, but mentally I wasn't at my best and you have to be, to beat the very best, like Andre Ward. I have no one to blame except myself for that night.

CHAPTER 15

As I landed back in England I was just happy the Super Six tournament was finished. The final against Ward was such an anti-climax, especially from what I had been led to expect. It was supposed to be a massive tournament which would redefine boxing. It didn't.

My immediate thoughts headed towards a Kessler rematch because I was pretty sure he wouldn't want to fight Ward again after what happened to him the first time they met in California. I got a text message from Mikkel when I was out in America saying 'Don't worry, Carl, what Ward does is not fighting ... you are better than him.' It was heartwarming to receive and it showed that Mikkel had experienced the same thing when he fought Ward. That made me feel good. A couple of days after getting back he phoned me and we chatted about a re-match, just knocking things around a bit and agreeing with each other over our opinion of Ward.

Lucian Bute wasn't really in the picture as I was under the impression he would fight Ward. But then I heard Ward saying on TV he had no intention of fighting Bute. A few days later, Eddie rang me up to say Bute's team had been in touch about a possible fight. Straight away I was on a bit of a high because I fancied facing Bute big time. Over Christmas Eddie reassured me there were plenty of big fights out there he could make. I enjoyed the festivities even more knowing that, and in early January the Bute fight was made.

Why did Bute come looking for me? To be honest, I don't think he fancied fighting Ward and, secondly, he and his team wanted someone like me, who had just lost a close one in the Super Six final, a tournament Bute hadn't entered. Beating me would be a great win for Bute and would have set up a real blockbuster against Ward.

I don't know exactly how Eddie persuaded Bute's team to come over here first of all, before a re-match in Canada, but it worked a treat. It's fair to say I didn't get a fortune to fight Bute in Nottingham first, but that was part of the deal. I had to pay to bring the champion over to England, but by beating him I knew I would then be in a much stronger position as I would have the IBF world title belt around my waist. And the deal worked well for Bute too; he was happy as he got paid more than me and had the safety net of knowing he had a re-match clause if he lost.

I couldn't wait to fight the first leg of a two-fight deal in Nottingham. I was sick and tired of travelling abroad all the time to fight. I could stay at home and train and not have to pack up and leave weeks before the fight. I was really pleased to be back fighting on Sky Sports, in my hometown and I felt confident from day one of my training camp, convinced that nothing could go wrong.

If Bute had said the only way this fight could go ahead was if I went to Montreal first I would have done so, but it never came to that. You can get frozen out in this sport very easily and I was prepared to do anything to get back in the top level frame. Losing out financially by fighting in Nottingham didn't bother me as I box because I love it, not for money. Rob thought Bute's team was being over-confident and reckoned he was just going to come over here and walk all over me. They hadn't got a clue what they were up against and were expecting the same fighter who boxed Ward in a stinker to turn up. Rob said that if I just made sure I was fit and strong I'd beat him. I thought to myself, too right, I'll prove it.

I never really rated Bute that highly and I still don't. I stand by what I said when the fight was first made. He is obviously a very good fighter, no doubt about that. You can't win that many fights without knowing what you are doing. But I never thought that he was the best fighter on the planet at 12-stone. Before the fight he had not fought anybody in the elite level like Ward, Kessler, Abraham, Pascal and Taylor. I'd fought all of them, and comparing them to Bute I was convinced that he was in no way a level above that lot.

I didn't want to go out of the sport on the back of the Ward fight. I was always going to fight again. If I'd lost this time I would have jacked it in because if I could not beat someone like Bute on home soil then that would have been the end for me. I wasn't interested in going back to small hall fights boxing for the British title. That was a big motivation. I wanted to go out in style. I was always going to go out swinging the lead.

I wanted to get back on the bike and get winning again. Fighters who I respect like Oscar De La Hoya had lost, but they bounced straight back up, never ducked anyone and got stuck into the next in line. Roy Jones Jr in his day was the same. The Argentine Sergio Martinez these days is very good for fighting the best out there consistently, one after another.

I didn't feel for a second I was finished at the top level. I've earned a lot of respect inside the game and nobody I spoke to thought for a minute that I didn't belong at the very highest level of the sport. But I wanted to prove it to myself that I was still right up there amongst the best. Rob didn't need convincing. We both agreed Bute was a great fight for me.

Eddie was 100 per cent behind me. We had some heart to heart conversations and he was always very supportive. Rachael just thinks I am the best fighter since Sugar Ray Robinson! She has been with me since I fought Jermain Taylor and agreed with me that the Ward display wasn't really me. She backed me all the way as well.

Before Bute and I stepped in the ring I had a few days of feeling a bit nervous about the outcome – just a few butterflies, which often happens in the build-up to a big fight. Eddie calmed me down, as did Rob. I read a piece by an American sports writer called Dan Rafael – a huge man-mountain of a bloke – and it basically just slagged me off. I'm human and of course I did ask myself a few questions, but it also helped, because there was a bit of nervous energy about me this time and I was very switched on and ready for action. I trained as hard as I had ever done and I was determined to shock the world, which is what would happen when I beat Bute.

One thing was very different about the build-up to the Bute fight and that was the small matter of the Olympics looming large. Rob's job as head coach of the Great Britain side meant he was in the gym in Sheffield every day, training the Olympic lads and girls.

My sparring went well with the tall and rangy light heavyweight Bob Ajisafe and Ryan Aston. Funnily enough I also sparred quite a bit with the Welsh Olympian Fred Evans, a brilliant young boxer who went on to get a silver medal, and Anthony Ogogo, who won a bronze. Training with Team GB was great as it gets really competitive on the running track, and being in the gym with all the youth and enthusiasm kept me switched on and constantly pushing the physical boundaries. I trained mostly on my own with Rob when it got down to the nitty gritty, but having all these youngsters around was a real boost.

I got on well with them all. They were all very different characters. Tom Stalker was the skipper of the side and was always ready for a chat, as were the two Anthonys, Joshua and Ogogo. Evans is a quieter lad, but we did work out quite a bit and I rate him as a fighter. Luke Campbell and I became good friends, and still are to this day. Brothers Kal and Gamal Yafai were both really impressive young fighters, and Kal is now a promising professional under my promoter Eddie Hearn.

Scotsman Josh Taylor and Wales's Andrew Selby made up the men's team of seven. There were no idiots down in the gym because Rob just won't have it. Rob spots idiots a mile away – those who aren't prepared to put in the hard work required – and he just gets rid of them. He won't have that type of character anywhere near the gym.

Rachael even did a bit of sparring with fellow Liverpudlian Natasha Jonas, who came so close to beating Katie Taylor in the Olympics, and should be very proud of how well she did. Savannah Marshall and Nicola Adams made the women's team and Nicola put the cherry on the cake by winning the gold medal – a brilliant, superb performance.

I'm not just saying this because the team did exceptionally well at the Olympics, but everyone got on really well. I don't want to sound soppy but it was like one big happy family.

Every day at the English Institute for Sport was brilliant. As well as all the Olympians, there were Rob's other coaches, strength conditioners, nutritionists, sports scientists – everybody. I made the weight four weeks before the fight, thanks to good training and good advice on what to eat and when by the nutritionist. On the night I left my house for the fight I was two pounds over the 12-stone limit. I'm usually about seven pounds over. It just underlines the fact that putting weight on very quickly after the weigh-in is no advantage at all. On this occasion I was much happier with the small amount of weight I put on after the weigh-in.

I later found out that on the morning of the fight Bute only just passed the IBF's 10 lbs rule, whereby a fighter has to be no more than 10 lbs over the 12-stone limit on the morning of a bout. He jumped on the scales in his pants and was about nine and a half pounds over. It was that close to being called off.

The build-up to Bute was perfect for me. I couldn't really go shopping around Nottingham or even step out of the house as I got mobbed, but I loved the fact that it was a big fight coming up and in my hometown. You could feel it in the air, the sense on anticipation, so much better than my last two fights in Atlantic City. It was a great feeling to be back home.

I'd met Bute at a couple of press conferences in Montreal and Nottingham. He was a good bloke, quite reserved and unassuming. We couldn't really chat too much as he speaks French-Canadian and of course he originally comes from Romania. You could tell he was a big name in Canada as I was on Canadian national TV when I went over there. We both gave each other a lot of respect, which is how boxing should be really. He was a gentleman and I regard myself as a gentleman, so we gave each other the regard that was due.

Although Bute was unbeaten in thirty fights leading up to our clash, he had taken a real battering when facing Librado Andrade in 2008 and was only saved by the final bell and a very generous referee, as he was out for the count. Maybe that was a wake-up call for him as he responded very well by beating Andrade easily in a re-match, then stopping the likes of Brian Magee, Edison Miranda and earning a wide points win over Glen Johnson.

I was super-charged, really confident and feeling very similar to the way I felt before I boxed Jean Pascal for the world title. I was up for it and felt nothing would stop me. That mentality stayed with me all the way to the changing rooms before the fight. Apart from a few pre-fight nerves as I mentioned earlier, I felt relaxed and chilled, just knowing I was going to win. I couldn't wait to get out there.

The ring walk was amazing. Sometimes it is like walking 'The Green Mile' – as in the movie with Tom Hanks, where he leads death-row prisoners to the electric chair. You know what is coming when you get in the ring and it's not going to be pretty. This time I felt fantastically sharp and focused.

I stepped into the packed arena and stood on a raised platform with the crowd all looking at me, ready for it to kick off. All I could see was a sea of faces, all cheering for me, so I soaked up the energy from them and felt electric.

The national anthems boomed out, then it was fight time. Rob pressed home the fact I had to box with educated aggression. I started off perfectly from the first bell and kept the pressure on throughout the opening round, looking to land whenever there was a chance. I remember he hit me flush on the end of my nose with a right upper cut and I felt it. It went down to my boots, so I knew he had some power. I wasn't deterred. He could punch but I already knew that, and it didn't bother me. I certainly showed my own intentions because I bounced back at him and fired some shots of my own which maybe made the round a draw. He knew he couldn't push me around and I was hoping he was sitting in his corner after the first round thinking, 'I wish I hadn't come here and agreed to this.'

He was stepping up to a higher level in fighting me, but in the second round I rammed home my advantage when I caught him with a couple of rights before a peach of a short left hook landed. It caught him on his chin and I felt him go. I jumped on him. I'd hurt him and I could tell. He tried to hold on to me. I wasn't thinking about anything else, other than getting Bute out of the ring sharpish. From that point in round two, I knew with absolute certainty I would win as I had hurt him with a short hook, not even one of my biggest shots.

In the third, I wasn't going to get big-headed. I threw more punches, but with less power. I wasn't going to let him get off the hook, but I was going to show him at my own pace that I was in there to spark him out. I threw punches in bunches, attacking him with controlled, raiding assaults. Then I would come off again and have a look. I think the referee must have been close to stopping it towards the end of the third as Bute couldn't take much more and was clearly in a load of bother.

As the third round finished Bute looked completely beaten. His confused face said 'Is the fight still on?' Fair play to him, he had balls as he came out for round four. I thought I'd take a bit of a breather, then as soon as he got in range I'd let him have it. You could argue that his corner shouldn't have sent him out for the fifth round because you could see he was done and dusted. However, I think Bute's corner said to him he didn't have to go out for the fifth and he answered that he wanted to face the music. The corner was going to throw in the towel, but Bute is a proud warrior and he was determined to get back in there.

The finish was clinical. Round five was one-way traffic. In the fourth round he got saved by the bell as I left it too late to finish him. It wasn't going to happen this time as I went to work straight from the off. I had to get him out of there.

As soon as the fifth started I let my shots go. In my opinion the referee should have stopped it earlier. I think the official tried to give the champion every chance to keep his title, which is fair enough, but when I had him on the ropes towards the end the ref should have jumped in. In the final attack I hit him with some clean, sickening shots and his head bounced around. I felt it was getting a bit dangerous, so when the ref jumped in to separate us I thought 'Great, that's it.' Little did I know he was giving Bute a count. It was confusing because before the bout the ref said there was no standing eight-count rule under the IBF.

I pulled away and celebrated, running towards Bute's corner. Next thing I know, someone is giving me a bear hug around the waist. I assumed it was Rob and the fight was over. By the time I turned round to see who it was, he was gone. I found out later it was Eddie! He assumed, like I did, the fight was off, so he jumped into the ring, charged full of excitement and adrenalin to start the celebrations. You could tell by the look on Eddie's face as he bear-hugged me how much it meant to him – pure passion was etched on his face. Then he turned around to see the referee standing above Bute and counting! Bute was clearly out on his feet and only upright because the ropes were holding him up. As far as I could see Bute was a beaten man and, in fairness, his corner had thrown in the towel. I just knew it would happen and it did.

There are no short-cuts in boxing, or any sport for that matter. The hours and hours in the gym had been worth it. I was the IBF world super-middleweight champion and another chapter of my career was about to begin.

I celebrated afterwards by heading to a Nottingham night-club, where I had a couple of vodkas, then a few days later I touched up the bathroom floor lino in one of my properties!

A few weeks later we went to Disneyland in Paris with Rocco, to celebrate Rachael's birthday on 24 June. My mum Carol then looked after Rocco for us and Rachael and I went to Marbella on our own. It was a fantastic little break, just the two of us.

After we got back I watched the Olympics like everyone else in the country, did a bit of commentating for Sky TV and loved every minute of it. I'd missed out on the Olympics by one point when I fought a final qualifier for Sydney 2000, but that didn't matter now, although at the time I was pretty upset about it. I was just delighted with how well the team did.

The Olympics certainly gave Audley Harrison and Amir Khan a big leg up in the popularity stakes, but everything happens for a reason and perhaps if I had fought at the Olympics I wouldn't have become the fighter I am now. You get fame and fortune very quickly with an Olympic medal around your neck and that doesn't work out for the best for all boxers. I came through the hard way and maybe that's why I am a three-time world champion now. If I had got a £1 million professional signing-on fee, having won an Olympic gold, I may not have achieved anything near to what I have done. I don't begrudge missing out and wouldn't have it any other way.

I was over the moon with the success of Team GB. Anthony Joshua – what a lovely, big lad. He is still a novice in boxing terms as he has only been doing it a couple of years, but he so deserved that final victory.

A couple were close, especially when he fought the Cuban Erislandy Savon earlier on, but why shouldn't the decision have gone our way? Hairline decisions have gone against us often enough in the past. He earned his gold medal by fighting the best and he definitely won the final as he finished very strongly. Josh has got a lot of guts, as he showed in the final when he believed in himself. He could have walked away behind his jab and picked up a silver medal, but he went for the Italian Roberto Cammarelle in the closing stages and deserved the gold. It just shows what a bit of self-belief can do for you and yet Anthony, by his own admission, is not the finished article by any stretch.

I'm close friends with Luke Campbell and he did a fantastic job. My prediction on Sky TV before the Olympics was that if we only got one gold medal it would be Luke. He just does what he needs to do to win. He is a lovely counter-puncher and is just a very, very accomplished fighter.

Nicola Adams was a packet of fireworks throughout the Olympics and it was an amazing day when she won our first ever women's gold. Again, all the hard work paid off for Nicola. A great girl and someone who deserved everything she got.

CHAPTER 16

My career had endured a torrid time in recent years, what with the Super Six World Boxing Classic and then going straight into a big world title clash with an unbeaten star of the ring.

Since Jean Pascal I had been fighting back-to-back monsters, so after the Bute fight Eddie ventured the opinion that maybe it was time to move down a gear, with a steady opponent. Not one I could relax about, but someone who wasn't going to give me too much trouble. We both agreed that we didn't want anybody useless next up as that wouldn't do me any favours and would be an insult to fans paying good money to come and watch. We wanted a world-rated, decent fighter.

Yusaf Mack's name cropped up very early on in the conversation as a possible opponent. He had a good, though not outstanding, record.

'Mack Attack' was from the proud fighting city of Philadelphia and had been around the block, having already turned the corner into his thirties. He had gone eight rounds before losing to Tavoris Cloud, who he had out-boxed for much of their fight before getting stopped. In my opinion he was ranked somewhere around the world's top ten at super middleweight, so he was certainly no pushover. He looked the part as well as Yusaf was seriously muscled, a big lad who had also fought at light heavyweight as well as super middle, and had fast hands. Altogether he was exactly what Eddie and I wanted.

Eddie suggested we should stay in Nottingham and to continue to build up my fan base in my hometown following the blistering win over Bute. I had received a great reception from the Nottingham fans and I was keen to give them another memorable night against a big, strong opponent. All fights are potentially dangerous and I was well aware of that when I saw footage of Mack boxing, but I was adamant that so long as I prepared well, like I did for Bute, Mack wouldn't be able to cope with me and I would be able to show off some of my skills.

At the press conferences before the fight Yusaf certainly looked tough and dangerous and, while remaining respectful throughout, promised to give me a whole load of trouble on the night.

Mack didn't represent the level I was used to, and wasn't about to let my title go against him. I didn't feel under too much pressure in the build-up and I was loving the fact I could train in Sheffield and get back to Nottingham on a regular basis to be with my family.

The fight at the Nottingham Arena could not have gone any better and I like to think the fans got value for money.

Basically I finished Mack off good and proper. A body shot had him in all sorts of trouble in the first round and I don't think Mack laid a glove on me. I ended the contest in the third round, underlining my belief that I belonged in the elite level.

I suppose the Mack fight emphasised perfectly the difference between the very best in the world and boxers who are very good and are just that one level below. I'm absolutely certain Mack would give a lot of domestic level fighters a really tough examination. He is probably British-title class. He is a capable fighter, but there are levels in boxing, just as there are in other sports.

I had got used to fighting the really top boxers, so it was a bit of a move sideways for me but it served its purpose, to build up my profile having only just moved to Sky television, as the ultimate aim was to be on pay-per-view.

I had faced Mack because of the gruelling match-ups I had been used to, one after the other. It all went according to plan and now I was ready for the next stage in my career: the unfinished business with a certain Mikkel Kessler.

In the meantime, though, life at home was changing. Rachael played a joke on me when she revealed she was expecting again, coming into our bedroom looking all disappointed with her bottom lip sticking out. She gave me the pregnancy testing stick, which had a cross on it – positive – and I said, 'Whoa, hang on a minute, does that mean you are then?' Her face transformed into a great big smile and we gave each other a massive hug.

Rachael's pregnancy was fantastic news as we were both excited about extending our little family. Although Rocco was unplanned, our latest addition wasn't entirely. We just decided to let nature take its course with the newest recruit to the Froch fold. We both attended the twenty-week scan and the nurse said she knew the sex of the baby. Did we want to know? I think Rachael was keen to find out, but we agreed to wait until Christmas Day. What we got the nurse to do was to write the sex down on a piece of paper and place it in a card. We put the card on the top of the Christmas tree, to the side where the angel sits.

We were looking at it for about four weeks with both of us saying every day, should we open it, should we open it? We managed not to take a peek and opened it on Christmas Day morning. The nurse had written in the card 'Congratulations – it's a girl!' How amazing is that? Rachael wanted a little brother for Rocco, while I was hoping for a girl, but we were both absolutely delighted.

After Christmas I painted the nursery pink. I papered one of the walls and got my 'Handy Manny' cap on! He's a cartoon character for kids for those of you who don't realise who he is. I did a lovely job of it as well, even if I do say so myself.

After the festivities were over the three of us, me, Rachael and Rocco – well, three and a half if you include our new baby – went away on holiday in January to get a bit of winter sun in Dubai. It was great to have a rest but I was ready to get back into action stations again. I was really eager to get back into the ring.

After Yusaf Mack I was determined to make a statement, so that meant a big challenge was needed. The two boxers who really came into that category were the two I had previously lost to: Mikkel Kessler and Andre Ward.

I had only recently boxed Ward and it was a fight that had not exactly set the world alight. He is a very skilful boxer, but not someone I was massively keen on stepping back into the ring with because of the way he fights. His cautious, safety-first style is just not me.

I spoke to Rob and Eddie and we agreed Ward had never been a big draw, not even in America. So it made sense to fight Kessler in a re-match. Mikkel was at ringside in Nottingham when I destroyed Bute, so I told Eddie to speak to Mikkel's promoter Kalle Sauerland and see if we could get it on.

Strangely, Kessler then did a bit of a disappearing act and nobody could get hold of him for a few weeks. The prospect of a fight with Mikkel seemed to be receding as no one could get an answer from him. For a while I thought the fight was not going to happen and so Eddie suggested I get in touch with Mikkel personally.

I had Mikkel's number in my phone and we had stayed in touch since I fought him in Denmark with text messages here and there. I texted him again and said I hoped he was fit and healthy and came out straight with it saying, 'Look, why don't we get this fight on?' I told him it was the only fight that really made sense for either of us. It didn't hurt that we've always have a very friendly relationship, with respect on both sides. Mikkel is money-orientated, no harm in that, so I mentioned that it would make a few quid for both of us and we would give boxing fans what they wanted: a clash not just between two fighters at the top of the game, but a re-match between him and me.

Mikkel texted me back immediately saying he was in great nick and Kalle would be in touch. That's when the negotiations between Kalle and Eddie started in earnest. I suppose the crucial thing – as it often is – was the money and that got sorted very quickly. Eddie mentioned to me that as champion, having just beaten Bute and Mack and with Sky TV on board, I could go for a 60–40 split. That made some sense but Mikkel was a warrior, like me and I felt it was important just to say to him, let's start by going straight down the middle – 50–50 on everything. I felt anything less than that wouldn't be right. Kessler would appreciate the offer and the fight could be made quickly and without any mucking around. Without Mikkel on board the fight that I wanted – a challenge between two evenly matched boxers – wouldn't happen. I didn't mind one bit giving him half the pot because he is a friend, a true fighter and someone I will always look up to and admire for the way he conducts himself in and out of the ring.

Eddie agreed that was the way forward, then told me Sky Sports television, through their boss Barney Francis, was definitely very interested in putting this re-match on pay-per-view. The last PPV fight had been my old mate David Haye versus Wladimir Klitschko and Sky were talking about this one being the next.

PPV was the only way the Kessler re-match was going to happen, as a lucrative deal was the crucial factor in enticing Mikkel back to the ring. I got paid relatively poorly for the Bute fight because it was not on PPV. It was a big step backwards in terms of my earnings from the Super Six World Boxing Classic, but I knew it was for a reason: to get me back in the big time. For Kessler II, it was clear PPV was going to give us all a very good payday.

As it happened the PPV sales for Froch–Kessler II were good, not as big as my two subsequent clashes with George Groves, but certainly enough to make it a very healthy show-down for both of us. I'm not fighting for money any more, because I've got enough of it to be comfortable for life but, of course, it helps.

The fight got made between Eddie and Kalle pretty quickly and I think one of the reasons was because both sides had a lot of respect for each other. Mikkel and I will always be friends, twenty, thirty years after we have finished in this game. Obviously, Mikkel was taking a risk coming to England but he is an intelligent bloke and, since I had trav-elled to Denmark to face him, it was only fair if he came over to my part of the world for a re-match. After beating me in Herning all those years ago he did say he would give me a re-match in England and he stayed true to his word. That's the kind of fair-minded person he is.

Nottingham was never really an option. To ask him to come to my hometown wouldn't have been right and I don't think Mikkel would have fancied coming to Notting-ham, especially after seeing what I had done to Bute, so London was the natural choice. After all, I hadn't fought him in Copenhagen, which Mikkel calls home, and in any case, the biggest indoor arena in Nottingham only holds 9,000. It's a fantastic venue but the O2 Arena in London can accommodate 20,000 fans. We knew the clamour for tickets would be such that we needed as big a venue as we could get.

The negotiations were done, I was fighting Mikkel at the end of May in the capital. I had been all around the world as a pro – Helsinki, Denmark, Atlantic City, California – but hadn't boxed in London since beating Brian Magee in 2006 for the British and Commonwealth super-middleweight title at Bethnal Green's York Hall, the small hall 'home' of the fight game. Mind you, 20,000 fans rammed into the O2 Arena would be a world away from York Hall, or, for that matter, the Goresbrook Leisure Centre in Dagenham, where I also fought earlier in my career!

When Mikkel found out Rachael was pregnant he sent me his best wishes. I think he must have thought there was something very strange going on as every time I boxed him Rachael was expecting! All joking aside, it was also a concern to me because we were given a due date of the first week of May and I was fighting Mikkel at the end of May.

The timing wasn't ideal, but in the build-up to any big fight there is always going to be something going on. The good thing was Rachael had done an amazing job with Rocco, with my mum Carol there whenever she needed help, and so that made me much more comfortable with taking a fight of that magnitude with another little one coming along.

It's fair to say I was very nervous about the Kessler re-match as it was a dangerous fight. This was someone who had previously beaten me and I had experienced enough of Mikkel in twelve rounds in Herning to know that our sequel was going to be one hell of a battle. Kessler can really fight and my other concern was that he might have been looking at it as his last bout before retirement. That would make him even more of a risk because fighters who are looking at retiring can go one of two ways – they can either go in there for a last decent payday without really giving it full throttle, or they can opt for the final hurrah, leaving every last drop of effort in the ring. Knowing Mikkel, I suspected it was going to be the latter.

I was convinced Kessler was going to have a real ding-dong with me to prove that the first fight wasn't a mistake, that he was the superior boxer. He was going to bring his best, so I made sure in training I went at it with all guns blazing.

A couple of weeks before the start of proper twelve-week intensive training I was already ticking over with two or three runs a week and ten rounds on the punch bags in my garage gym and at the Phoenix gym. I also cycled a few times with a pal of mine, Andy, and did some sprinting work as well. I was taking it ultra-seriously.

Monday, 4 March 2013, was the official start of my training camp and I was already in decent shape when I turned up to meet Rob in Sheffield. I did twelve rounds of pad work with Rob in that first week, which just shows I was pretty fit already. I did some 'technical' sparring, which is proper sparring, but you just don't let your shots go full throttle. It is more about working on specific punches and getting the timing absolutely right.

I stayed in Sheffield a lot during the build-up for Kessler and I was fully aware how vital this fight was for the rest of my career. I regularly sparred with a few of the amateurs up at the English Institute for Sport as well as the professionals, the likes of Anthony Ogogo, Tony Bellew and Callum Smith.

It was a tremendous camp and it shows how totally committed I was that the sparring was so intense and physical against some terrific fighters. Against the amateur lads, without being disrespectful, I can get my own way, but against top boxers like Bellew and Smith, I did get a bit nervous when going in with them as they can really bang and have technical skills as well. David Haye and I have talked about sparring many times and we agree that you have to have really high-level sparring when you go in there for the big fights and that's what I did. I may not have been massively enjoying it, but it needed to be done if I was going to have any chance of avenging my defeat to Kessler.

Callum is only young but he has got bags of ability and Tony Bellew is a seasoned pro who knows his way around a ring. Callum is part of the famous boxing Smith family, who are all absolutely top professionals and I'm convinced, like a lot of knowledgeable fight people, that he has a great future ahead of him. The Smiths are a lovely family, all very close, which is great to see. I know Paul the best and he is a true gentleman. They can all really fight, but I think Callum is a bit special. I don't think he'll be a super middleweight for all of his career as he has the body of a light heavy, but he is one hell of a prospect and I know having sparred with him many times.

I had the real 'Eye of the Tiger' for Kessler. My camp was as intensive as any I had ever done in my career because I knew what was coming. I knew you don't get anything for free against Kessler. I certainly didn't think I was going to win by stoppage against Kessler so I constantly pushed myself to my limits. Knowing that Kessler had beaten me before made me a lot more focused and driven. I also knew Mikkel could take my best punch as he had done it in Herning when he shipped a big shot in the fifth round, chewed down on his gum shield and won the fight.

I never thought about the prospect of losing and retiring, which I had for the Bute fight. Had I lost against Bute I would have called it quits because two defeats in a row is too much of a kick in the balls. I didn't go into the rematch thinking, if I lose, that's it, all over. Retirement wasn't remotely in my thinking; I was 100 per cent focused on winning ...

Only a few weeks before the fight there was a bit of a diversion, otherwise known as Natalia!

Before I travelled up to Sheffield for training just three weeks before the fight, Rachael was pretty convinced the contractions had already begun. I spoke to Rob and he said this close to a fight, it was vitally important I didn't miss a session of sparring and circuit work so I said I would shoot up to the English Institute of Sport in Sheffield, do my sparring, then gun it back down to Nottingham. I was pretty cool with this as Rocco took ages to pop out, twenty-eight hours to be precise.

Unknown to me, as I always have my phone switched on to silent when I spar, Rachael had been trying to get in contact. Rachael even rang Laura, PA in the office at the EIS, saying she was about to give birth. She told Laura the contractions were really close and painful and had gone to the City Hospital in Nottingham, but I was oblivious to it all. Rob waited until after I had done all my sparring and circuits, then said 'Rachael has been calling and is in the labour suite so you had better go.' I asked him when she rang and Rob replied, 'Oh, about an hour and a half ago. She's been going mental down the phone, but you had your sparring work to do so there it is.'

I bolted down to the hospital and got there about ninety minutes before Rachael gave birth to Natalia. Actually, I arrived at just the right time because Rachael had taken all her birthing drugs so she was in cloud cuckoo land, happy and smiley. I was at the business end of the birth, while my mum was busy stroking Rachael's head and trying to comfort her. I cut the umbilical cord, which was a great feeling. Just like with Rocco, seeing what a woman goes through in labour is very primitive and barbaric, but at the same time the most wonderful, amazing occasion anyone can ever experience, to see the birth of your own flesh and blood.

Natalia was born on Friday 3 May, which was perfect timing as it meant that I could spend a couple of days with Rachael and our new baby and then get back to my day job. In a sense it spurred me on even more to beat Kessler as I now had another mouth to feed. My emotions were a bit jumbled up as meeting your daughter for the first time was heavy-duty stuff and an emotional rollercoaster, especially as I was in selfish fight mode, as Rachael calls it, where the only thing I was trying to concentrate on was Mikkel Kessler and finding a way to beat him.

I had my last spar, six rounds, with Callum Smith on Monday, 20 May, and went down to London the following day. My final spar was a bit cagey as I didn't want to do anything silly, like picking up a hand injury or a cut.

Tickets for the Kessler re-match in the O2 Arena in London sold out in a matter of minutes, showing the high level of interest and anticipation from the public. I think it was my victory over Bute, which was my first big fight in England for a number of years, that put me on to another level with sports fans. Fighting in America is all well and good, but only true fight fans in the UK watch it because half the time the fight is broadcast live in the middle of the night. However, after this big fight in the UK I started to notice that even non-fight supporters were beginning to recognise me.

By the time I got down to London, staying at an apartment in Canary Wharf, I was not sleeping very well, underlining how nervous I was. In fact, the days before the re-match got me into the worst sleep pattern I've ever had. I took my stopwatch to bed with me to see how much kip I got and I remember only managing two hours here and two hours there. I just kept waking up, nervous as hell. I didn't want to let myself down, or Rob, or Eddie, or Sky. All these things kept waking me up.

Fight week in London went slowly. I stayed in the apartment just with Mark Seltzer. He kept me company and walked around the shops with me. Mark is funny, a great character. He will do anything to help and in fight week he is there doing whatever he can to assist.

I saw Rob at the various press conferences at the O2 Arena and he kept telling me I should be super confident because all the work had been done. However, I got in a bit of trouble for making a comment about Mikkel in front of the press lads. One of the journalists asked if I would find it hard in the ring to take on someone I had so much respect for as a person and a fighter. I said words to the effect of, 'This is do or die and means everything to me. Regardless of the fact Mikkel is a proper gentleman, I want to "kill" him in the ring.' Obviously, I didn't have any intention of wanting to kill Mikkel, but it was just a crap choice of words. I was talking metaphorically. What I meant to say that was that there would be only me and him in there in the ring and one of us was going to lose.

It was the wrong thing to say at the wrong time. With Kessler, even at my very best, I knew I could still lose the fight, because he is such a tough, strong man. He will keep going to the end. There was a lot at stake for both of us: we're friends but we're also fighters, and we respected each other too much to go soft in the ring. I knew how much of a challenge I was facing, and while I had trained too hard to let him get the upper hand, during that press conference I had never suffered from nerves before a match as much as I did on this occasion, and I think the combination of this and lack of sleep made me say something I regretted almost instantly. The BBBC rightly pulled me up on the comment after the fight, so I made a donation to their charity as a gesture of goodwill. I also apologised.

On the Friday before the fight I woke up at 167 lbs and had a bowl of porridge. I rested until the weigh-in with my best mate Adam and felt good that at last it was getting close.

As nervous as I was, it was nearly fight time now and the adrenalin had kicked in. I got to the changing rooms two and a half hours before the bout. I watched a bit of the George Groves fight against Noe Gonzalez Alcoba in my dressing room and thought, you never know, I might be fighting Groves one day. Little did I know ...

There was a toss of a coin for who would go into the arena first as I was the IBF champion and Kessler held the WBA crown. I didn't mind one bit heading in there before him. The place was packed, absolutely rammed. I entered the arena by being raised on a platform. The crowd was within touching distance, and they were all shouting positive things for me so I did a bit of shadow boxing, only to feel the platform wobble, so I stopped that straight away! I thought, this wouldn't look good if the platform collapsed with me on it.

The O2 Arena is twice the size of the stadium in Nottingham and it felt like it that night. All I could see was a sea of people looking at me. I was amazed at how big it was, not knowing then that I was going to fight at Wembley stadium one day soon. The noise was intense and I could feel my body really fired up. I was shaking a bit and my legs were full of nervous tension, but not in a scared way, more from sheer electricity. All the energy I had was honed into the fight. In my head I was thinking, this is unbelievable, this place is packed and going nuts, all for me and Mikkel Kessler. This is why I am in boxing, to soak up that feeling and enjoy it This was big-time boxing and I was the main attraction so I wasn't going to shy away from it, I was going to revel in it and prove I was the better fighter.

At its best, nothing beats boxing. You don't get that kind of crackling tension with anything other than two warring boxers going head to head. Even now it makes the hairs on my arms stand up on end because I love it so much.

When you do the training hard and you know you haven't cut any corners it makes you more confident and that's how I felt standing on that platform in front of 20,000 baying fans. I had a feeling it would pan out well when I was standing there as Michael Buffer announced for the first time in my career ... *'Let's get ready to rummmmmmmble!'*

It was important to concentrate and focus and from the first minute to the last. I knew I had to use my jab to its full effect. I had to keep the jab on his chest, on his shoulders, on his arms or in his face. I had to aim anywhere on his body where it was going to land and not miss him, otherwise I would be open to a big counter. If the ramrod jab I possess was working well I knew I would be in business. Before the fight Mikkel said my jab was a potent weapon and that it was deceptive in its reach. He is dead right. I was born with long arms. I'm like an albatross. I've got a 75-inch wingspan, from fingertip to fingertip, which is huge for my size. It's a real advantage. Where I get that from I don't know, but it comes in very handy as a boxer.

Everything had to be behind the jab. The jab would win or lose the fight for me. It had worked beautifully against Arthur Abraham, mainly because he is shorter than me, and it would be the key to winning against Mikkel.

I had worked on jabbing in sparring for hours and hours and early in the fight I knew it was working as I planned. It was important not to just paw out the jab, but to actually punch with it as it would keep Kessler off me.

The fight was going my way and I genuinely thought to myself after three or four rounds that this is too easy, Mikkel is going to do something drastic about this. Rob told me to carry on doing exactly what I had been as it was clearly working and I was winning round after round, but after round three I said to Rob, 'Does this look all right?' meaning, are the crowd enjoying this? I knew that Sky customers paid out lots of money on pay-per-view to watch me against Kessler and that there had been some poor fights lately on it, so for some reason I decided it was too easy and I had to give more value for money. That was stupid and daft as it put my whole game plan at risk. I started staying in Kessler's range a little bit longer so we could have a proper scrap. But I can't take all the credit for turning the fight into a memorable dust-up because Kessler clearly realised he was getting beaten behind my jab, so he understood he had to open up more and do something different.

When he saw what was happening Rob went mad at me and said, 'What are you doing Carl? What are you doing?' Instead of out-jabbing Kessler I was getting involved in a tear-up, which was crazy. Rob was right. If you can win a fight by using your jab and clocking up the rounds that's exactly what you should do. Remember, this is boxing, it's not a pub brawl. It's what Roy Jones Jr did for years and what Floyd Mayweather Jr does now. In fact, a lot of top fighters do it because they know that is how you keep winning.

But being me, a bit of an animal in the ring, I decided I wanted to get a couple of right hands off and give the crowd something to cheer about. You can land one-two-three decent jabs and that doesn't get the audience going, but as soon as you start mixing it up and throwing jab, right hook, jab, left hook, jab, upper cut, you can hear the crowd getting into it. That's what I did. Kessler got in a couple of shots and I could tell the crowd was really beginning to enjoy it.

I didn't do myself any favours by changing my tactics as I was starting to get hit. Rob was doing his nut, but there you go. Rob is right when he says if you land two jabs and he lands none, you win the round. If you land ten power punches and he lands nine, you win the round, but you also take a risk of getting knocked out. It is then pretty much a fiftyt-fifty fight, so why risk it? I don't know. All I know is that's the way I fight. Rob tells me until he is blue in the face: this is boxing, not brawling. The job is to hit and not get hit, use your attributes and maximise your chances of winning every time. He is dead right, only I often get caught up in the moment and just let go. I can't help myself. It's not so much a case of not listening to Rob, it is just my natural instincts taking over in the heat of the battle. If I get hit with something, you're getting it back.

Human beings are made this way – they either get hit and they want to run, or they get hit and they fight back. I'm most definitely the latter.

Kessler is born the same as me and whenever I hit him I got a wry smile from Mikkel as if to say 'You're getting that back.' Kessler's defensive skills that night were also very impressive, because whenever I caught him he always knew what to do to survive and hang in there. He would turn a little to one side to make himself harder to hit. It worked, as I couldn't stop him.

To force a stoppage against Kessler would have been so much harder than, say, Bute, because Bute just sat there waiting to get hit again, convinced he could take my power punches. He couldn't. Mikkel ships a couple, then turns you and before you know it he is out of trouble and taking a breather, ready to come back at you. He is a very clever boxer.

The energy from the terraces was electrifying. I could hear them going bonkers as Mikkel and I traded blow after blow. We banged away at each other and I kept telling myself, somebody is going to go down here and it isn't going to be me.

It was the heat of the battle, which I love and is the reason I carry on in the fight game because that sort of showdown is what you live for. They are the moments you enjoy more than anything and I remember thinking, this is amazing, this is what I do this for.

In the eleventh round I shipped a right pisser of a shot as I did what I had told myself a thousand times not to do. I pawed out a lazy jab and, wham, Kessler spotted it straight away because he is such a class fighter. He jumped on me with a big right-hand counter that landed flush on my chin and shook me down to my boots. One of the biggest shots I've ever taken. My left leg wobbled a bit, then I showed what an amazing chin I have because I sucked it up. Kessler could see I was hurt, he is that good, and tried to finish me off with a decent combination, but my powers of recovery are strong and by the end of the round I was giving as good as I got. We both stood in the middle of the ring banging back at each other, then the bell went.

The twelfth was more of the same as we both took turns in landing power punches. I was aggressive without taking too many risks and yet I think I got pretty close to halting him as a few times I could see Mikkel was in trouble. The bell finally went. What a fighter Kessler is. I've got massive respect for him for our two supreme battles and always will.

I was in control all through the fight and although I lost a couple of rounds and maybe split a few others I could hear the crowd throughout the contest and I really enjoyed it as much as they did. It was close-ish fight but it was also a contest that I knew I had won. I had a great start and a good finish and so I was never in any doubts.

I was convinced I had the fight in the bag and so it proved as the judges made me a unanimous winner. One judge had me winning 118–110, which was very wide, while the other two made it 116–112 and a too-close 115–113.

The Kessler fight showed more than any other in my career what I am like as a boxer. Let me make an assessment. Before going in the ring with me, fighters will say things like: 'Froch is slow, he's easy to hit.' Then they realise my jab is landing flush in their face without them even knowing it. After boxing against me I've heard opponents say, 'I didn't think Froch was that quick and, by the way, he punches very hard.' Kessler said something like that to me after the fight, giving me a lot of respect for being much more skilled than he initially gave me credit for. I've heard similar things from fighters and sparring partners over the years.

I'm one of those fighters who a lot of my rivals think they can beat, but when they get in with me they realise they are in big trouble. I am one of those boxers who is better than I look. I get plenty of credit now, especially after Kessler, but that wasn't always the case earlier in my career. You land your best shot on me and I'm still coming at you. I proved that for the umpteenth time in my boxing career against Kessler and I would prove it again in my next fight.

I've only just started dissecting my attributes and ticking boxes for what I am good at and not so good at. A lot of my strengths are centred around my sheer toughness. It's not as if I haven't got some ability, after all, I was a very decent amateur so that proves I have technical skills, but I'm not Sugar Ray Leonard. I'm not the fastest, I'm not the most skilful, I am a bit awkward and unorthodox, but I'm also a four-time world champion so I know what I'm doing. My engine is phenomenal and I think my main strength over the years has been my chin, because I can walk through someone hitting me with a lump hammer.

Not having a decent chin can be the difference in class. It's not all you need, but if you have got everything else in your locker but no chin, then fight over. You're going to lose, eventually. Also, if you've got a great chin and no ability you are going to get damaged.

The best boxers are the all-rounders, the ones who have a bit of everything and can take a shot as well as give it, like Kessler and like me. I hit Kessler with a hell of a shot in Herning and he felt it but he came straight back. I hit him with some crunching shots in our second fight and I know they hurt, but again, he swallowed them up and came back at me.

At world level, as I've found out when facing Ward, Kessler, Pascal, Abraham, Taylor and Johnson, they stand up to heavy shots and take them. Glen Johnson especially walks through howitzers. In his prime, you could hit him all day long and he would still be standing there.

After the fight I did a urine test and by that time it was stupid o'clock in the early hours. You're not going to believe what I did that night after beating Kessler. I went back to the apartment I had been staying in. Rachael wasn't there to comfort me as she had stayed behind at home to look after Natalia. It was about 4 a.m. and although I was tempted to go to the post-fight party in a Canary Wharf hotel I realised that anyone still awake at that hour would be pissed out of their brains, or knackered and stumbling around.

It was getting light as the sun was coming up, so I decided to start tidying up my apartment, forgetting that a cleaning service came as part of the price. I was still wide awake, so I killed a couple of hours cleaning, hoovering and doing the pots and pans. I even cleaned the cooker and took my stuff out of the fridge. The flat was absolutely spotless.

I took a few photos with my phone with my new WBA belt and the IBF one as well and I rang my driver to take me back to Nottingham at about 7.30 a.m. He said he had not slept, so I told him neither had I, just take me home!

We went up the M1 back to Nottingham to Rachael, my son and my new daughter and I was the happiest man in the world. That defeat in Herning all those years ago, which had ended my unbeaten record as a pro, had been avenged.

CHAPTER 17

After the Kessler fight I spent some precious time with Rachael, Rocco and his new little baby sister. It was fantastic, absolutely brilliant, to be back home with the belts and having avenged my loss to one of the modern-day greats in the super-middleweight division. I left Mikkel that night on good terms, as we always do when we meet, and who knows? At one to one, maybe somewhere down the line there is one more left in us.

However, it was the next chapter of my boxing career that was to have huge implications ...

It was about three weeks after Kessler and I was sitting in my car outside Paul Smith's clothing store in Nottingham, about to pick up a nice new suit for an appearance on Sky. I was on the phone to Eddie, talking about where to go next.

Eddie Hearn is a terrific bloke and I admire both him and his dad Barry for what they have done and achieved. We talked about where to go next, and he told me straight, this is what we have ahead of us: I could fight George Groves or vacate the title. Or I could fight Andre Ward again, or maybe even Kessler for a third time. This last option was the most unlikely; Kessler didn't fancy it straight away and neither did I. Ward didn't particularly interest me either. That left Groves, who, Eddie informed me, was now my mandatory challenger for the IBF belt. I genuinely thought Groves would not be a big enough fight for me. It would be a case of coming back down to a domestic-level fight as I didn't particularly think he was that good. I had seen him fight a few times and had noticed a lot of flaws and weaknesses in his work, especially his chin.

I had sparred with him at the English Institute for Sport in Sheffield before the first Kessler fight and I just didn't rate him highly. He was a tough-enough kid but there were obvious limitations to his game. Sparring with him wasn't like sparring with Tony Bellew or Callum Smith, it was below that level.

David Haye was watching when I put him down on his arse when we sparred as David and Groves both trained in those days under Adam Booth. Groves has got a bit of heart as he stayed in there and finished the spar, although I slowed down as I didn't want to deck him again. A few weeks later Groves came back to my gym in the Phoenix in Nottingham in what would be my last proper spar before the Kessler fight. I was pretty much in second gear and it was probably a lot closer between us as I was wary about how near it was to the real fight in Herning.

I was in control throughout but it's fair to say I got caught by a couple of his shots because that's what you expect in sparring, as that's what it's there for: to get you ready. Later on, amongst the hundreds of other ridiculous statements and claims Groves subsequently made, he revealed he had 'schooled' me in that sparring session. Nobody schooled anybody. I was taking it relatively easy on him and we had a decent spar, that's it, nothing more, nothing less. It was a good workout. But then, as I found later on, George Groves likes to make up stories to boost his enormously out-of-proportion ego.

Anyway, I said to Eddie in the car park that day, are you sure this is a big enough fight for me? Eddie wasn't sure himself and told me so. He reckoned it would do pretty good numbers as it was a domestic clash, but it's fair to say he had similar reservations to me.

The final option was to vacate the IBF belt and Groves could fight someone else for it. I mulled it over At this stage I didn't really fancy Groves up next as I was absolutely convinced it was an easy fight.

It was quite an amazing set of events that had led to Groves becoming the mandatory challenger for the IBF crown. When I won the title Adonis Stevenson was the number one mandatory but he had decided to move up to light heavyweight to fight Chad Dawson for the WBC crown. The next fighter in the IBF rankings was Lucian Bute, but he was nursing an injured hand. Then it went down to Thomas Oosthuizen, but he was already in training for another bout that had already been made. Next was Edwin Rodriguez, who was also set to fight Denis Grachev and then, the next on the IBF rankings after that, was George Groves, with James DeGale one place behind him. Groves became mandatory by default.

A week later Eddie rang me again and said he had just spoken to Barney Francis, the head of Sky Sports. Eddie told me Barney was convinced it would be another Sky Box Office fight on PPV. However, I still wasn't sure it was worth it, and the conversation ended with me saying to Eddie, OK, I'll vacate the belt rather than fight Groves. The title I had won against Bute would no longer be mine.

Then I began to think about it. Many years ago Joe Calzaghe had vacated the WBC belt rather than fight me, a young gun and his mandatory challenger. Joe had done that rather than face me and to this day I've criticised him for it. Joe has never got anything nice to say about me as I've given him plenty of stick for his decision, so there was no way I was going to risk looking like a hypocrite.

Although the conversation with Eddie ended with me saying I would vacate, I phoned Rob and had a chat with him. Rob didn't particularly fancy the Groves fight as well for the same reasons as me, he just felt he hadn't earned his shot at an elite-level boxer like me. However, Rob said to me, whatever you do, don't vacate a world title. You earned it, you are the champ and a belt is a belt, not to be tossed away after you worked so hard for it.

What clinched the fight was simple: pay-per-view. When I'd had chance to think about it, that call from Barney to Eddie was the difference because it was going to be pretty lucrative for me and I was totally sure that as soon as I cracked Groves on the chin he would go down. I knew he could box a bit and had grown in confidence as he had won every fight as a pro, but I didn't take him seriously from day one of the match-up being made. Two weeks before I started my proper twelve-week training for Kessler I was already on it, already knuckling down, but in comparison it was nothing like that for Groves. I did a bit of cycling and running on the treadmill and other than that I was travelling to and from London for ITV's dancing competition *Stepping Out* hosted by Davina McCall. In other words, I was doing precious little proper fight training.

At the start of week one of training on 2 September I worked out in my gym at home on the treadmill and did fifteen minutes on the bag. The rest of the time I was doing dance workouts with Rachael and at the end of my first week of training I was at the studios in London dancing an Indian bhangra routine. Not something that's ever been part of my twelve-week build-up before!

At the end of week two of training Rachael and I also did a dance routine in London at the weekend and got voted the best of the show, but I had tweaked a muscle in my back so we both had to pull out of the rest of the competition. This was just ten weeks before I was due to face Groves on 23 November. I had focused on the dance competition for the first two weeks of a twelve-week training camp and now I had got a sore back as well.

All this adds up to one obvious conclusion: I was guilty of under-estimating Groves completely because I just did not take his threat seriously. I didn't take him seriously as a person either. Psychologically it was hard to get pumped up for a fight I knew I would easily win.

That's a bad attitude to have, as I subsequently discovered, but I'm only human and every single person I knew – press, family, friends, supporters – were telling me it was going to be a straightforward payday.

Rob's opinion was the same for Groves as it has been for every fight I've gone into: you have to take them all seriously. However, he was also convinced that Groves posed no realistic threat to me. He gave me a few kicks up the arse but he was adamant it would turn out all right for me on the night.

For Kessler, I had spent loads of time up in Sheffield at the EIS, staying over with the other boxers and putting in the hard yards in the gym. For Groves I spent only a single night in Sheffield as I preferred to head back down the motorway to be with my family. Again, another sure sign I wasn't taking it as seriously as I should, and I'll be the first to admit it now: I was under-motivated for what was to come.

At the end of week three and week four I had to go back to London to be there in person for the last two editions of *Stepping Out*, not as an active participant, but just to be on the show. It was good fun and pretty hard work doing all the dance routines, but I don't think John Travolta has got any serious competition from yours truly. Rachael loved it and it's fair to say she's a bit more of a natural mover than me.

In my first four weeks of training camp – the final *Stepping Out* show went out on Saturday, 28 September – I was flitting between Sheffield, Nottingham and London, never really focusing fully on the job in hand. I was trying to get ready to fight Groves by doing a combination of treadmill runs and working out on the bags. Instead of pounding the streets, because the nights were closing in around that time of year, I said to myself, 'I'll jump on the treadmill instead.'

This happened time and time again in my build-up to Groves I.

Groves kept coming out with comments that made him look like the local village idiot. In the various press conferences I said I would use his ridiculous words as a motivational tool, but in truth I didn't really do any such thing. Deep down his constant carping didn't motivate me to take him more seriously because I genuinely believed he was a proper clown.

Worse was to come. In my fight diary where I keep all my training notes, on 11 November I marked down – 'athlete's foot, infection, stuffy nose and flu-ey'. That says it all.

The athlete's foot problem had developed into an infection and because I don't take antibiotics it had got worse. I went to see a doctor about it and he told Rob at the English Institute for Sport, 'How important is this fight?' He was basically saying: if this fight isn't that vital to Carl's career, maybe he should call it off.

So just ten days before the fight I had a really bad cold and my body was fighting off a foot infection. My left arm started giving me problems and I couldn't straighten it. A lot of boxers have problems with their elbows and I'm no different. It's a long-standing injury but one which I live with.

Yes, I did consider postponing the fight because I hadn't done any intensive sparring in the last two weeks before the bout. I thought to myself, I shouldn't really be fighting this time because I know I am not that fit and my foot was killing me. But, unlike Joe Calzaghe, I don't pull out of fights. I decided it had to go ahead.

Despite the setbacks I was still as sure as I could be it would be all right on the night, even though I'd say I was at about 80 per cent. I convinced myself that would be enough against Groves. I've had painkilling injections before fights in the past and I was adamant that even with a half-hearted twelve-week training camp it would suffice. I just thought I would KO him, easily.

As I neared the final week I couldn't get my boot on properly due to my foot infection and Rob could see I was not at my best. On the Monday of fight week I did a brief four-round tippy-tappy spar with Anthony Ogogo as my foot was giving me that much pain I couldn't carry on. That's not a good enough level of preparation for any fight.

One thing I was pleased about was the fact the fight was taking place at the Manchester Phones 4u Arena, formerly the Manchester Evening News Arena, as I remembered Ricky Hatton beating Kostya Tszyu there on what was one of the greatest nights in British boxing history. Hatton was magnificent that evening and, although I didn't go there in person, even on TV you could tell that the atmosphere was electric. It's a massive indoor arena, about the same size as the O2 Arena in London, and it was packed to the rafters that night, with Tszyu failing to come out for the last round and the iconic picture of Hatton falling to his knees on the canvas before being submerged by his training team. It was a Wow! moment in our sport. Ricky Hatton did the business that night in a tough, brutal fight.

In the final build-up Groves did his 'Jack the Lad' routine. On one appearance on Sky's *Ringside* Groves asked me if I was going to cry. I responded by saying I didn't understand him, why would a grown man cry on television? In what circumstances would that happen? I know Oliver McCall famously cried when he was in the ring with Lennox Lewis, but he had just come out of rehab.

Whether Groves genuinely believed I was going to cry or not, or just said it because it was a stupid, obnoxious, little twerp thing to do, I don't know. It didn't wind me up. It just confirmed my opinion that he was a proper grade-A village idiot. I was annoyed by Groves and his ridiculous, childish antics, but not to the point where it would trigger me into delivering a proper performance. I was annoyed with him the way you get annoyed with a fly buzzing around in the car. You want to swot it away.

In the last few press conferences Groves started giving it even more lip, then turned up at one of them in clothes my granddad wouldn't have worn.

I only went up to Manchester on the Tuesday before the fight and although I knew in my heart of hearts I hadn't had a good training camp I was still certain Groves would pose no major problems for me. I was wrong.

When I got to the venue I wanted to get the fight out of the way and be done with it. I was in a big PPV fight on Sky in front of 20,000 fans and I had taken it for granted I was going to win, all I had to do was land a good, clean punch and this kid was going to fall over. If he didn't fall over from one punch I would just break him down and win relatively comfortably.

When you think that way you are not really as switched on as you should be. I fight at my best when there is a little bit of fear involved. I need to respect my opponent, like I did with the likes of Kessler, Taylor and Abraham. It's not a nice feeling, but the nerves and sense of fear do sharpen your senses. Say on a scale of one to ten, when I boxed Kessler I was right up there at about nine and a half. It was uncomfortable, nervous tension, knowing that I was in there with someone who can really fight. With Groves, I was on about two. When I boxed Ward I didn't want to be there. I wanted to be home for Christmas with Rachael and it showed in my performance. Earlier in my career I was ill-prepared in a similar way for Dale Westerman, when I fought him for the Commonwealth title. I had seen Westerman box and without being disrespectful to a fighter, because you have to be a brave lad to get in the ring, I thought he was useless and couldn't lace my boots. Again, I delivered, by my standards, a poor display.

Immediately before the fight in the dressing room I had a chat with David Haye and told him in no uncertain terms that I felt Groves was my Audley Harrison. David had made mincemeat of Harrison a few years earlier in a mis-match with Audley barely throwing a punch.

David phoned me up the day after the fight half laughing at me and half telling me I had been stupid. He told me he knew I wasn't switched on because of that comment. David knows Groves well, and knows he can punch hard and is dangerous as they have sparred hundreds of rounds. He also said the best of me beats the best of Groves every day of the week, but as I wasn't really as switched on as I should have been, David was convinced I was in for a surprise. He was absolutely right.

On fight night I remember briefly thinking, 'What if I get beat? Can you imagine losing to him and having to listen to his moronic patter all over again?' Then I reassured myself I had sparred with him and came back to the same conclusion. He was not in my class.

As I got into the ring I turned to my little brother Wayne and told him, 'Don't worry, I'm going to chin this little prick.' Groves was stood in the middle of the ring gawping at me and I was looking forward to just getting in there and knocking him out.

From round one I wanted to land the big shot that ended the contest. In doing that I neglected my jab and head movement and forgot where my feet should have been. Basically, all my boxing ability went out the window. All the skills and attributes I possess that had got me to the point of being a respected world champion had been left at home.

Towards the end of the first round I semi-connected with an upper cut and was convinced I had hit him nicely enough to have hurt him. That's when I decided now was the time to try and exert myself and chin him. I left my feet behind and leapt in with a right hand that I thought would land. It had no chance of finding the target as it fell well short, but in throwing the punch I had opened myself up and left a great big gap for Groves to walk through.

It was a gimme. You know when playing golf you allow your opponent not to take the putt that is sitting three inches from the hole? That's what I had done. I was there for the taking and he responded with a very solid, well-timed, right hand, straight on my chin and down I went.

It was an unusual circumstance for me, as only Jermain Taylor in my pro career had ever put me on the canvas. I knew I had gone over, knew I had shipped a tasty shot and, yes, there was probably a split second when I had blacked out. It was a flash knock down though, because as soon as my arse hit the canvas I got straight back up. My legs deceived me a little bit, which is there for all to see, but I got up and felt OK. It was probably what I needed to make me realise that Groves was a threat.

It was near the end of the round and I took another couple of big shots from Groves before the bell went. I walked back to my corner and I knew where I was. It may sound strange but I was also convinced he couldn't hurt me again because I had just taken his best shot and got back up.

I think rounds two and three were pretty even and could have gone either way with the judges. They weren't bad rounds for me and I felt I was doing all right, having just been flattened. I could see he was loading up, happy to swing away with big punches, but I largely evaded them. However, in rounds four, five and six I got hit by a fair number of his big shots. Why? I don't really know, but I was trying too hard to knock him over again with a single punch of my own. That's not really my style as I am not renowned as a one-punch concussive fighter. It was a tactic that failed in those three rounds.

The way I was fighting was totally wrong and Rob was telling me at the end of every round to get back to what I knew, fight behind my ramrod jab. Everything Rob was telling me I was doing the opposite. I think I was still slightly concussed and my memory still to this day is not particularly clear until about the middle of round six. I had experienced the same lack of clarity for several rounds when I beat Jean Pascal to win my first world title, so it had happened before.

For me, the end of round six was the turning point in the fight. We had both exchanged a lot of heavy artillery in the round and he had certainly got the upper hand, but I had stood up to it. It was the round that determined the outcome of the fight, because I came through on pure fighting instinct, mental strength and physical toughness, which is something you can't really learn, whereas he wilted.

We had both been hit with hurtful shots and both walked back to our stools knowing it had been a proper ding-dong. I had got frustrated towards the end of it as I had been caught with a couple of really big blows. I knew I had lost the round but I was still in there.

Groves would never admit it, but the round had just about finished him off as I felt from that moment on he was pretty much a spent force. I could feel he was very tired. He had given his all, landed his best shots and it still hadn't been enough to shift me. Now he was starting to feel the pace and unfortunately for him it was only the end of round six.

Groves had won the first half of the fight, but there was a second half still to come. As round seven started I began to feel more confident as I realised more and more of my shots were beginning to land to the body and head. I was starting to concentrate more, get behind my jab and put together telling combinations. I could feel him starting to crumble. Slowly at first, but it was there. He was increasingly weakening and I was getting stronger. It was by no stretch completely one-sided but it was enough for me to know that the tide was turning and I was taking over the fight.

At the end of round seven I saw Eddie looking at me and he clenched his fists. Rob was getting happier with my work and so was I. In round eight I got a small cut but wasn't remotely worried about it as I knew the fight was at last going the way I wanted it to and I really believe it made me box better as I didn't want to get hit on the cut again. As the round wore on I landed a couple of body shots, which made him wince.

In the ninth round I was continuing to take over and the really telling punch finally came with an overhand right. It was a bit of a sneaky punch as I moved to the right to throw it and it kind of crept through his guard to land on the side of his head. It stiffened his legs and he wobbled a bit.

He did the right thing and tried to close the gap and hold me. When he did that I could feel he was hanging on and hurt. I pushed him off me, ran towards him, shoving him with my body weight. The referee Howard Foster intervened a bit between us and I remember landing a straight right, followed by a left hook. He fired back with a left hook and I landed another straight right and another left hook, which wobbled his head. The ref looked at it and could see he had already been hurt by the earlier overhand right and now he was soaking up more shots. Groves's arms slumped and he leaned forward with his head looking down to the ground trying to grab me. It was then that I felt I had free shots. I threw right-left-right and Foster, a very experienced official, saw the follow-up punches and stopped the fight, doing Groves a massive favour as he was going to get totally finished off with the next couple of blows.

Foster called it as he saw it and certainly did not deserve some of the heavy stick he got. He was doing his job as he saw fit, end of story. Howard Foster is one of our best and most respected judges and as referee he is the sole person who can make a decision to stop a fight. He did so because he was convinced Groves was about to get seriously hurt, which he was.

The crowd reacted by booing the decision and me. On the night I initially didn't hear it because I was still in fight mode, but as the booing continued I began to realise some of it was directed at me. In retrospect, I can understand why people paying good money were pissed off with an inconclusive finish, but obviously I felt the booing was completely unjustified. I had got off the canvas to stop a fighter in only the ninth round. I'm a proud bloke so to be booed wasn't something I liked.

When I watched it back on video I accept that the fight could have carried on. If I was a paying customer, forking out good money for a world title fight, I would have felt short-changed. I can totally understand the disapproval of the stoppage, totally. But the way I look at it is without that we wouldn't have had such a fantastic re-match at a packed Wembley stadium. The sequence of events that night, with Howard Foster stopping the fight, was almost something out of a Rocky movie. A Hollywood writer could not have scripted it better. There was controversy and that's what made the second Groves clash such a massive occasion, the biggest ever in British post-war fight history.

It wasn't until the next day when I watched the tape, read the papers and saw some comments on Twitter that I fully realised what had happened. The backlash was pretty fierce. I had won the fight fair and square but the way it had ended had really tarnished my reputation, and my reputation means a heck of a lot to me, both as a fighter and as a person. I had a couple of days where I felt quite low about it all. Rachael was upset and kept asking me if I was all right. The abuse on Twitter was unbelievable. I'm usually not that bothered about what keyboard warriors think about the fight game, but the general feedback was pretty poor. Former England striker Michael Owen sent a tweet out saying it was disgusting I had got booed out of the ring, remarking that it was typical of us as a nation to build sportsmen up, then take great delight in knocking them down.

I don't want this next comment to make it sound as though I thought I'd suddenly become a big shot because I didn't, but I felt the abuse I got was similar to when David Beckham was sent off in the 1998 World Cup finals against Argentina. Suddenly everyone was at his throat telling him what a let-down he had been. Obviously what happened to me was on a much smaller scale, but for a few weeks that summer he was hated. Now he is loved by the public.

I had only ever been a boxer who delivered in the ring. I had won and lost world titles all around the world, both as an amateur and a pro, and by sheer hard graft I had pulled myself up by my boot straps. Before I stepped in the ring against Groves I was a hero and now I was getting stick everywhere.

Some of the newspapers criticised me, but thankfully not all of them. Some of the boxing press guys know what they are talking about and they saw what I saw: that Groves was in real bother when the fight was stopped. But everyone loves an underdog doing well in any sport and I'm sure Groves loved all the backing he received, convincing himself he had been robbed.

My post-fight interview on the ring apron didn't do me any favours either. Instead of burying it and saying well done to my opponent, it was a great fight, I reiterated that Groves had shown me no respect at all and I didn't like him or the juvenile games he played before the fight. I also said I felt the stoppage had come at the right time as Groves had been properly hurt. Before the interview Groves came over to shake my hand and I told him to 'Fuck off.' I didn't like Groves before the fight, or during the fight and I am a man's man who stands by his convictions, so I wasn't going to start telling the world what a great fellow he was after we had boxed. Fact is, I don't like Groves and I'm not about to pretend to anyone that I do just because I had beaten him.

For the good of the sport and to be the bigger man I should have shaken his hand, but I didn't feel like that at the time. I wanted to ask him a few questions and for him to explain himself. Maybe I wanted to hear him say that he was only saying stupid things to build up interest in the fight and that he didn't really mean it. Or I wanted him to say, 'I genuinely don't like you, Froch. You may be a champion boxer, but I think you're an idiot.' Instead I got nothing of the sort, no explanation, just a dumb, half-arsed look on his face.

I did a post-fight press conference for the newspapers later that night, perhaps an hour after the bout, with Eddie and Rob at my side, and I think I got the flavour of that about right. I hadn't given Groves any praise at ringside, probably because I had just come out of a tough, gruelling fight, but later on that night I got my head screwed on and I gave Groves some credit. If I had done that earlier on when the TV cameras were running it would have sounded a lot better, even though I stand by every word I said in both interviews: I meant every word in both of them.

The interview at ringside was spoken from the heart, but people didn't want to hear that. They believed I had just been gifted a decision and I think the consensus was I should have been more gracious in victory. That's what they were thinking and maybe they were right, I don't know. All I know is I said I didn't like Groves before the fight and still didn't.

Straight away Groves started whingeing and droning on about a re-match and maybe my post-fight ringside interview helped set up the phenomenon that was Wembley Stadium because the needle was genuine. For me, it's very hard to fake all that. Sometimes you need controversy to make the very best fights and that's what you got with me and Groves when we met. He told the world and his wife he was in control of the first fight throughout the nine rounds and was about to win, whereas the reality is I took his best punch, got up off the canvas and finished him off.

It's important for me to say that George Groves did well. He turned up ambitious, confident and fresh and there is no doubt he can punch quite hard. The knock down wasn't the hardest punch I've ever been hit with, but I have to give him some credit as a boxer.

But while Groves is a decent fighter, I'm above that level and in world class. The best he could throw at me wasn't enough for him to beat me at my absolute worst. There is no doubt about that. I was poor that night, mentally not at all at the races, and Groves took advantage.

I wasn't going to let it happen again.

CHAPTER 18

As George Groves would say, 'Everything for a reason.'

The Groves re-match was always going to happen. I had come close to having my legacy destroyed and with the way I beat him in our first fight I had certainly tarnished my reputation as a professional boxer. I received a lot of love from the general public after the Bute fight and the Kessler re-match and now I was getting the flipside.

After the first Groves fight I had to make sure whatever happened in the re-match I would go in there knowing I hadn't left any stone un-turned. I had to do everything in my ability to do the business. In terms of fitness, speed, stamina, power, endurance, footwork, you name it, I had to be 100 per cent certain it would be the best of me out there.

These thoughts were going through my head well before my training camp even started because I knew the fight was going to take place just a few days after our first clash in the ring. This time I wasn't going to leave anything to chance. The first thing I did was to take a look at my training regimes for Kessler II and the Arthur Abraham fight – in my opinion my best two camps. I looked at the detail and could see from day one I was on it.

In both those fights I felt great before the actual bout, in particular Abraham in Helsinki, where I remember feeling as light as a feather on my feet in the hours building up to the clash. That's what I wanted to feel like before Groves II and I was going to make absolutely certain I would be.

Even to this day the only time I'm ever really spoken to Groves outside of a boxing press conference, or a few brief words in the ring, was at the BBC Sports Personality of the Year awards in early December 2013, only a few weeks after we fought in Manchester.

He walked up, puffed out his chest and stood next to me at the pre-awards VIP party. He didn't ask me about my family or anything like that and was instead trying to be intimidating. I was with Rachael and my agent Luke and his wife, while Groves was on his own. He said, 'What are you doing then, what are you doing? What's going on?' I mentioned I was pretty tempted to fight Julio Cesar Chavez in Las Vegas as I had an offer on the table. He told me the Chavez fight wasn't available, it wasn't big enough and there was no interest, or money in it. He said the only fight out there for me was him.

It was annoying because I had this young pretender, who had just got beat, telling me what I should do with my career. Little did he know I had already made up my mind to fight him, but was just playing my cards close to my chest and making out there were plenty of options out there so that he didn't get to think he was Mr Billy Big Balls.

I shrugged my shoulders and kept it as amicable as I could before going on stage and giving Groves plenty of credit for the first fight, while saying, as succinctly as I could, that it would be different if we met again. I was respectful and it went down well with the crowd. If I had said he's not in my league and my preparation was really poor, I would have been roundly booed – and rightly so.

My mind-set that night was to be as chilled as I could possibly be. On another day if someone had come up to me in front of my missus and started telling me what I should or shouldn't be doing we would have had a roll around on the cobbles, as they say in Nottingham.

Let's not forget prize fighting is as much about business as it is sport. Eddie, Rob and I did an unbelievable job on the business negotiations and I was very happy with what I got from the deal, which was the most lucrative of my career in the ring.

We played a bit of poker with Groves's negotiators after he travelled to America and got himself made mandatory challenger with the IBF to be my next opponent. Mandatory or not mandatory, the fight was always going to happen, so although he didn't know it, Groves was wasting his time kicking up a stink.

Twelve weeks before the fight in May was Monday, 10 March, – the start of proper training – but it is a sign of how seriously and pumped up I was taking it this time that I was already working out in the weeks before that date.

A glance at my diary shows in the fortnight before of pre-camp I was running four times a week. I was also doing some technical sparring and light sparring work. I did ten rounds of that a couple of times a week and this was before proper training even began.

At the start of week one I did a press conference with Groves at Wembley, catching a helicopter down from near my house to London, but before then I did a five-mile run in the morning. I call it the 'Rocky Run' because it reminds me of a scene from one of the many Rocky movies where he trains in a rundown industrial area. I did it in around six and a half minutes a mile, again a sign I was already getting fit.

During that first press conference I was cool and relaxed. It didn't matter to me what Groves did because I knew in my own mind I was going to be a different fighter for our re-match. At one stage he pulled out a Rubik's Cube and started playing with it. He wasn't going to get under my skin. I just ignored him.

I had done a few sessions up at the English Institute for Sport in Sheffield with Chris Marshall, a sports psychologist, and they were paying off. Groves even tried to take the piss out of that, saying there was something mentally wrong with me. In fact, nothing of the sort as I'm as stable out the ring as any man could be. Like many top sportsmen and women these days I consult a sports psychologist to explore other ways of getting an extra half a per cent out of my perform-ance. I enjoy the sessions and they definitely helped me.

Groves brought with him to the press conference his ridiculous ten-strong security team. Later on when we were on the pitch at Wembley having our pictures taken, surrounded by his hired goons, he started whispering sweet nothings down my ear. I could feel the moisture in his breath and my ear was getting cold and wet from his spittle. I was still very composed but it didn't mean I had to listen to his crap, with Groves slurping in my earhole.

He kept repeating the same thing over and over again. 'Can you hold it together, Carl, can you hold it together?' I then shoved him and Groves went bright red. I'm sure it upset him and yet throughout it all I was as cool as a cucumber. He then looked really annoyed.

I told him I didn't want to listen to his childish, schoolboy taunts. I told him to grow up, while smiling at him.

Groves countered with, 'Don't ever do that again, or else.'

I replied, 'I've just done it and I'm stood here so why have I got to do it again? If you want to do something about it, then come on.'

He didn't. As far as I'm concerned Groves bottled it, big time. Schoolyard bullies say the same thing – 'don't do that again or I'll respond' – and yet they never actually do anything.

If someone had shoved me to the ground the way I did to him, I would have replied with my fists and I'll leave the rest to your imagination. Groves didn't, even though my 'entourage' consisted only of Rob, whereas he had half a platoon to protect him.

For the Groves re-match I did so much sparring – real quality sparring – that it was like taking a walk in the park. I sparred with Sunderland's heavyweight amateur Warren Baister, who is very good, very solid; Antony Fowler, from Liverpool, who over three or four rounds would give any fighter in the world a lot of problems; and Anthony Ogogo,

Olympic medallist and now an up-and-coming professional. All three have got really good futures ahead of them.

I had sparred before with Baister and Ogogo but this was the first time with Fowler, who I confidently predict will go a very long way in the sport. Everyone has big hopes for him. A Scouser, he is a genuinely good lad and a great workout for me. I'll be watching all their careers very closely as I think they have all got what it takes to succeed.

By the end of March I was mixing up the sparring between all three of them. There were no cutting corners. It was three sessions a day without fail. At the weekends I would go back to Nottingham and maybe have a little bike ride. For instance, to give you a snapshot from my training diary, on Monday, 1 April, I started with three rounds of heavy stuff with Daister, three with Fowler and four with Ogogo. I wrote in my diary that day the word 'tired', as I had also been running and had done my strength and conditioning weights work. There were no runs on the treadmill this time. I am a big believer that treadmills don't get you fit. They may keep you ticking over but as a boxer you need proper road work.

Training was painful and hard but this time I was fired up. I remember speaking to Adam about when we used to train with Ady Shepherd early on in my career in Nottingham. Ady is a personal trainer now, but has always been a weightlifter. In my early days I used to train with him for an hour and a half on Friday nights at the Utopia gym in Nottingham, when everyone else was going out for an evening on the town.

Ady would always punish me in weight training and I would need maximum effort to get through them. I used to dread and love those sessions in equal measure. Every time

I finished a session with him I almost needed to be carried home. For the start of the Groves II training camp I realised I needed to go back to that sort of level of training, where I nearly fell apart I was so knackered. Although I don't work with Ady any longer – we are still good mates – my mind-set had to be the same if I was going to bring payback time to Groves.

I did the long runs with my best pal Adam on Monday morning then travelled up to the English Institute of Sport for the rest of the week. The intensity level this time was different. Rob's take on it was simple: apply yourself properly and you'll win. He knew my head was not fixed right for the first fight with Groves and if I did the work then everything would be OK. He told me in no uncertain terms that nothing else was in important in my life right now, other than train-ing and my family. He was right.

Training was going brilliantly, there were no injuries or setbacks to speak of and on 1 May I again flew down to London from Nottingham by helicopter with a pilot, a bloke called Richard 'Dickie' Knocker. I kid you not; it's his real name. His parents must have had a sense of humour.

In *The Gloves are Off* and *Ringside* for Sky television Groves made a big deal about the fact that in our first fight he went in there believing, now he was going to go in there knowing. As usual it was a load of bollocks and I told him so. I saw in his eyes that he was a spent force at the end of round six and I have been around boxing long enough to know when a fighter has found the going too much.

I then said his best performance can't beat my worst performance and I drew confidence from that. He was playing

Jack the Lad, but most of it was the usual hot air and total garbage. For the benefit of Sky television and the viewers I was prepared to have a conversation with Groves, even though I didn't really want to listen to his version of events.

The Gloves are Off wasn't something I was contractually obliged to do and I could have said no, but had I done that it would have looked like I was worried. I wasn't. I also respect Sky's employees a lot as they are only trying to do their jobs, which is building up and putting on a massive boxing show.

I said I would prove that the first fight wasn't a lucky win for me. It was now a chance for me to further my legacy and show that I deserved the victory in our first dust-up. There was no robbery. This time, because of everything that happened in the first fight, I would put it right at Wembley Stadium in front of 80,000 boxing fans.

Nothing Groves said or did bothered me one bit and I thought the programme went really badly for him as he just embarrassed himself by talking rubbish. He was stuck for words several times and didn't know how to respond. I think when Groves goes into a press conference he enters into it with a script already written for him. Whether it is playing with a Rubik's Cube or repeating over and over again the same sayings like 'Everything for a reason', it's all very unnatural. When he hasn't got a script, he's lost for words.

Groves was asked by Johnny Nelson, 'What does every-thing for a reason mean?' Because he didn't have a pre-planned script in front of him he just mouthed a few silly words about knowing he was going to win this time, last time he only believed it. When it is face to face, mano a mano, Groves doesn't have a clue. I'm old school because I'm perfectly prepared to go into a conversation with any fighter and say what I think. Groves, on this occasion, looked like a rabbit in the headlights.

I ran rings round him and then as we shook hands he tried to pull me towards him. I just pulled him back and made him look like the child he is. The whole scenario was perfect. Mentally I knew I had him where I wanted him.

After the show I kept getting messages from Groves on Twitter saying: 'Round one to me.' Then another: 'Wembley Stadium – second round to me.' Then: 'First press conference – third round to me.' In the end I just un-followed him so he couldn't send me any more daft messages. I wasn't in the least bit bothered about them and wanted Groves to know that.

Then Groves started sending general Twitter messages out saying: 'Seven weeks to go, tick tock. Six weeks to go tick tock.' By week four they stopped and I thought Groves now knows reality is closing in on him.

He had told everyone who would listen the re-match was going to be easy and he had been robbed. However, four weeks before the bout I think he must have thought, hell, I've got to fight Carl Froch, who has only had one unavenged defeat in his career, to Andre Ward, who is second on every pound-for-pound list of boxers in the world, behind only Floyd Mayweather Jr. I'm sure the reality of his situation kicked in and Groves couldn't lie to himself when his head hit the pillow. All of a sudden he went very quiet on his social media outlets.

I suppose it's fair to say I was surprised by the enormity of the fight at Wembley stadium. I was shocked the first fight between us sold out so quickly and I was even more gobsmacked when the numbers started coming in for the re-match. When Eddie told me he was thinking about using Wembley stadium I said it was too ambitious. Surely we couldn't sell that many tickets. Then at the first press conference at Wembley we had already sold 60,000 tickets. I couldn't believe it.

At that stage I knew it was going to be massive. At first I thought it would do about 50,000 tickets, about the same as when Ricky Hatton fought Luis Collazo at Manchester City's ground. But when 60,000 tickets were sold it was clear this was way above even that.

Eventually Eddie and the fantastic Matchroom team sold 80,000 and it would have been even more had the capacity not been limited due to transport concerns. The first fight had set up a massive re-match. While I'm proud of the size of the fight and flattered by it, at the time all my focus was on fighting George Groves, to restore my faith in boxing and to make sure fight fans restored their faith in me.

I hadn't exactly fallen out of love with boxing, but I certainly wasn't enjoying the abuse and feedback I had been getting after my first fight with Groves. For the first time in my career I thought: this is horrible. It wasn't what I went into boxing for, the sport I absolutely love. I played the first fight over and over in my mind. I'd got dropped in round one, shipped far too many blows, especially right hands, but as the bout wore on I forced a stoppage then got booed out the ring. It didn't seem right to me.

As the re-match drew closer Rob and I had a few chats. He assured me that with the training regime I had gone through there would be only one outcome. He was certain I would win.

I had my final training sessions at the EIS all day on Monday and Tuesday and then wrapped it up on Wednesday morning. I had rented an apartment in London, finally driving down to the capital with my brother Lee and a pal Karl Beard on the Wednesday night before the big day. Lee drove a sponsored Mercedes-Benz and I chatted in the back seat with Karl, as chilled as I could possibly be.

I checked into my apartment on my own and Mark Seltzer joined me later, while Lee and Karl went to their hotel. I had a good feeling about Saturday night even then as it was Rob's birthday that day and Lee's as well. Surely they were good signs of what was to come?

The apartment was fantastic and I had been lucky in training because other than a cold just before I started my twelve-week camp I didn't have any physical setbacks. I hadn't even taken any diclofenac, which I tend to live on when I'm in training as it is a good and effective anti-inflammatory tablet.

The afternoon of the fight I spent time in my apartment trying to visualise how the night would go in front of a massive crowd, which was going to be the biggest post-war turnout for a boxing show in Britain. As I visualised my ring walk at Wembley I felt very calm inside, knowing that all the hard work was done and that the fight had already been won through the commitment of a hard training camp. However, as soon as I visualised Groves's gawping stare as I climbed into the ring my heartbeat would race. I could feel it pounding the inside of my chest. Just the thought of him standing there giving it large made me angry. But it was this emotion that had hindered my performance in our first fight and I wasn't going to let that happened again. It was then I decided I was going to climb into the ring and show him my back. Years earlier I had fought Middlesbrough's amateur legend John Pearce, a former Commonwealth gold medallist, in the semi-finals of the ABAs and he did the same thing to me. I was just an naïve kid back then and it really ruffled my feathers, so I thought, if that worked for Pearce back then, I'm going to try it myself this time.

It made me feel at peace when I was sitting there in my apartment relaxing and visualising the fight, because the only thing that had bothered me up to then was getting in the ring and seeing Groves giving it the full tough-guy stance. My psychology sessions had been worth it because I mentally felt incredibly strong.

In the build-up to our re-match Groves had been going to the opening of every envelope. He was dining out on his ten minutes of fame from the first fight by turning up to all the red carpet dos. I thought, excellent, just keep doing what you are doing. He even went on a London bus tour with a cardboard cut-out of me. Again, I was delighted with the financial deal. Not only had I secured the lion's share of the revenue, Groves was now selling the show like a man possessed. This enabled me to concentrate on the important side of boxing: getting fit and winning. I simply put this down to being involved in championship-level boxing for many years, as opposed to the naïve young cub who thinks he knows better.

I slept very well, another good sign, and then it was fight night. As soon as I got to the venue the sound from the crowd was different because it was my first open-air show. Adam said, 'This is your night, Carl, you're a gladiator tonight and this is your coliseum.' I love the TV shows *Spartacus: Blood and Sand* and *Gods of the Arena*, as well as the film *Gladiator* with Russell Crowe, and have watched all of them over and over again. Getting to Wembley made me feel like I was in ancient Rome.

As I got to the stadium our Olympic gold medallist Anthony Joshua was pummelling some poor bloke and the show had about 10,000 people in their seats. Even with only an eighth of the eventual crowd it still made the hairs stand up on my arms in anticipation. I was imagining what it would be like when the place was packed to the rafters.

I was happy, relaxed, unworried and although I was a bit nervous, like I am with all my fights, it was 'healthy' nerves, if you see what I mean. There was no apprehension about what was going to happen in the ring.

I knew it was my time to put the record straight and there is no better feeling in boxing, knowing that I was about to cross the line having put in all that graft and dedication into my training. I don't believe in luck in boxing, or in other sports for that matter and I was about to prove that this two-horse race was going to go my way.

I was asked what sort of entrance I preferred by the Sky team and I said I just wanted to keep it simple, no platforms or flying carpets, no buses, just me and the lights on full blast. Groves decided he wanted to be the showman so opted for a London bus, whereas I was happy with just coming out and getting down to business.

I'm an old-school fighter so I reflected that by wearing a 'Team Cobra' T-shirt. I soaked up the amazing atmosphere in Wembley Stadium that night and felt as cool as I've ever felt walking into a ring, even with 80,000 fans watching me.

As I climbed through the ropes I did what I'd decided to do and showed Groves my back. It worked a treat as Rob told me later Groves didn't know what to make of it. I felt great as I then got myself into fight mode. I had to concentrate on what I wanted to do, take the centre of the ring and start employing my jab to good effect. In the first Groves fight I started poorly by not taking the centre of the ring and as such I got pushed on to the back foot. It wasn't going to happen a second time. My plan was to meet him in the centre and keep stepping around him, with no straight-line attacks. If I could do that for the majority of the bout I was sure it would end in victory.

Just before the bell went I opened my mouth up and showed Groves my gum shield. I did that for a reason too. I discovered before the fight that Groves wanted to use a new-fangled gum shield that was supposed to realign your jaw. It was also meant to speed up your reflexes, although I'm not sure exactly how it does that. But the creators of this new gum shield had offered it to me first so I dived in there and took it. I tried it a few times and it was comfortable enough. Groves had later asked the makers to do another one for him as he wanted it as well, only to be told, no, sorry, Carl Froch has already taken up the offer.

So the bell was about to go, the referee told us to touch gloves and I gave Groves the full wide grin so he could see the maker's name, the logo, on the front of my gum shield. I knew it was just the sort of petty little thing would piss him off and get to him. I saw Groves had spotted it; I had got the gum shield he wanted.

As for the fight, it was quite simple. I clearly dominated and it was one of my easier fights. I controlled it throughout. It was all about me doing what I wanted to do and executing my game plan perfectly.

Rob and I split the fight up into three parts. The first four rounds, don't take a step backwards, control the ring centre and use your sharp jab cleverly and with menace. Oh, and don't get hit like I had been in the first meeting. That was it. That was the plan and actually when you know what you are doing in the ring that's not particularly difficult. Groves was trying to throw a few bombs, but when you have got a killer jab with the long range I have got, it's pretty easy to control the bout and not get hit. When he threw, I would just skirt around him, then throw a few counter shots of my own.

The second part of the fight, rounds five, six, seven and eight, Rob and I called 'closing the gap'. The idea was to get a bit closer to him, don't go head hunting, but throw in a couple of meaningful body shots.

If you notice in this stage of our fight, whenever I had Groves on the ropes I would throw some stuff to his body. This was done to back him up and methodically slow him down.

The last four rounds I would have closed the gap even further and gone for the gold-plated finish, with him half-knackered and his defences all at sea. As it happened, it never even got that far.

I would have been quite happy going into round seven even on the judges' scorecards because I knew that was where I could really take over. As it was I was ahead with the judges. At that half-way stage I was sure that I was in front by at least two to three rounds. I didn't feel as though Groves had won a single three minutes. When I watched it back, I admit a couple of them were close and he could have nicked them, but when we were in the ring I felt I was comfortably in control.

My plan to be at least level at half way was working to a tee and in fact I was so comfortable in there I knew I had the fight in my hands if I carried on concentrating and working off the jab in the centre of the ring. Rob and I agreed that if the fight got to round seven – if Groves even lasted to round seven – there was only going to be one winner.

The end came swiftly and decisively. I backed Groves up into his own corner and threw two lefts before delivering a left hook, which I hoped would open up a chance to throw a booming right hand. The left hook landed just exactly where I wanted it to, on the glove by the side of his head and teed up the right hand, which came straight down the pipe with full power. Naïvely, he tried to throw a left hook. Whether he did so because he told the world before the fight he would knock me out with a left hook you would have to ask him, but by throwing that punch of his own he opened the door even more for me to take full advantage. I did.

As I was in the process of delivering my right hand I could see Groves trying to respond with his left hook counter. Big mistake, as my big right hand landed flush on his chin, perfectly timed, as he was triggering his left hook. It was a terrific combination thrown by me, which conclusively ended the argument.

It was probably one of the best single punches of my career on the biggest platform I could have wished for. It's gone down in folklore. I've thrown good punches and landed with them against top-level opposition, but nothing gave me so much pleasure as that one.

If you watch it back now, and you can see my feet were in the perfect position, my timing was spot on and Groves walked right into the trap. If I had said, 'Groves, stand there, don't move and lift your chin a bit while I hit you as hard as I can with my biggest shot' I still couldn't have hit him any more perfectly than I did that night at Wembley Stadium.

I landed the shot in a split second and as soon as it hit the mark I knew it was a heavy blow. I thought, beautiful, great punch. But I was convinced he would get up because I always get up. As I walked a few steps back to the neutral corner I took a little glance over my shoulder and could see there was no chance of Groves getting up. His knee was cocked at an oblique angle and he was absolutely out of it. Even if he did get up, which looked unlikely, the fight was over and Groves was gone, gone, gone.

At the time I was willing Groves to get up and take some more punishment, for my own satisfaction and love of the sport. Call it a sick pleasure, call it what you want, I wanted Groves to continue. I wanted to hit him with more shots and beat him up a bit more. I didn't want to do any damage, I have never wanted that in any fight I've been involved in, but I definitely wanted to dole out a few more reminders to him that I was boss. I wanted the satisfaction of giving Groves a bit of bad medicine for his constant lack of respect before both fights, but I'll take the stoppage any way it comes and the single punch finish was the way it ended. Against Bute it was a different kind of ending as I pummelled him for quite a while until the ref stepped in but, with Bute as well as Groves, I never wanted either of them to get hurt. This is boxing, it is a sport, you do your best, win or lose, and you come away healthy.

Groves did well to stagger to his feet, but from where I was standing he was absolutely finished. He stumbled back to his corner, sat down on his stool and a minute after the fight he tried to stand up, only to slump into the arms of Gavin 'Paddy' Fitzpatrick. I think the bright orange bandana Gavin was wearing may have acted as a homing beacon for Groves as he seemed only semi-conscious. He was then given oxygen, so was clearly in a bad way.

The referee made the only decision he could and subsequently, the one-punch finish has gone down in history, hugely enjoyable for the thousands watching it live at Wembley and the millions at home or in the pub.

The fight with Groves was one that a lot of non-boxing fans watched. They'd ask questions like: 'How do you throw a punch like that? What do you have to do?' A few weeks after the fight someone said to me, 'I read you were working on that punch for an hour beforehand in the dressing room.'

For those who don't know the sport too well, I'll explain, it was just a right hand, a good right hand, but just a right hand. There was no hour-long preparation. I saw the opening and took it, but it is a punch I have thrown thousands of times over the years in the ring, albeit not as sweetly as that.

CHAPTER 19

Family is important to me, the most important thing in my life, and I have been very lucky that my career has meant that I've been able to support my family while competing in the greatest sport in the world. I'm also proud to live in Nottingham, the place where I grew up. A lot of Frochs have gone through the doors of the City Hospital. I was born there, as were my brothers Lee and Wayne, and when it was time for Rocco to be born, that's where we went. The staff there are fantastic – very professional and always incredibly helpful and friendly. Natalia is just the last of the Frochs to have been born there, but who knows?

How can I describe Natalia? She is a gorgeous, beautiful, adorable little girl. She has now passed her first birthday and has already started taking her first baby steps, albeit pretty doddery ones! Of course, she is different to Rocco, but in some ways they are also quite similar. They are both very boisterous, and when the pair of them have a play fight she doesn't waste any time pushing him away when he gets too much for her so she has plenty of the Froch fighting spirit within her.

She is also clever because she will scream the house down when Rocco goes near her. I'll walk into the room and he'll be standing there with a look of complete innocence on his face, protesting he has not even touched his sister. Natalia has already learned that attack is the best form of defence or, more correctly in her case, screaming is the most effective way to keep Rocco off her.

Rocco is now four years old and is a real people person. He loves being around others, be they adults or other kids. He'll talk for England to anybody who'll listen. I often pop into a café in Nottingham called Fratelli's, which is run by a pal of mine called Tony, and Rocco will, if he is only with me, just go and sit outside with the old boys, or move himself over to another group of people and just start chatting to them. He is so out-going, such an extrovert and will think nothing of saying to other café customers, 'What are you doing here? Shall I join you?'

Rocco loves it at nursery and is very forward. I wouldn't have him any other way. There is not an ounce of shyness or reserve about him and maybe that has got a bit to do with my mum as he loves spending time with his grandma. I think Natalia will be very similar when she grows up as she is showing all the signs of being very confident in herself as well. She started at a local nursery when she was about ten months old and has already settled in very quickly. On the first day I took her and dropped her off I wondered how she would settle and when I picked up her up later that day she crawled over to me as if to say 'Thank you, Daddy, for rescuing me.' Now, a few months down the line, she smiles, looks up and carries on playing with her toys or with the other little ones. It is so important to let your kids interact with other children as it widens their horizons so early in life.

I'm very lucky as Rachael and I live in a lovely village on the outskirts of Nottingham and there are excellent state schools on our doorstep. I firmly believe that going to a decent state school can be better for kids than sending them to a private school. Being a good parent is just as important, if not more important, than which school your kids go to. Discipline, education and teaching your child to be a good human being start at home and I'm absolutely determined to be a very good father to Rocco and Natalia. I read to Rocco every night I'm at home and will do the same with Natalia. Rocco can already recite the alphabet and he can even count to thirty in Spanish, even though he is only four!

The senior school nearby which my kids would go to has got a fantastic reputation as one of the best in the country. One of the reasons I'm not a massive believer in the private education system is that I believe kids have got to have a bit of 'street' in them. I was born on a tough council estate and it certainly didn't do me any harm. I was bought up with a streetwise mentality, which I'm sure helped me in my life and will also help my children.

I want to teach Rocco and Natalia not only how to behave well to other people, but also the value of money. When Rocco is a bit older I will have him raking the leaves in the garden every autumn for two hours for a tenner. I'm going to bust his balls a bit, but ultimately it will do him good to understand the ways of the world. You have to work for everything. I have a very working-class mentality, which has given me a brilliant grounding in life. It was the way I was brought up and it is one of the reasons I have got to where I am now. And I appreciate the nicer things in life now because I have had to work for them.

I remember I had a hard paper round when I was a kid! Maybe I won't expect Rocco to do that, as I recall lugging those papers around Nottingham for hours, just for a few quid. On Sunday, the bag was so heavy I had to make two trips to the newsagent because I couldn't carry them all in one load. Getting up at 6.30 a.m. wasn't an awful lot of fun either!

I think the way I bring up my kids will be a natural extension of the way I was brought up. My mum worked hard all her life to feed and clothe her kids and she always made us boys appreciate what we were getting from her. Rachael is very grounded as well, which is due to the amazing job her parents did raising her.

At this point I'd like to pay proper credit to my mum, as she plays a huge role in my kids' upbringing. I think it is safe to say without my mum I wouldn't have enjoyed the success I have had in the ring – it's as simple as that. She has helped enormously with both our children from day one and I know Rocco loves spending time with his grandma, just as Natalia will in due course. Mum is nothing short of the perfect grandparent. I often say to Rocco, 'Do you want to come home with your daddy and watch a movie or pop over and see your nana?' I know the answer pretty much every time will be 'Nana, Nana.' He loves my mum, as do I. She has been one of my biggest fans ever since I became a fighter, worrying before the contest, then celebrating with me when I win.

I spend quite a lot of time driving – usually up to Sheffield and back – and there are countless occasions when I've rung Mum for a bit of advice, or just to tell her my feelings and emotions. She always knows the right thing to say and I can't remember a time when I have not listened to her advice and ended the conversation a lot happier. Without my mum I would not have achieved what I have. Everyone who is successful in whatever they do needs someone they can rely on for help, advice and sometimes just a listening ear. She does all of that and a lot more.

The job of being a boxer is so demanding and hard that I've been very fortunate because I never have to worry for a second about my kids. Also, Rachael and my mum get on superbly, which is so important. They agree on pretty much everything. I have unconditional love for my mum and it goes both ways. Mum's partner Steve, my stepdad, is a terrific person as well and has become over the years someone who I can truly rely on. He makes my mum very happy, which in turn makes me happy. Steve has been around since I was about 19, so he's been in my life for many years and I know he has my mum's best interests at heart in everything he does. I look at Steve nowadays as one of my best mates.

My mum is the reason why my morals are good. I try to treat people how I would like to be treated and that fundamental decency was ingrained into me from her.

Boxing has given me so much in life but it has also meant I have earned well enough from it to be financially comfortable for the rest of my days. I'm lucky to be in that position due to the achievements I have enjoyed in the ring.

Needless to say, the most important people in my life are Rachael and my two kids Rocco and Natalia, but I also hope my brothers, who I love dearly, will benefit from what I have done in the ring. Along with my mum, my brothers have been my biggest supporters since the day I became a fighter. Now I've got the means, I want to show them the same support, but I want to do it my way, the sensible way.

My brothers are hard workers. My elder brother Lee is a building project manager who knows how to get the job done. He has his own business called the 'Whole Project' and he has been very successful. He will do anything within the trade: kitchens, bathrooms, extensions, you name it. Anything in the building industry that needs doing, Lee knows how to get it done, from the foundations to the last tile in the bathroom. And he is brilliant at what he does. Lee has been involved from start to finish in a number of the property investments I've made over the years. When I retire from boxing I want to become a property developer, with my elder brother in charge of the day-to-day operations and Wayne also working for the company.

I've got a passion for old buildings, be they Victorian or Georgian. I like the idea of restoring these places back to their full grandeur. I want to carry on doing that, while at the same time I will carry on expanding my property port-folio, which is centred around Nottingham. I can't do that on my own, but with Lee and Wayne helping me, I can expand the business five times quicker and we can all make money out of it. That is the way forward for me, so that my brothers and their families also reap the benefits of what I have done in the ring. I'll make the initial cash investment – I don't need to go to the bank to ask for a loan – but then Lee and Wayne can use up some of their blood, sweat and tears and I like the idea that we can all build something together.

Other than being a world champion, I can think of nothing that would make me prouder than helping set up my brothers in life. They have got the opportunity to create for themselves and their families a really nice lifestyle and I know they will take it and work hard. Lee has two daughters, Scarlet and Sienna, while Wayne has twins, a boy and a girl named Mason and Maya, and I know the future will be bright for of all them when our business takes off.

When my career in the ring is finally over – and I genuinely don't know when that day will come – I would like to stay involved in the sport as my passion for boxing will never leave me, but only as a commentator. I enjoy immensely the summariser role I do for Sky television. Going to fights and analysing them is great work and I feel very relaxed and confident in front of a camera because I know what I am talking about. I've spoken to people inside the game and they seem to appreciate my opinion, because I am obviously talking from experience.

I don't think I have got the patience for coaching fighters. I see Rob in the gym day in day out and you know what, I just don't think that is something I want to do with the rest of my life. You have really got to love the sport inside and out to do the sort of job Rob does – and I do – but I just think I would rather use my time elsewhere. That's not a criticism of the sport, I am just saying how I feel, and patience, the trait of the best coaches, has never been my strongest virtue. I don't want to go through the ups and downs with another fighter as a coach as that would almost be like reliving my career again. That's not something I want to do; I want to keep moving forward.

What else is there in my life? Rachael, of course, and I am going to make an honest woman of her one day! I've asked her to marry me and she has consented, so next up I've got to give her an engagement ring at a romantic location. The plan is to get married in the summer of 2015 and I'll be the happiest man in the world on that special day.

Rocco has started school and Natalia is already at nursery for a couple of days a week so Rachael is getting broody again. I came out and asked her if she wanted any more additions and she admitted she does so I definitely think there will be more Froch kids along the way. Kids keep you very young as well and I enjoy every minute with them, even the nappy-changing!

Boxing has brought me many things over the years and I have learned a lot from competing in the ring. It's an intense sport, requiring skill and agility, mental strength and finely honed focus. I learn something new about myself each time I face an opponent, and that keeps the sport fresh and exciting. I will keep boxing until the day comes when I don't enjoy it. Right now, I still enjoy it just as much as I did the first day I walked into a gym.

CARL'S
ACKNOWLEDGEMENTS

Thanks go to all my stable mates over the years, there's far too many from my amateur days to mention all of them, but you all know who you are. Special thanks though, to close friend and training partner from my amateur days Jason Yarnall, you helped strengthen me, physically and mentally. Thanks also to all the boys I trained with every day for the very start of my professional career. The Class of 2002 was an exciting time. David Walker, Lee Meager, Matthew Thirlwall, Bill Corcoran, John O'Donnell and Lenny Daws. The Lennox Lewis College in Clapton, north London, was my gym and second home for four years and without you all coming in daily to train, I definitely would not have enjoyed this period of my life. Thanks to my amateur coaches Dale McPhilbin, Dominic Travis and Ray Windress.

Thanks to my professional coach and very close friend Mr Robert McCracken, without you I would not have even considered turning professional. It's never really been a business relationship, we've never needed a contract, you've simply been a real friend. What we have achieved is amazing and we're not finished yet.

Thanks also to my promoter Eddie Hearn and his team at Matchroom Sport, who are the best in the business.

Thanks to Niall for all the help with the book.

Now, on to my family. Mum, you always are a voice of reason, encouragement and support, no matter what. You believed in me even when maybe I didn't believe in myself. My brothers Lee and Wayne, I know you are both my biggest fans and having you there supporting me makes me feel very special. Thanks to my stepdad Big Steve for all your support, nothing is ever too much trouble when I need your help. Thank you to my best friend Adam, you are in the family section as you are more like a brother to me, you are always there where ever and whenever I need you.

Now on to those to whom I dedicate this book, my beautiful partner Rachael and my children Rocco and Natalia. Rachael, your first time watching me fight live was against Jermain Taylor and it's a fight we will never forget. That was a turning point in my career and you went through all the mixed emotions that night with me and the rest of my family. That's when you became a part of my family. We first met in 2009, but it feels like I've known you forever. The bond and love we share cannot be defined with words and the birth of our two gorgeous babies has sealed that bond forever. Thank you for being you.

NIALL'S ACKNOWLEDGEMENTS

First and foremost, I have to express my heartfelt thanks to Carl Froch for all his time, patience and consideration. Not only a fine boxer, but a wonderfully warm-hearted person, who is the most cheerful part-time DIY enthusiast I've ever met. Frank, Lee and Wayne Froch, Carl's mum Carol and his partner Rachael have also been hugely supportive, the latter of whom makes a lovely brew!

Carl's amazing story would not have been possible without my wife Lynn's tireless support. In future I'll be more careful, as we always seem to produce children while finishing a book! Others I must thank include John Matthews, Paul Branagan, Mark Sylvester, Alun Palmer, Jason Advocate, Darren Pitt, Des O'Hare, Barry Pearce, Chris McGhivney, John and Sue Arrand, the Cattermole family, Leon and Andrea Hickman, Jon Sevink and the Levellers, Ralph and Ali Ineson, Mick Hennessy, Vicky and Lee Squirrell, my fellow boxing writers, Tom at Hellaby Hall Hotel near Rotherham, David at the Frenchgate Hotel, Richmond, North Yorkshire, the Hatton family and Rob McCracken, the best trainer in the business. All the sports team at the *Daily Express* under our editor Bill Bradshaw and Andrew Goodfellow and Liz Marvin at Ebury Press, who deserve special praise for their unceasing support.

Finally, I hope when Rocco and Natalia grow up they can sit down one day and read about their father's wonderful achievements. Carl Froch – a great boxer, a proud son of Nottingham and one hell of a bloke.

CARL FROCH'S VITAL STATISTICS

Sex	Male
DOB	02/07/1977
Nationality	British
Reach	75"
Birth Name	Carl Martin Froch
Stance	Orthodox
Home town	Nottingham
Height	6'
Rated at	Super Middleweight
Trainer	Robert McCracken

W 33 (24 KOs)

L 2 (0 KOs)

D 0

Total **35**

RING RECORD

Date	Froch's Weight (lb)	Opponent	Opponent's Weight (lb)	W-L-D
31/5/14	167½	**George Groves**	166¼	19-1-0

Location: Wembley Stadium, London, UK

Result: **W** **TKO** **8**

Referee: Charlie Fitch

Judges: Michael Pernick, David Singh, Alejandro Lopez Cid

IBF Super Middleweight title

WBA Super World Super Middleweight title

Date	Froch's Weight (lb)	Opponent	Opponent's Weight (lb)	W-L-D
23/11/13	167¾	**George Groves**	166½	19-0-0

Location: Phones 4u Arena, Manchester, UK

Result: **W** **TKO** **9**

Referee: Howard John Foster

Judges: Dave Parris, Waleska Roldan, Massimiliano Bianco

IBF Super Middleweight title

WBA Super World Super Middleweight title

Date	Froch's Weight (lb)	Opponent	Opponent's Weight (lb)	W-L-D
25/5/13	167½	**Mikkel Kessler**	166½	46-2-0

Location: O2 Arena, London, UK

Result: **W**   **UD**   **12**

Referee: Pete Podgorski

Judges: Carlos Sucre, Jean-Francois Toupin, Adalaide Byrd

IBF Super Middleweight title

WBA Super World Super Middleweight title

Date	Froch's Weight (lb)	Opponent	Opponent's Weight (lb)	W-L-D
17/11/12	167½	**Yusaf Mack**	168	31-4-2

Location: Capital FM Arena, Nottingham, UK

Result: **W**   **KO**   **3**

Referee: Phil Edwards

Judges: Patrick Morley, Francesco De Ruvo, Steve Gray

IBF Super Middleweight title

Date	Froch's Weight (lb)	Opponent	Opponent's Weight (lb)	W-L-D
26/5/12	167¼	**Lucian Bute**	167 ¾	30-0-0

Location: Capital FM Arena, Nottingham, UK

Result: **W** **TKO** **5**

Referee: Earl Brown

Judges: Howard John Foster, Benoit Roussel, Steve Weisfeld

IBF Super Middleweight title

Date	Froch's Weight (lb)	Opponent	Opponent's Weight (lb)	W-L-D
17/12/11	167½	**Andre Ward**	168	24-0-0

Location: Boardwalk Hall, Atlantic City, NJ, USA

Result: **L** **UD** **12**

Referee: Steve Smoger

Judges: Craig Metcalfe, John Keane, John Stewart

WBC Super Middleweight title

WBA Super World Super Middleweight title

Date	Froch's Weight (lb)	Opponent	Opponent's Weight (lb)	W-L-D
4/6/11	167½	**Glen Johnson**	166½	51-14-2

Location: Boardwalk Hall, Atlantic City, NJ, USA

Result: **W**   **MD**   **12**

Referee: Earl Brown

Judges: Mark Green, John Stewart, Nobuaki Uratani

WBC Super Middleweight title

Date	Froch's Weight (lb)	Opponent	Opponent's Weight (lb)	W-L-D
27/11/10	167	**Arthur Abraham**	167½	31-1-0

Location: Hartwall Arena, Helsinki, Finland

Result: **W**   **UD**   **12**

Referee: Frank Garza

Judges: Burt A. Clements, Oren Shellenberger, Max DeLuca

Vacant WBC Super Middleweight title

Date	Froch's Weight (lb)	Opponent	Opponent's Weight (lb)	W-L-D
24/04/10	167¼	**Mikkel Kessler**	167	42-2-0

Location: MCH Messecenter Herning, Denmark

Result: **L**   **UD**   **12**

Referee: Michael Griffin

Judges: Guido Cavalleri, Daniel Van de Wiele, Roger Tilleman

WBC Super Middleweight title

Date	Froch's Weight (lb)	Opponent	Opponent's Weight (lb)	W-L-D
17/10/09	167¼	**Andre Dirrell**	167½	18-0-0

Location: Trent FM Arena, Nottingham, UK

Result: **W**   **SD**   **12**

Referee: Hector Afu

Judges: Alejandro Rochin, Massimo Barrovecchio, Daniel Van de Wiele

WBC Super Middleweight title

Date	Froch's Weight (lb)	Opponent	Opponent's Weight (lb)	W-L-D
25/04/09	167	**Jermain Taylor**	166	28-2-1

Location: Foxwoods Resort, Mashantucket, CT, USA

Result: **W**   **TKO**   **12**

Referee: Mike Ortega

Judges: Nobuaki Uratani, Omar Mintun, Jack Woodburn

WBC Super Middleweight title

Date	Froch's Weight (lb)	Opponent	Opponent's Weight (lb)	W-L-D
06/12/08	166½	**Jean Pascal**	167¾	21-0-0

Location: Trent FM Arena, Nottingham, UK

Result: **W**   **UD**   **12**

Referee: Guido Cavalleri

Judges: Predrag Aleksic, Herminio Cuevas Collazo, Tom Kaczmarek

Vacant WBC Super Middleweight title

Date	Froch's Weight (lb)	Opponent	Opponent's Weight (lb)	W-L-D
10/05/08	167¼	**Albert Rybacki**	168½	15-0-0

Location: Nottingham Arena, Nottingham, UK

Result: **W**   **TKO**   **4**

Referee: John Keane

Date	Froch's Weight (lb)	Opponent	Opponent's Weight (lb)	W-L-D
09/11/07	167½	**Robin Reid**	167¼	39-5-1

Location: Ice Arena, Nottingham, UK

Result: **W** **RTD** **5**

Referee: Dave Parris

Judges: Howard John Foster, Ian John-Lewis, Terry O'Connor

BBBofC British Super Middleweight title

Date	Froch's Weight (lb)	Opponent	Opponent's Weight (lb)	W-L-D
23/03/07	167¼	**Sergey Tatevosyan**	167	26-7-0

Location: Ice Arena, Nottingham, UK

Result: **W** **TKO** **2**

Referee: Terry O'Connor

Date	Froch's Weight (lb)	Opponent	Opponent's Weight (lb)	W-L-D
24/11/06	166½	**Tony Dodson**	166	20-3-1

Location: Ice Arena, Nottingham, UK

Result: **W** **KO** **3**

Referee: Phil Edwards

BBBofC British Super Middleweight title

Commonwealth (British Empire) Super Middleweight title

Date	Froch's Weight (lb)	Opponent	Opponent's Weight (lb)	W-L-D
26/05/06	167¼	**Brian Magee**	167¾	25-2-0

Location: York Hall, London, UK

Result: **W**   **KO**   **11**

Referee: Richard James Davies

Judges: Ian John-Lewis, Terry O'Connor, Paul Thomas

BBBofC British Super Middleweight title

Commonwealth (British Empire) Super Middleweight title

Date	Froch's Weight (lb)	Opponent	Opponent's Weight (lb)	W-L-D
17/02/06	167¾	**Dale Westerman**	167	15-5-0

Location: York Hall, London, UK

Result: **W**   **TKO**   **9**

Referee: John Keane

Judges: Marcus McDonnell, Terry O'Connor, Ian John-Lewis

Commonwealth (British Empire) Super Middleweight title

Date	Froch's Weight (lb)	Opponent	Opponent's Weight (lb)	W-L-D

| 02/12/05 | 166¾ | **Ruben Groenewald** | 167¼ | 19-4-3 |

Location: Ice Arena, Nottingham, UK

Result: **W**   **TKO**   **5**

Referee: Howard John Foster

Judges: John Keane, Terry O'Connor, Paul Thomas

Commonwealth (British Empire) Super Middleweight title

| 09/07/05 | 167½ | **Matthew Barney** | 168 | 21-5-1 |

Location: Ice Arena, Nottingham, UK

Result: **W**   **PTS**   **12**

Referee: Phil Edwards

BBBofC British Super Middleweight title

Commonwealth (British Empire) Super Middleweight title

| 21/04/05 | 167 | **Henry Porras** | 167¾ | 30-4-1 |

Location: The Avalon, Hollywood, CA, USA

Result: **W**   **TKO**   **8**

Referee: Pat Russell

Judges: Ray Corona, Max DeLuca, Lou Filippo

Date	Froch's Weight (lb)	Opponent	Opponent's Weight (lb)	W-L-D
24/09/04	167	**Damon Hague**	168	23-2-1

Location: Ice Arena, Nottingham, UK

Result: **W** **TKO** **1**

Referee: Mickey Vann

BBBofC British Super Middleweight title
Commonwealth (British Empire) Super Middleweight title

Date	Froch's Weight (lb)	Opponent	Opponent's Weight (lb)	W-L-D
02/06/04	167¾	**Mark Woolnough**	168	14-3-1

Location: Ice Arena, Nottingham, UK

Result: **W** **TKO** **11**

Referee: Dave Parris

Commonwealth (British Empire) Super Middleweight title

Date	Froch's Weight (lb)	Opponent	Opponent's Weight (lb)	W-L-D
12/03/04	167¾	**Charles Adamu**	164¼	11-1-0

Location: Ice Arena, Nottingham, UK

Result: **W** **PTS** **12**

Referee: Marcus McDonnell

Commonwealth (British Empire) Super Middleweight title

Date	Froch's Weight (lb)	Opponent	Opponent's Weight (lb)	W-L-D
30/01/04	170	**Dzmitry Adamovich**	176	9-7-0

Location: Goresbrook Leisure Centre, Dagenham, UK
Result: **W**   **TKO**   **2**

28/11/03	167	**Alan Page**	167	8-0-0

Location: Derby Storm Arena, Derby, UK
Result: **W**   **TKO**   **7**
Referee: John Keane

Vacant BBBofC English Super Middleweight title

04/10/03	171½	**Vage Kocharyan**	174½	10-7-1

Location: Alexandra Palace, London, UK
Result: **W**   **PTS**   **8**

16/04/03	171	**Michael Monaghan**	166½	12-7-0

Location: Ice Arena, Nottingham, UK
Result: **W**   **TKO**   **3**
Referee: Terry O'Connor

Date	Froch's Weight (lb)	Opponent	Opponent's Weight (lb)	W-L-D
05/03/03	172¼	**Varuzhan Davtyan**	177	3-5-0

Location: York Hall, London, UK

Result: **W**   **TKO**   **5**

Referee: Ian John-Lewis

Date	Froch's Weight (lb)	Opponent	Opponent's Weight (lb)	W-L-D
28/01/03	171	**Valery Odin**	177¾	6-5-0

Location: Ice Arena, Nottingham, UK

Result: **W**   **TKO**   **6**

Referee: Shaun Messer

Date	Froch's Weight (lb)	Opponent	Opponent's Weight (lb)	W-L-D
21/12/02	171¼	**Mike Duffield**	166	9-15-1

Location: Goresbrook Leisure Centre, Dagenham, UK

Result: **W**   **TKO**   **1**

Date	Froch's Weight (lb)	Opponent	Opponent's Weight (lb)	W-L-D
25/10/02	170	**Paul Bonson**	191	16-55-6

Location: York Hall, London, UK

Result: **W**   **PTS**   **6**

Date	Froch's Weight (lb)	Opponent	Opponent's Weight (lb)	W-L-D
23/08/02	167	**Darren Covill**	169	8-28-1

Location: York Hall, London, UK

Result: **W**   **TKO**   1

Date	Froch's Weight (lb)	Opponent	Opponent's Weight (lb)	W-L-D
10/05/02	171	**Ojay Abrahams**	168	19-36-4

Location: York Hall, London, UK

Result: **W**   **KO**   1

Referee: Lee Cook

Date	Froch's Weight (lb)	Opponent	Opponent's Weight (lb)	W-L-D
16/03/02	170	**Michael Pinnock**	181	4-52-8

Location: York Hall, London, UK

Result: **W**   **TKO**   4

Referee: Mark Green